DETROIT
ACROSS THREE
CENTURIES

RICHARD BAK

Sleeping Bear Press

Sleeping Bear Press
310 North Main Street
P.O. Box 20
Chelsea, MI 48118
www.sleepingbearpress.com

Printed and bound in Canada.

10 9 8 7 6 5 4 3 2 1

Library of Congress Cataloging-in-Publication Data

Bak, Richard, 1954-
Detroit : across three centuries / Richard Bak.
p. cm.
ISBN 1-58536-001-5
1. Detroit (Mich.)—History. 2. Detroit (Mich.)—History—Pictorial
works. I. Title.
F574.D457 B35 2001
977.4'34 dc21
2001002870

▲ *Above photo:* Spirit of Detroit.

For my parents,

Edward and Lillian Bak;

and to the memory of my grandparents, Alexander and Theresa Koscielny and Stanley and Julia Bak

CONTENTS

◄ Interior of the Wayne County Courthouse in Detroit.

CADILLAC'S VILLAGE

If trees could talk, *le grand arbre* on Windsor's Riverside Drive presumably would be spinning stories in fluent French. One can only imagine what tales the venerable pear tree—planted by Jesuit priests not long after *habitants* settled both banks of the Detroit River—could tell. Perhaps they would echo the observations of Bela Hubbard, who in his old age recorded his impressions of the *ancien regime* he and his fellow New Englanders helped supplant in Detroit.

"Seldom have I witnessed a more animating spectacle," Hubbard wrote in 1877, "than that of a large canoe belonging to the Hudson Bay Company, manned by a dozen *voyageurs*—the company's agents seated in the center—propelled with magic velocity, as if instinct with life, every paddle keeping time to the chorus that rang far and wide over the waters."

Although the tree's rotted trunk has been filled in with cement to help keep it erect, its arthritic branches continue to blossom in the spring and to bear fruit in the summer—a cycle of stubborn rebirth that mirrors the three centuries of boom-and-bust history it has quietly watched from its vantage point a few blocks east of the Ambassador Bridge.

This towering sentinel, among the largest of several 18th-century fruit trees to be found between Windsor and Monroe, is one of the few surviving traces of old French Detroit. Nearly everything else from that period has been either destroyed or paved over, including a cemetery under Cobo Arena where the bones of many anonymous French settlers are scattered.

◄ *Traces of old French Detroit: a pear tree in Windsor.*

➤ *Cadillac arrives in Detroit.*

The virtually complete eradication of the city's beginnings is a shame, said Brian Dunnigan, who can trace his own roots to a canoe-paddling ancestor named Jean-Baptiste Bausom.

"One of the things I find most interesting about Detroit is that most people assume its history begins with the automobile," said the curator of maps at the University of Michigan's William Clements Library. "By that time, however, the city was already 200 years old. Few people have any conception of it as a colonial settlement."

It was the summer of 1679 when the first sailing vessel on the Great Lakes glided up the deep, clear waters now known as the Detroit River into Lake St. Clair and the St. Clair River beyond. On board the *Griffon* was Recollect Father Louis Hennepin. The natural beauty of this waterway linking Lake Erie and Lake Huron, called *le detroit* ("the strait") by the French, moved him. "The banks of the strait are vast meadows," he wrote rapturously, "with some hills covered with vineyards, trees bearing good fruit. . . . Groves and forests are so well disposed that one would think Nature alone could not make, without the help of art, so charming a prospect."

It was that sort of gushing that kept explorers, missionaries, and traders coming to the New World some three centuries ago. Modern Michigan cities like Port Huron, Niles, St. Ignace, Sault Ste. Marie, and Mackinaw City all got their starts as isolated toeholds on the great North American continent that England and France struggled so mightily to dominate and to exploit. Here was a vast, verdant, pristine wilderness that had the added value of being practically uninhabited. Anthropologists estimate that, prior to the arrival of the Europeans, no more than 100,000 Native Americans lived in the area that constitutes present-day Michigan. On the other hand, the region held an estimated 10 million beaver—the web-footed, paddle-tailed, aquatic rodents whose valuable fur impelled French exploration into the Great Lakes region in the early 17th century. The French ultimately lost their bid for empire, but not before leaving a legacy of French names on the contested forests and lakes.

One of the most influential figures in the story of New France was Antoine Laumet de la Mothe Cadillac, a short-tempered, high-spirited adventurer of middle class origins who also was a bit of a

➤ *Ambitious, ruthless and imperious, Cadillac envisioned a permanent settlement growing out of the one-acre-square stockade his men built on the bank of the Detroit River.*

➤ *Opposite page: Cadillac's landing was re-enacted on July 24, 2001, as part of Detroit's year-long tricentennial celebration.*

rogue and a poseur. Born Antoine Laumet in the tiny village of St. Nicholas de la Grave in southern France in 1658, he first came to the New World as a young army officer in 1683. He was an excellent fencer, owning as many as 18 swords. While at Port Royal, Nova Scotia, he became associated with a seagoing trader named François Guyon. Through Guyon, he became a topflight navigator and possibly a privateer. Ever the opportunist, he married Guyon's 17-year-old niece, Marie Therese Guyon, a member of one of the most prominent families in Quebec. In order to boost his standing in high society, the up-and-coming Antoine Laumet fabricated claims of nobility and turned himself into Antoine de la Mothe, Sieur de Cadillac. A land grant gave him 187,000 acres in an area that now includes Bar Harbor, Maine.

As an expert on the Atlantic coastline, Cadillac was recalled to France to serve as an advisor to King Louis XIV. His schmoozing abilities won him the favor of the French court, including the king's chief minister, Count Pontchartrain. Within five years he was awarded a captaincy and given command of Michilimackinac in northern Michigan, the most important of the various French forts in the upper Great Lakes. There he supervised all military and missionary matters, while at the same time making a tidy profit on the fur trade.

While stationed at Michilimackinac, Cadillac first heard tales of the "deep, clear river" that Fr. Hennepin and others had marveled over. When he returned to Paris in 1699 to discuss plans for fortifying French claims in the lake country in anticipation of a war with England and Spain, Cadillac made the case for establishing a colony at *le detroit.* Where the court saw Detroit as only another in a series of way stations sprinkled strategically around the shorelines of the Great Lakes, Cadillac envisioned a permanent settlement—one populated by farmers, artisans, and their families, as well as soldiers and priests. He was driven as much by avarice and the lust for power as he was for shaping some Eden out of the wilderness. But he clearly was infatuated with a land that he described as "delightful and advantageous." He later wrote: "This country, so temperate, so fertile and so beautiful that it may justly be called the earthly paradise of North America, deserves all the care of the King to keep it up and to attract inhabitants to it."

Cadillac left Montreal on June 2, 1701 with just over 100 men—half of them

⋏ Hart Plaza in downtown Detroit has a historical marker, written in French and English, identifying the site as "Landing of Antoine Laumet de la Mothe Cadillac."

◄ *A view of Detroit in 1701, shortly after Cadillac's men erected a stockade named Fort Pontchartrain.*

▼ *On the third floor of the Detroit Public Library at 5201 Woodward Avenue is a 1921 mural,* The Arrival of Mme. Cadillac and Mme. Tonti, *painted by Detroit artist Gari Melchers. It depicts the arrival of the wives of Cadillac and his chief aide, Pierre Alphonse de Tonty.*

soldiers—jammed into 25 canoes. Members of the expedition tended to be short-legged and barrel-chested, the better to squeeze into and propel their crafts. A little more than seven weeks later, after an arduous trip that included several back-breaking portages, the expedition arrived at Grosse Ile late in the afternoon of July 23. The following day, July 24, 1701, Cadillac and his men struck camp and paddled back to a narrower stretch of the river, a spot overlooked by 20-foot bluffs. It was an excellent defensive position. The group beached their canoes on the north bank of the river, at a site now occupied by the Ford-UAW National Training Center (formerly the Veterans Memorial Building) at Jefferson and Shelby.

Under Cadillac's direction, woodsmen unpacked their axes and began taking down nearby conifers and oak and maple trees to build a palisade that was about 15 feet high and 200 feet square. Cadillac named it *Fort Pontchartrain du Detroit*, in honor of his principal sponsor. Its boundaries today would roughly be Griswold, Jefferson, Larned, and Shelby. Trees also were felled for the first building—St. Anne's Church, the cornerstone of a parish that, after one in St. Augustine, Florida, is the second oldest in the country. "All of this is no easy task," Cadillac wrote, "as everything has to be carried on the shoulders, for we have no oxen or horses yet to draw loads, nor to plough, and to accomplish it, it is necessary to be very active." That fall, Cadillac's wife arrived; a couple of years later their daughter became the first white child born and baptized in Detroit.

THE WHITE AND RED NATIVES MIXED TOGETHER AS ONE PEOPLE. THEY SOMETIMES INTERMARRIED, BUT ASIDE FROM THIS, THE EARLY WHITE MEN WHO WERE TRAPPERS, HUNTERS AND TRADERS IN THE WOODS, LIVED WITH THE SAVAGES ON TERMS OF PERFECT EQUALITY AND THEIR TRAITS AND HABITS OF LIFE BECAME SIMILAR. — *Clarence Monroe Burton,* When Detroit Was Young *(1951)*

∧ *This drawing shows Detroit as it looked in 1705, four years after Cadillac's arrival.*

Detroit quickly became the center of the Great Lakes fur trade, as high-smelling trappers came in from out of the woods to trade the pelts of elk, bear, raccoon, minks, lynx, muskrat, wolf, opossum, fox, deer, and the ubiquitous beaver for such items as gunpowder, blankets, and liquor. Cadillac got a piece of the action on each pelt shipped to Montreal.

Cadillac's profiteering was unremarkable among high government officials. What helped distinguish him was his administrative abilities. Like any good supervisor, he had already developed a detailed plan for creating and maintaining a colony on the Detroit River. Much to the horror of missionaries, with whom he had always feuded, Cadillac promoted marriage between the French settlers (known as *habitants*) and Indians. It was "absolutely necessary," he explained, to allow his men "to marry the savage maidens when they have been instructed in religion and know the French language, because they always prefer a Frenchman for a husband to any savage whatever. Marriages of this kind will strengthen the friendship of these tribes, as the alliances of the Romans perpetuated peace with the Sabines through the intervention of the women whom the former had taken from others." Illegitimate French-Indian children became common and were known as "natural children."

Soon more than 2,000 Indians—principally of the Huron, Ottawa, Potowatami, and Miami tribes—had built camps near the fort, attracted in part by the rum and brandy stored in a central warehouse. Some referred to the settlement as "Yondotiga," which meant "great village."

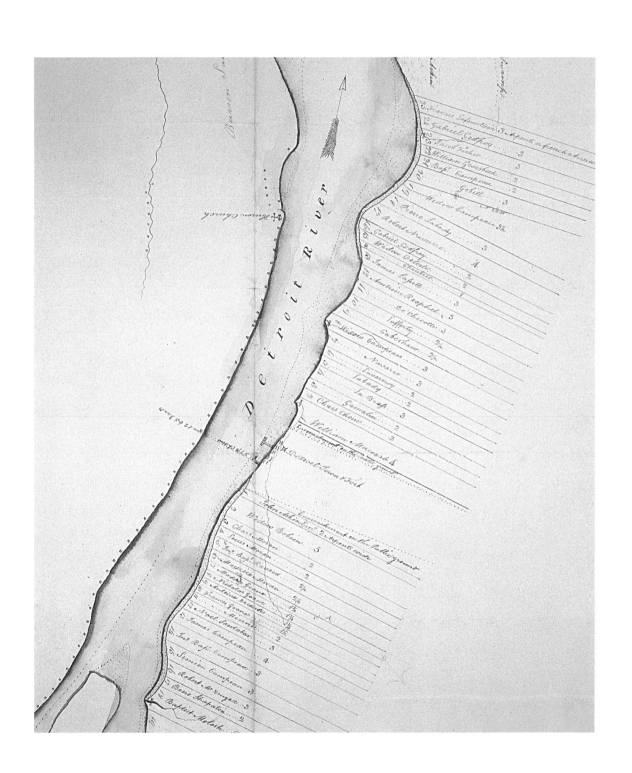

◄ In order to ensure that all French settlers had access to the riverfront—the highway system of the time—land grants in early Detroit were as narrow as 200 feet across but as deep as two or three miles inland. The boundaries of some of these so-called "ribbon farms" live on in streets carrying the names of their original owners: St. Aubin, Beaubien, Chene, St. Antoine, Cadieux, Livernois and others.

St. Anne's today.

St. Anne's Church

Just two days after Cadillac founded Detroit on July 24, 1701, the French explorer and his men hastily constructed a log building for worship. From these humble beginnings sprang St. Anne's Parish, a Catholic congregation that still exists as the second oldest continuous church in the United States.

Since 1886, St. Anne's Parish has been centered around the twin-spired, French neogothic church located on Howard Street, near the Ambassador Bridge. This is the parish's eighth location. Despite the many changes in venue, St. Anne's significance was never measured in mere brick and mortar.

According to Frank Rashid, a Marygrove College professor who has researched St. Anne's history for many years and was married there, the parish is important not only because of its long history, but because of its commitment and service to the community. "The priests and people of St. Anne's established the city's first schools, oversaw the first feeding programs for the poor, established the first orphanage, and gave sanctuary to those immigrants seeking refuge. This proud legacy of service continues today."

As the French influence in Detroit gradually faded away, St. Anne's role as the community's only cultural and religious institution was diminished. Nonetheless, the church, mindful of its mission, became a point of entry for waves of Catholic immigrants from Germany, Belgium, and Ireland. Today the congregation is about 75 percent Hispanic.

The historic parish survived a number of church closings by Catholic officials over the years. The most serious was in 1966, when the archdiocese wanted to raze the church because it needed $750,000 in repairs. Thanks to a grassroots effort, supporters and preservationists convinced the archdiocese to save it. The effort was one of the first and few examples in Detroit where citizens saved a historic landmark.

Today, St. Anne's has a strong congregation and continues to be a cornerstone of the community. Some credit the parish for inspiring a multi-million-dollar building boom in southwest Detroit. Others cite the never-ending quest for social change. In 1996, for example, Father Robert Duggan brokered a truce among several warring gangs. Not only did St. Anne's priest exact promises from gang members that they would not cause damage on Devil's Night, he influenced them to take to the streets and help fellow citizens fight arson that evening.

Rashid believes St. Anne's continuity makes it important to Detroit. "It's the first and only institution we have had since the beginning," he said. "In a city where the automobile culture is based on annual change, the parish has been a central, stabilizing force for three centuries."

In an attempt to encourage settlement, Cadillac granted *habitants* strips of farmland on both sides of the river. In the absence of roads and horses, water access was crucial. In order to provide as many riverfront lots as possible, the farms were as narrow as 200 feet across but as deep as two or three miles inland. The boundaries of these so-called "ribbon farms" and the names of their owners live on in such streets as St. Aubin, Riopelle, Beaubien, Chene, St. Antoine, Cadieux, Livernois, and Dequindre.

The *habitants'* farmhouses were made of rough logs and overlooked the water. Meadows of grass and wildflowers sloped gently to the river's edge, where the principal mode of transportation, canoes, were beached. The *habitants* were indifferent farmers, but they grew enough to supplement their diet of fish and wild game. In the back of the houses were vegetable gardens and apple, cherry, and pear orchards; behind these were corn and wheat fields, pasture land and wood lots—an orderly progression

The Pilette family of Detroit, circa 1912, one of many local families who can trace their ancestry to the original group of French colonists—in this case, Jacques Pilet, a Quebec soldier who sailed to Detroit with Cadillac.

➤ *Detroit in 1766, now under British rule.*

of natural resources intended to give each settler everything needed to develop a permanent home. Beyond that was the wilderness: dark, vast, and teeming with deer, wolves, black bear, otter, beaver, pheasant, quail, and turkey.

During his nine years in Detroit, Cadillac ruled with the rights of a feudal lord. The *habitants* were required to pay him annual fees and to work for free on his farm. A blacksmith named Joseph Parent grumbled that he had to kick back 600 francs, two hogsheads of ale, and the free shoeing of all Cadillac's horses. Even Count Pontchartrain was moved to chide Cadillac in 1709 for exhibiting "too much greed." The following year Cadillac was ordered to leave Detroit to become governor of the Louisiana territory.

The jury is still out on Cadillac, who returned to France in 1717 and died there in 1730. W.J. Eccles, the noted Canadian historian, has called him "one of the worst scoundrels ever to set foot in North America."

But later generations have largely been kind to him, honoring his memory by naming everything from a western Michigan city to a luxury sedan after him. In 1972, Detroit history buffs stepped in at considerable expense to preserve his birthplace. Whatever history's verdict, this much seems clear: without Cadillac's foresight and energy, the city by the straits probably would have never been born, much less prospered and lived to see its 300th birthday.

Little changed over the ensuing decades, save for Fort Pontchartrain being renamed Fort Detroit in 1751. Even the French and Indian War of 1753–60, whose outcome would decide which European power would control this land of natural beauty

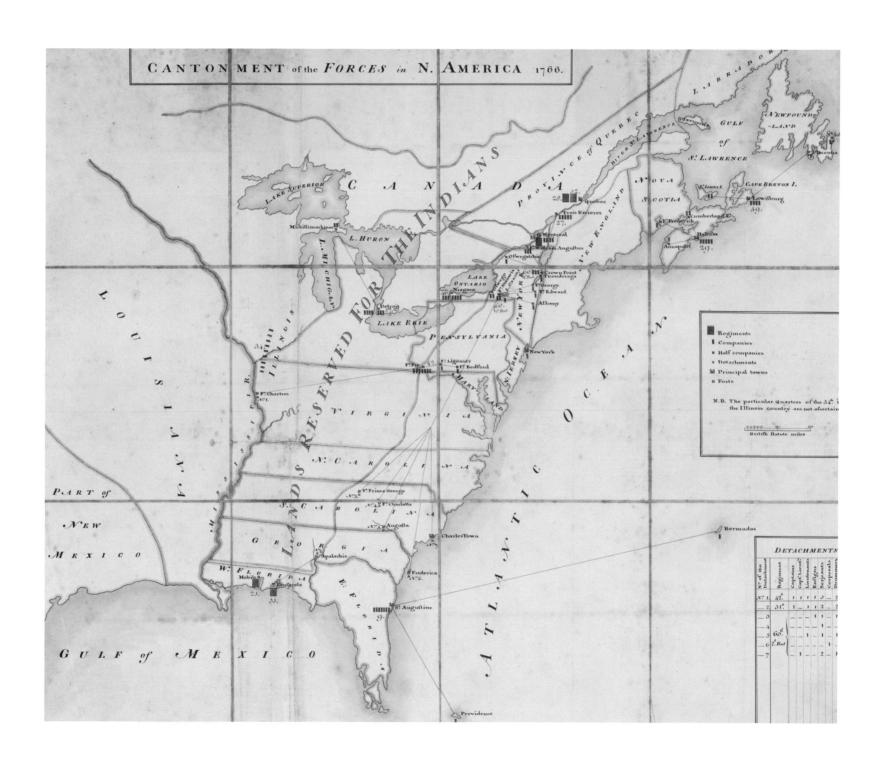

and riches, hardly touched Detroit until the fort was peacefully turned over to the British on November 29, 1760. The ceremonious surrender was the result of a French capitulation following the disastrous losses of Montreal and Quebec. That day 38 French soldiers marched through the fort's gates for the last time. With their departure, the former citadel of New France officially became a British possession.

A stroke of the pen could not as easily wipe out the animosity that existed between the Indians and the British. Unlike the French, the British did not care to mingle with the natives; they also showed a predilection for cheating them at trade. When rumors spread among the Indians that the British were going to try to starve them to death by limiting sales of gunpowder, a statesmanlike warrior named Pontiac decided it was high time for his people to do something about it.

The legendary Pontiac, recognizable to modern readers as the namesake of a city in Oakland County and an automobile division, was in 1763 the 43-year-old chief of the Ottawas. He had fought against the English in the French and Indian War and held a simmering hatred for them. Demonstrating an unprecedented knack among Indian leaders for pulling together the interests of diverse and distant tribes, he methodically forged a coalition whose mission was a general uprising that would throw the British out of the Northwest. Each tribe was assigned a specific fort, to be attacked simultaneously so that no garrison could reinforce another. Pontiac reserved Detroit as his target.

In a community that has experienced its share of murderous events, the insurrection that came to be known as Pontiac's Conspiracy remains the deadliest and most dramatic. Pontiac's plan was to enter the fort for a council with the British and, at a prearranged signal, have his companions turn on the garrison. Legend has it that a young Indian maiden tipped off Major Henry Gladwin, the fort's commander, to Pontiac's plot. Actually, news of what was brewing was fairly common knowledge among the French families, and word soon got back to Gladwin.

Gladwin was prepared for Pontiac and his followers when they entered the gate on May 7, 1763. As the Indians filed in, their robes hiding tomahawks and sawed-off muskets, they found themselves surrounded by heavily armed troops. Pontiac, realizing an attack under these circumstances would be suicidal, had to endure a severe tongue-lashing from Gladwin, who afterward had the Indians escorted from the fort.

Humiliated, Pontiac turned his fury on the Brits living outside the stockade fence. Over the next several days, scores of unwary settlers, traders, surveyors, and soldiers were massacred on Belle Isle and in the surrounding countryside. Three weeks into what would become a five-month siege, a relief expedition was ambushed; 18 men and a woman were tortured and mutilated before being tied to logs and floated down the river, past the horrified eyes of the fort's defenders. The atrocities even extended to Captain Donald Campbell, second-in-command of the garrison and a demonstrated friend of the Ottawas. When he attempted to negotiate with Pontiac under a flag of truce, he was seized and ultimately butchered, his dripping heart ripped out of his chest and devoured by the Chippewa chief.

Meanwhile, Indians had launched their coordinated attacks on the other forts. One by one, the posts fell, their garrisons either slaughtered or taken into captivity. Only Detroit held out. In July, reinforcements arrived.

◄ *Despite failing to take Detroit during a prolonged seige, Pontiac is widely recognized as the greatest Indian leader of the 18th century. His tomahawk is displayed at the Detroit Historical Museum.*

◄ *Opposite page: According to legend, Pontiac's plot to spring a surprise attack on Fort Detroit on May 7, 1763, was foiled when Major Henry Gladwin was tipped off by a young Indian maiden.*

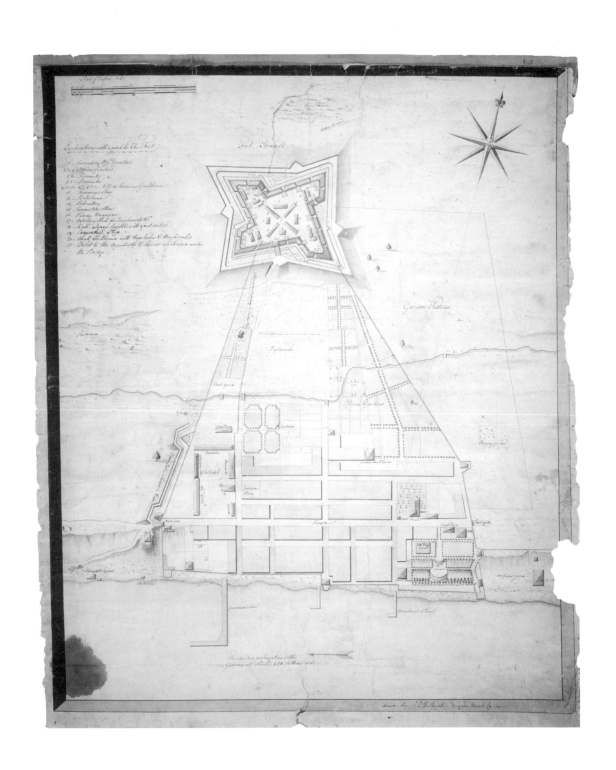

On the last day of the month, 250 men under the command of a glory hound named Captain James Dalzell marched north of the fort along the river road (now East Jefferson Avenue) in an ill-advised attempt to lift the siege. While crossing Parent's Creek near present-day Mount Elliott, the column was surprised and nearly annihilated. The creek ran red with blood, causing it to be known forever after as Bloody Run.

The siege stretched into the autumn. Suddenly, after 153 days, Pontiac made a peace offer to Gladwin. Before the embattled officer could respond, Pontiac—his unique coalition rapidly dissolving with the onset of cold weather and news that France had finalized their peace treaty with Great Britain—pulled up stakes. He left the territory, dying six years later in East St. Louis when another Indian plunged a knife into his back. Despite his ignominious death and the failure of his confederacy to oust the British from the Northwest, Pontiac stands as the most important Indian leader of the 18th century.

During the uprising many of the *habitants* living up and down both sides of the river had openly sympathized with the Indians, but after the fighting ended the French and British resumed their strained but cordial relations. Everyday life went on as it had for decades, the *habitants* scratching out a living from the lakes and their farms. "The people here are generally poor wretches," a visitor, George Croghan, wrote in 1765, "and consist of three or four hundred French families, a lazy idle people, depending chiefly on the savages for their subsistence."

Detroit's French did demonstrate an unmatched zest for life, an élan evident in the dances, horse races and other social activities that helped break up the monotony, especially during the long winters that closed off navigation and turned Detroit into a frozen, isolated community. "This was the season for French gayety and resource to display themselves," remembered one citizen. "No aid from foreign sources was needed to make the winter pass pleasantly. And who could surpass the French for parties, balls, and merry-makings!"

In 1775, with the onset of the American Revolution, Captain Henry Hamilton arrived to serve as the fort's lieutenant governor. The British officer soon became known as "Hamilton the Hair Buyer," as he organized Indian raids on American communities in Kentucky, Pennsylvania, and New York. As many as 2,000 men,

◄ Opposite page: Over a two-year period beginning in 1777, the British commander at Detroit, worried over a possible attack by Americans, had a second fort built to the north of the original stockade. Fort Lernoult was centered on present-day Fort Street and featured 11-foot-high earthen ramparts and several cannon. Later renamed Fort Shelby, it wasn't torn down until 1826.

women, and children had their scalps lifted by Hamilton's war-painted mercenaries.

Hamilton, anticipating an American attack on Detroit, later was defeated at Vincennes, Indiana, by a force under the command of George Rogers Clark. Clark never did mount his planned assault on Detroit, which after Hamilton's defeat was strengthened by the construction of a second fort a few hundred yards north of the original stockade. Fort Lernoult was centered on present-day Shelby Street and named after Hamilton's second in command, Captain Richard Lernoult. (Its name later was changed to Fort Shelby.) Even when the Treaty of Paris was signed, the British stubbornly stayed put, happy to reap the benefits of the fur trade while the two governments wrangled over technicalities. Their American landlords finally evicted them on July 11, 1796, nearly thirteen years after the war ended. Captain Moses Porter had the honor of being the first person to raise the stars and stripes over Detroit.

For the first time a part of the United States, Detroit saw its population plunge dramatically. Nearly 2,300 soldiers and civilians had lived there in 1783. Now, with the arrival of Lieutenant Colonel John Francis Hamtramck and a small contingent of soldiers, many residents eschewed American citizenship and joined the exodus of British troops relocating to the Canadian side of the river. The 1796 census showed only 500 people in Detroit.

For the next couple of decades, the settlement was stagnant. Activities remained basically those of a trading post, and its rustic complexion changed little from Cadillac's day.

This all went up in smoke on July 11, 1805. That summer morning, baker John Harvey innocently tapped his clay pipe against his boot—and before anyone knew it, the glowing plug had ignited an out-of-control fire. Residents were able to

➤ *Detroit burns to the ground on July 11, 1805.*
Although no lives were lost, the only structures left
standing were a stone building and Fort Lernoult.

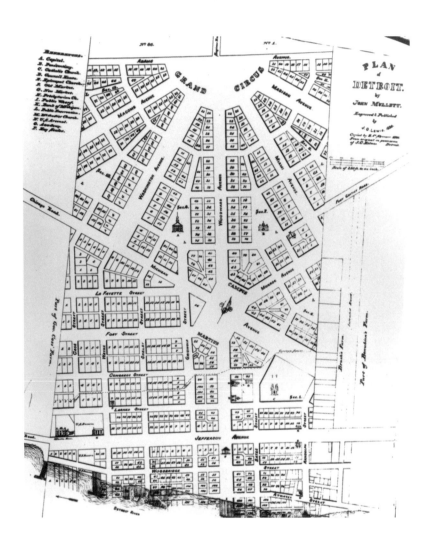

▲ A fragment of Judge Woodward's ambitious plan to rebuild Detroit in a series of wide boulevards and intersecting parks called "circuses."

flee to safety, but the blaze quickly consumed all but one of the settlement's 300 closely packed wooden buildings. "In the course of three hours," one observer wrote in his journal, "nothing was to be seen of our city except a mass of burning coals and chimney tops, stretching like pyramids in the air."

A few weeks after the fire was finally put out, Judge Augustus Brevoort Woodward, one of three federal appointees sent to govern the newly established Territory of Michigan, arrived from Washington. The tall but stooped 31-year-old judge with the hooked nose and brusque manner had been trained in the classics at Columbia University and was a close friend of President Thomas Jefferson. Woodward was a bit obsessed with ancient Greece. As part of the committee charged with rebuilding the blackened ruins on federal land east of the fort, he envisioned creating a "modern Bosphorus" near "immense Mediterraneans." He also was infatuated with the work of Pierre Charles L'Enfant, the French-born architect who had laid out the streets, parks, and boulevards of the nation's capital. Woodward's idea was to lay out Detroit in 200-foot-wide boulevards and intersecting parks called "circuses," a pattern of circles and spokes that could be repeated *ad infinitum* as the community grew.

The displaced frontier folks, who wanted to rebuild in the old style—cramped lots, narrow streets—before the snow fell, thought Woodward was nuts. Much of the opposition to Woodward's grandiose plan stemmed from distaste for the judge's personal habits. He was noted for his body odor, which, considering the level of personal hygiene then, is really saying something. He rarely bathed, preferring to sit outside on a chair during rainstorms. He was known to keep a glass of brandy next to him on the bench, and he admitted to once spending $300 on wine trying to bribe a congressman.

Idiosyncrasies aside, Woodward today is recognized by some scholars as one of America's most creative urban planners, though most of his original plan never became reality. "You have well named that main avenue Witherell," he complained to one of the judges who felt compelled to narrow some streets and arbitrarily cut off others, "for you have withered my beautiful plan of Detroit and have spoiled the beauty and symmetry of the city of Detroit for all time." Over the following decades, the community grew along conventional grid street patterns.

Woodward remained a controversial figure in Detroit until leaving in 1823. In 1817 he enacted a plan of public education that established the "Catholepistemiad" in Detroit—a university that called for subjects like "iatrica" and "physiognostica" to be taught by "didactors." Such polysyllabic Greek verbiage confounded Lewis Cass, Michigan's leading politician of the 19th century. Cass referred to the school at Bates and Congress streets as "Cathole-what's-its-name." The academy later was relocated to Ann Arbor and became the University of Michigan.

It was near Ann Arbor that Woodward purchased 700 acres of land in 1822, intending to erect a model metropolis named after Prince Demetrios Ypsilanti, then a hero in Greece's war to win independence. Before this latest dream could be realized, Woodward was reassigned to a district bench in Florida, where he died in 1827. However, in a final strike of philhellenic homage, Woodward got around the new owners' desire to name the property "Springfield" by imperiously registering the area as "Ypsilanti."

While Judge Woodward is best remembered for his ambitions and eccentricities, one of his contemporaries, General William Hull, gained infamy as a coward whose actions during the War of 1812 caused Detroit to become the only major American city ever occupied by a foreign army.

Hull, a Revolutionary War hero who had accompanied Woodward to Detroit in 1805 to serve as territorial governor, reluctantly accepted command of some 1,600 soldiers and volunteers after a second war broke out with England in 1812. While cautiously organizing an attack on undermanned Fort Malden, located across the river in Amherstburg and ripe to be taken, Hull heard reports of the fall of Mackinac and of his supply lines being breached near Monroe. He ordered a retreat back to Detroit.

A British force of several hundred regulars and militiamen,

∧ *Lewis Cass was the most prominent Detroit politician of the 19th century. He arrived in 1813 as the 31-year-old governor of the Michigan Territory and became rich through land speculation. He later served as the minister to France, as a U.S. Senator, and as secretary of state in President James Buchanan's administration. In 1848, he ran unsuccessfully for president on the Democratic ticket, the closest any Detroiter has ever gotten to the White House.*

∨ *The sword of Lewis Cass.*

➤ *General "Mad Anthony" Wayne, a Revolutionary War hero, passed into local lore in the summer of 1794, when his U.S. troops defeated a combined British and Indian force determined to keep the Americans out of the Northwest Territory. The Battle of Fallen Timbers, fought in northern Ohio, convinced the British to finally surrender Detroit—13 years after the treaty formally ending the American Revolution was signed. General Wayne subsequently became the namesake of Wayne County (established July 15, 1796), the city of Wayne (originally called Derby's Corners), and Fort Wayne, the 82-acre fort erected on West Jefferson in the 1840s to protect the city against Canadian attack.*

their ranks swelled by about 500 Indians, approached. Although the Americans outnumbered their foes, General Sir Isaac Brock had the upper hand when it came to gamesmanship. The British commander whipped up rumors of exaggerated troop strength and dropped hints that, should Detroit fall, the Indians could be expected to massacre every last American. While Hull pondered all this, British cannonballs began raining down. Civilians joined troops in hunkering down inside the palisaded walls. Several men were killed, and even Judge Woodward was sent scurrying for cover when one shot crashed through his bedroom wall and landed in the fireplace.

Hull, a corpulent, good-natured 60-year-old who enjoyed the better things in life, lost his nerve. Among those whose fates he had to consider were those of his own son, daughter, and grandchildren. On August 16, 1812, he surrendered his superior and well-armed force to Brock. And he did it without delivering a single shot in defense of Detroit. It was one of the greatest debacles in U.S. military history and nearly cost Hull his life—by American musketry. At war's end he was court-martialed for cowardice and neglect of duty and sentenced to be shot, but President James Monroe, remembering Hull's Revolutionary War service, spared him. Hull returned to his native Massachusetts, where he died in disgrace in 1825. Detroiters, who endured a painful year-long occupation by the British because of Hull, felt the shame for decades to come.

With the danger of Indian attacks largely gone, Detroit's image as a military outpost evaporated. In 1826 Fort Shelby was torn down, leaving Detroit without palisades for the first time in its history. Meanwhile, the Erie Canal was completed. The 363-mile waterway from Albany, New York, to Buffalo drastically cut the time and expense involved in settlers moving west. It quickly made Cadillac's original vision of Detroit as the "gateway to the West" a reality. "We can now go from Detroit to New York in five and a half days," marveled the *Detroit Gazette*. "Before the war, it took at least two months more." By the middle 1830s, hundreds of people each day were being funneled through Detroit into the heartland. More than a few—many of them merchants from New York and New England—opted to put down roots. Collectively, they were known as "Bostonians." As the population mushroomed, these easterners—more serious and literate than the old-line

▲ *In 1818, Walk-in-the-Water became the first steamship on the Detroit River, offering regular passenger service to Buffalo. Steamships, coupled with the opening of the Erie Canal a few years later, encouraged immigration to Michigan and expedited Detroit's growth.*

Clarence Monroe Burton

It's an old saw that any institution is the lengthened shadow of one man, and nowhere is that more true than at the world-famous Burton Historical Collection, housed inside the main branch of the Detroit Public Library. Containing an estimated half a million items of immense historical and genealogical importance, this repository was the result of the single-minded quest of Detroit attorney Clarence Monroe Burton to preserve as much of the past as possible, before time and neglect inflicted their usual damage.

The scope of Burton's interest encompassed Detroit, the Great Lakes, Michigan, New England, and New France, with many of the materials dating as far back as the 1600s. Included are maps, newspapers, diaries, military records, wills and probate records, baptisms and cemetery inscriptions, obituaries, census schedules, scrapbooks, business records, photographs, and numerous other items gathered by Burton between 1874 and 1914.

During this period Burton outlived his first two wives and married a third time, siring a total of nine children. He also created a very successful abstract title company and still found time to serve as city historian and in several other civic posts. Generally speaking, Burton demonstrated little passion outside of his bed, business, or books. He disdained drink and nonworking vacations. But although he was known during his adult life as a rather stiff, no-nonsense type, Burton had an early life that rivaled any French *voyageur* for adventure.

He was born in 1853 in a log cabin near the mining town of Whiskey Diggings, California. His father, a physician and founder of the *Battle Creek Journal*, had impulsively hauled his family west to mine gold. While Clarence was still a baby, the family sailed from California to Panama. On the second day of the voyage, criminals hidden aboard the ship robbed the passengers and sank the vessel. Several people drowned. The Burtons, however, were rescued and relocated to the old Spanish town of San Diego. From there they drove a team of oxen and a wagon north to San Francisco. Within a year the peripatetic Burtons were on the move again. After settling for a short while in New York City, the family eventually made its way back to the small community of Hastings, Michigan.

Burton came to Detroit in 1874 after earning a law degree from the University of Michigan. He didn't receive a diploma because he refused to pay a few cents for the actual sheepskin. Burton's penurious nature was evident throughout his life; even when he could well afford it, he would walk rather than ride a streetcar.

The young lawyer didn't scrimp on books and other materials related to his major field of interest: history, particularly documents relating to the exploration and settling of the Old Northwest (today's

▼ *The many historical works of Clarence Monroe Burton included* Landmarks of Detroit.

Midwest). When he was making $100 a year and sleeping on a cot inside the office of his first employer, the law firm of Ward & Palmer, Burton somehow found a way to set aside a few dollars for purchases. By the time he started the Burton Abstract Company in 1891 to examine land titles, he had already gathered an impressive library of books and original documents inside his house on Brainard Street. Always eager to share what he had, Burton threw open the doors of his fireproof library to scholars and casual researchers.

They were apt to find just about anything: a diary of "Mad Anthony" Wayne, for example, or a letter written by George Washington. Burton spared no expense or effort in recovering documents, regularly traveling to remote overseas locales or forwarding blank, signed checks to dealers. The thrill of the hunt drove him. Once, he found the valuable 200-year-old papers of fur trader John Askin moldering in an abandoned chicken coop.

Much of what Burton uncovered appeared in an endless stream of books and pamphlets. His first book, a biography of Antoine de la Mothe Cadillac, appeared in 1895 and was followed by several more volumes of history and biography. Most of Burton's works were self-published ventures that ate up even more of his money. His abstract company, however, expanded with the city, eventually growing into one of the country's largest and providing Detroit's number one historical collector with a ready source of capital. By 1914, however, the magnitude and expense of his passion threatened to overwhelm him and his house, so he donated his collection to the city. As city historian, he continued to contribute time, money, and materials.

Burton died in 1932, but his original library has continued to grow. Notable additions over the years have included Ernie Harwell's collection of materials on the early days of baseball, as well as the 550,000 files of the Detroit Police Department's infamous "Red Squad."

The benefactor's unselfish legacy was best summed up by an admirer, who said that the man who spent his life preserving integral data about Detroit's past "has revealed to us the historic associations of the place wherein we dwell."

⋀ *Thanks to Burton's diligence, Detroit's Main Library houses one of the finest collections of materials about the Great Lakes and the Old Northwest.*

The Mayors of Detroit

Moreso than in most places, Detroit's evolving image is embodied in the personalities and policies of its political leaders. In fact, when respected urban historian Melvin G. Holli recently published his book on America's most influential big-city mayors, no less than three Detroit office holders made the list: Hazen S. Pingree, Frank Murphy, and Coleman Young.

The first took the brand-new office in 1824. John R. Williams, a judge and county commissioner, wrote the original city charter. Citizens showed their appreciation by electing him mayor several times and naming not one, but two streets—John R and Williams—after him.

Early mayors had little clout. Decisions were made by the common council, whose number grew with the city. At its peak, Detroit was run by 42 aldermen, all of whom were beholden to the real keepers of the keys—the saloon owners, who typically controlled the wards. "Boodle" remained the time-honored grease of local politics until 1918. That year, after decades of scandal and corruption involving aldermen and ward heelers, Detroiters adopted a new charter that provided for a nine-member at-large city council and gave greater power to the mayor.

To date, 59 Detroiters have been called Hizzoner, and they have been a mixed bag. Many have their names adorning streets, freeways, and public buildings, a tribute to their efficacy or inoffensive natures. Some were so crooked they could drink soup with a corkscrew. At least one was flat-out apathetic about the office. "I never wanted to be mayor of Detroit," admitted John C. Lodge, who lost his reelection bid. "The result was no disappointment to me, and when it was known the following morning I remarked to my sister at breakfast that I was genuinely glad of it."

A choice few put a real stamp on the city, in the process helping to define this schizophrenic metropolis to the rest of the country. From the first to the present, here are Detroit's main men:

John R. Williams (1824–25, 1830, 1844–46)

Henry J. Hunt (1826)

Jonathon Kearsley (1826*, 1829)

John Biddle (1827–28)

Marshall Chapin (1831, 1833)

Levi Cook (1832, 1835–36)

C.C. Trowbridge (1834)

Andrew Mack (1834*)

Henry Howard (1837)

Augustas A. Porter (1838)

Asher B. Bates (1838*)

De Garmo Jones (1839)

Zina Pitcher (1840–41, 1843)

Douglas Houghton (1842)

James A. Van Dyke (1847)

Frederick Buhl (1848)

Charles Howard (1849)

John LaDue (1850)

Zachariah Chandler (1851)

John H. Harmon (1852–53)

Oliver M. Hyde (1854, 1856–57)

Henry Ledyard (1855)

John Patton (1858–59)

Christian H. Buhl (1860–61)

William C. Duncan (1862–63)

Kirkland C. Barker (1864–65)

Merrill I. Mills (1866–67)

William W. Wheaton (1868–71)

Hugh Moffat (1872–75)

Alexander Lewis (1876–77)

George C. Langdon (1878–79)

William G. Thompson (1880–83)

S. B. Grummond (1884–85)

M. H. Chamberlain (1886–87)

John Pridgeon Jr. (1888–89)

Hazen S. Pingree (1890–97)

William Pickert (1897*)

William C. Maybury (1897–1904)

George P. Codd (1905–06)

William B. Thompson (1907–08, 1911–12)

Philip Breitmeyer (1909–10)

Oscar B. Marx (1913–18)

James Couzens (1919–22)

Frank E. Doremus (1923–24)

Joseph A. Martin (1924*)

John C. Lodge (1924, 1928–30)

John W. Smith (1924–27)

Charles Bowles (1930)

Frank Murphy (1930–33)

Frank Couzens (1933–37)

Richard W. Reading (1938–39)

Edward R. Jeffries Jr. (1940–47)

Eugene I. Van Antwerp (1948–49)

Albert E. Cobo (1950–57)

Louis C. Miriani (1958–61)

Jerome P. Cavanagh (1962–69)

Roman S. Gribbs (1970–73)

Coleman A. Young (1974–93)

Dennis W. Archer (1994–2001)

indicates acting mayor

WE HOPE FOR BETTER THINGS; IT WILL ARISE FROM ITS ASHES —*Official motto of Detroit by Fr. Gabriel Richard*

French families—came to dominate local cultural and commercial affairs.

The Michigan Territory was granted statehood in 1837, and for the next ten years Detroit served as the state capital. During this remarkable period of growth Detroit bloomed from a village into a city. In 1850 the census showed 21,019 people living in the former trading post, a tenfold increase in just two decades. Today that figure is surpassed by the population of nearly every suburb in Metro Detroit. But 150 years ago—a time when the overwhelming majority of Americans still lived on farms—only a score of other U.S. cities were larger.

For good and bad, Detroit took on the characteristics of an urban community. For the first time, public safety was a major issue, as citizens wrestled with the proliferation of grog shops, brothels, and transient crime. Land speculation was rampant. The need for safe water, reliable roads, effective education, and other basic services increased. Detroiters accepted the challenges, forming militias and volunteer fire companies and grumpily paying taxes to support the better good. However, along with all that was being gained in the rush of progress, something intangible also was being lost.

One September day in 1832, Detroit's most beloved citizen, Father Gabriel Richard, died. He had contracted cholera while ministering to the sick during one of the outbreaks that periodically gripped the city. Father Richard, born into a prominent French family in 1764, was a pioneer in every sense of the word. After surviving the French Revolution and several years as a missionary in New France, he arrived in Detroit in 1798 to serve as St. Anne's assistant pastor. Four years later he was named pastor. Fr. Richard, who could write and speak in seven languages, brought the first printing press to Michigan and in 1809 published Detroit's first newspaper, the short-lived *Michigan Essay or The Impartial Observer*. He started four small schools and in 1823 became the first Roman Catholic priest to be elected a U.S. Congressman.

But it was his unflagging devotion to the community and his religion that set him apart. His optimistic words in the wake of the 1805 fire— "Speramus meliora;

⋏ *Father Gabriel Richard—missionary, publisher, congressman—was the most influential religious leader in the city's history.*

⋏ Michigan entered the union in 1837 and Detroit served as the state capital for the next decade. After the legislature relocated to Lansing, the original Capitol Building on Griswold Street was turned into a high school.

➤ Opposite page: A view of Detroit from the Windsor side of the river in the late 1830s.

resurget cineribus"—survive as the official motto of Detroit: "We hope for better things; it will arise from its ashes."

During his years on the frontier, Fr. Richard had traveled far and wide to tend to the poor, the hungry, and the sick. As a man who routinely neglected his own health, his death from a highly contagious disease, while not entirely unexpected, still was a shock to the citizenry. "During his sickness," reported the *Detroit Free Press*, "his room was filled with all classes, every one wishing to aid their worthy and departing friend. His funeral was attended at 4 o'clock in the afternoon, by a numerous concourse; and by estimation more than two thousand people, of all ranks and denominations, followed the remains of this profound scholar, and firm supporter of the Catholic faith and true lover of American liberty, to the cold and silent grave."

As much as any other single event, the priest's passing fore-shadowed the vanishing of the old French society in Detroit. The future could be seen everywhere one looked. The first passenger train appeared, followed by the first hospital and public school. Hundreds of brick buildings were built. Churches and temples of various faiths were constructed. Gaslights and telegraph wires became part of the landscape. Shipbuilding and heavy industry sprang up along the shoreline, the *voyageurs*' song replaced "by the shriek of the steam-whistle and the laborious snort of the propeller," lamented Bela Hubbard. Minor streams once favored for fishing were either filled in or converted into covered sewers. Fur ceased being a major part of the local economy, and many of the original ribbon farms were subdivided. By the approach of the American Civil War, Cadillac's village had been rebuilt along modern lines, and peopled by newcomers from foreign lands, and amidst all this hubbub the simple world of the *habitants* soon faded from the busy city's collective memory.

See You at the Michigan State Fair

For two weeks at the end of every summer, tens of thousands of people from throughout Michigan congregate at the State Fairgrounds on Woodward, just south of Eight Mile, to celebrate the Michigan State Fair. For years the fair has featured everything from thrill rides and band concerts to pie eating contests, barnyard animal races, and agricultural exhibits. Fair director John Hertel once called the experience tantamount to "going to Cedar Point, Pine Knob, and your grandfather's farm—all in one day."

The country's oldest state fair began in 1849, just 12 years after Michigan gained statehood. In an effort to promote agricultural products and implements and to foster communication between the rural and urban populations, the Michigan Agricultural Society sponsored a three-day exhibition on grounds on the west side of Woodward, between Columbia and High streets. Except for 1893, when a lack of funds prevented the fair from being held, and during the World War II era, the fair has returned every year since its inception.

Until the fair found a permanent Detroit home, numerous cities throughout the state— including Lansing, Grand Rapids, Kalamazoo, and Jackson—hosted what many considered to be *the* state event of the year. In 1905, Joseph L. Hudson, Detroit's leading retailer, gave 135 acres of farmland seven miles north of Detroit to the Michigan Agricultural Society in order to create a permanent state fairgrounds. After acquiring more land, the society gave the property to the state in 1921.

At the time, more Americans lived on farms and in small towns than in cities. An expedition to Detroit in those days represented a considerable investment of time, money, and trouble, but the payoff for fairgoers was a chance to be educated and entertained. In an era when excitement on an everyday basis was in short supply, the fair was always good for a few thrills. This was especially true in the early days of the automotive and aviation industries, when tinkerers and daredevils could be found showing off their specialties to open-mouthed visitors.

Although it has often failed to turn a profit, and attendance has varied due to weather and economics, the state fair is a tradition that Metro Detroiters have embraced and eagerly anticipate. For many, it is their only exposure to farm animals and a way of life that their great-grandparents once took for granted. City dwellers learn about their country roots, rural traditions, and where their food comes from, while country folk are exposed to an urbanized lifestyle of large crowds, noisy thrill rides, and splashy big-time entertainment.

The Michigan State Fair of the 21st century may be highlighted by gut-splitting rides like the Turbo-Force and the Mega Drop, or the nightly entertainment of acts like the O'Jays, Alice Cooper, and Bob Dylan, but it is the old-time agricultural exhibits and festivities that continue to draw the core group of visitors.

∨ / ➤ Young picnickers and an exotic looking belly dancer were all part of the scene at the State Fair, circa 1900. Today's fair boasts thrill rides and big-name entertainers while still staying true to its rural roots.

WHERE LIFE IS WORTH LIVING

By the time of the Civil War, many of the economic cornerstones of preindustrial Detroit were in place: warehouses, docks and wharves, railroad lines and shipping vessels, a growing immigrant workforce. The former fort was evolving into a manufacturing and commercial center, with hundreds of companies, large and small, producing such diverse items as shoes, stoves, paints, varnishes, cigars, drugs, patent medicines, boats, hoopskirts, railroad cars, steel rails, soap, brass fittings, and seeds for local consumption and for export.

"Detroit will resolve into one of the greatest industrial islands on earth," the city's first millionaire, self-made tycoon Eber Brock Ward, predicted at the time. "With immense supplies of iron and copper to the north, coal to the south, the Detroit River in front and canals on either end, the city cannot miss." When Ward (whose many accomplishments included turning out the first Bessemer steel in America at a Wyandotte mill) dropped dead on a downtown street one winter day in 1875, the 63-year-old entrepreneur was worth $5 million—just one of several fortunes made during this big-shouldered, transitional stage of Detroit's history.

The citizenry considered itself morally progressive. In 1830, the controversial hanging of a murderer at a downtown gallows prompted a movement that led to Michigan becoming the first state to outlaw capital punishment. On several occasions between 1834 and 1859 self-righteous mobs took it

◄ *Woodward Avenue in the 1890s.*

➤ *Eber Brock Ward.*

STOCKHOLDERS
OF THE UNDERGROUND
R. R. COMPANY
Hold on to Your Stock!!

The market has an upward tendency. By the express train which arrived this morning at 3 o'clock, fifteen thousand dollars worth of human merchandise, consisting of twenty-nine able bodied men and women, fresh and sound, from the Carolina and Kentucky plantations, have arrived safe at the depot on the other side, where all our sympathising colonization friends may have an opportunity of expressing their sympathy by bringing forward donations of ploughs, &c., farming utensils, pick axes and hoes, and not old clothes; as these emigrants all can till the soil. N.B.—Stockholders don't forget, the meeting to-day at 2 o'clock at the ferry on the Canada side. All persons desiring to take stock in this prosperous company, be sure to be on hand.
By Order of the
Detroit, April 19, 1853.   BOARD OF DIRECTORS.

upon themselves to burn down houses of prostitution. Temperance and antislavery societies flourished, with Detroit becoming the last major stop for escaped slaves fleeing to freedom in Canada. The "underground railroad" was a secret network of houses, churches, barns, haystacks, attics, cellars, and other hiding places that stretched from the southern United States north to Canada. Several Detroit-area communities, including Farmington, Wyandotte, Rochester, Plymouth, Mount Clemens, and Birmingham, were way stations on this clandestine freedom road, over which an estimated 50,000 African Americans traveled between 1830 and 1860.

Detroit, like many northern cities in the decades leading up to the Civil War, had a very active antislavery movement. While a handful of slaves existed in the city until about 1830, these were owned by citizens who had originally bought them during the period of British occupation. After Detroit raised the stars and stripes above its stockade walls in 1796, no new slaves were brought here. The new state constitution, signed in 1835, specifically outlawed slavery in Michigan. After that the abolition movement grew quickly, and incidents between abolitionists and slave hunters became more common and sometimes very severe.

On one occasion, in 1833, a mob of mostly black Detroiters surrounded the jail on Gratiot where the sheriff was waiting to haul a slave couple back to Kentucky. A sympathizer was somehow able to exchange clothes with the imprisoned woman, allowing her to flee to Canada; the husband was freed a couple of days later when another mob attacked the sheriff en route to Kentucky.

Because of its proximity to Canada, Detroit naturally played a vital role in the protection and transportation of escaped slaves, who by the 1840s were worth as much as $1,800 apiece to their owners. There were several stations in the down-town area, including the city's first two black churches, St. Matthew's Episcopal at Woodward and Holbrook, and Second Baptist, located on Monroe near Greektown. Second Baptist was founded in 1836 by 13 former slaves, just a small percentage of the hundreds of black freedmen and freedwomen who decided to put down roots in the city.

"On any night of the week, the church could expect the arrival of passengers on the railroad," wrote historian Arthur M. Woodford. "The pastor would receive a note from one of his members which might read: 'Pastor, tomorrow night at our 8 p.m. meeting, let's read Exodus 10:8.' In Underground language, that meant Conductor No. 2 will be arriving at 8 p.m. with ten slaves, eight men and two women."

The busiest station was the livery stable of Seymour Finney, who operated the Temperance House at the corner of Woodward and Gratiot (today the site of the Kern Block). Finney's stable was a block away at State and Griswold, where the Detroit Bank & Trust branch office now stands. A bronze plaque on the bank's wall marks the spot where countless escapees were fed, hidden by day, then spirited away at night across the Detroit River in canoes and barges.

A couple of important historical events had their roots in Detroit's antislavery activities. In 1854, local merchant Zachariah Chandler helped organize political rallies in response to the Fugitive Slave Act, which was designed in part to derail the Underground Railroad. A larger meeting of similar committees from around the state was held that July in Jackson. There the Republican Party was founded.

Five years later, the fiery abolitionist John Brown delivered 15 escaped slaves from Missouri to the city on the very day the noted orator Frederick Douglass visited local black leader William Webb. That night, inside Webb's house on Congress

◄ *Opposite page: Detroiters anxious to honor veterans of the Civil War raised $75,000 to erect the Soldiers and Sailors Monument on Campus Martius. It was unveiled on April 9, 1872, the seventh anniversary of the end of the war. The new city hall (background) had been opened just nine months earlier.*

▼ *The Civil War created several local heroes, including General Orlando Willcox (who received the Medal of Honor) and Private Robert Hendershot, one of the most famous drummer boys in the Union army.*

"DETROIT IS THE HANDSOMEST CITY IN THE WORLD."

— Robert Woods, Joliet, Illinois

near St. Antoine, the bearded, wild-eyed Brown outlined his radical plan to lead a series of slave revolts throughout the South. Brown then crossed into Canada, picking up recruits for his infamous and ill-fated attack on the Union arsenal at Harper's Ferry in Virginia.

Detroiters did their part in preserving the Union. Between 1861 and 1865, 6,000 men from the city joined another 3,213 from other parts of Wayne County in heeding the call to serve in Mr. Lincoln's army and navy. The first to leave for the front were the 780 members of the First Michigan Volunteer Infantry, who on May 13, 1861 were presented with their colors in a grand ceremony in Campus Martius. Three days later it became the first western unit to arrive in Washington, prompting Lincoln to proclaim, "Thank God for Michigan!" The regiment was bloodied at Bull Run, but like all of the subsequent units mustered into service—including the First Michigan Colored Infantry—it proved its mettle amidst the cannon shot and whizzing minié balls at such distant battlefields as Antietam, Fredericksburg, Chickamauga, Gettysburg and Cold Harbor. Six Detroiters received the Congressional Medal of Honor for heroism, while another, Lieutenant Julian Dickinson of Michigan's 4th Cavalry, helped capture Confederate president Jefferson Davis at war's end.

Veterans returned to a city whose progress had barely been impeded by four years of war. While the soldiers were away, the Detroit Police Department was formed (though it wasn't until after the war that the first uniformed patrolmen worked a beat) and the first horse-drawn streetcars clop-clopped down Jefferson Avenue. Harper Hospital, built in 1864 on land donated by a reclusive eccentric named Walter Harper, started off as a government-run military hospital caring for Civil War wounded before maturing into a private facility and medical college. In time, the original wooden barracks were replaced by a modern building on John R Street. Today Harper and its neighbor, Grace Hospital, are integral parts of the Detroit Medical Center.

The evolution of the fire department also was a wonder. Fire companies in the 19th century were highly competitive fraternal organizations that often fought

⋏ *The city's fire-fighting apparatus remained at least partially horse-drawn through 1922.*

⋏ *The main boat landing at the river entrance to the Detroit International Exposition, held September 17-27, 1889.*

◄ *Opposite page: The corner of Lafayette and Michigan avenues in the 1890s.*

each other instead of the fire they were responding to. About the time war broke out, the volunteers were replaced by a paid municipal department. By century's turn it had evolved into one of the best in the country, using such modern equipment as water towers (to fight fires in tall buildings) and, beginning in 1908, motor vehicles in place of horse-drawn engines.

The thunder of horse-drawn engines attracted its share of "sidewalk chiefs," like business executive William Ducharme. According to the memoirs of John C. Lodge, Ducharme "would run to a fire at any time of the day or night." There were others, like attorney John W. Anderson. "No matter how important the client sitting in his office might be, Anderson would slam down his roll-top desk, pull out his watch, and exclaim, 'I am due in court right now,' and depart for the fire."

Characters like these stood out in what essentially was still a small town. In 1880, Detroit's 120,000 citizens lived within a three-mile radius of the original riverfront settlement. The neighborhoods featured block after block of single-family frame homes, typically painted green or white. Unlike other growing cities hemmed in by geographical obstacles, Detroit did not have to expand vertically in the form of tenements. There was plenty of land to subdivide and develop.

∧ *July 4, 1871: City council members get ready to move from the old city hall to a new one across the street.*

The city was a sight to behold, to judge by the comments of Robert Woods of Joliet, Illinois, who visited in the 1880s. "Detroit is the handsomest city in the world," he rhapsodized. "Its handsome boulevard, bordered with broad green grass plots fringed with beautiful flowers and canopied with the foliage of contiguous trees, its electric towers with their silver light; its broad, deep river, its charming suburbs and numerous retreats for pleasure and recreation, and above all the spirit and disposition of its people combine to make it an attractive and desirable place of residence or for business." The leafy avenues and orderly neighborhoods gave Detroit its first national identity— "the Paris of the West." In September 1889 the city was feeling so good about itself that it held the Detroit International Fair and Exposition on a 14-acre site just south of Fort Wayne. A grand exhibition hall—at the time the largest in the world—was built to show off the city's industrial and agricultural capabilities.

⋏ *The Edison Illuminating Company began installing street lights in Detroit in 1884, five years after the first experimental electric lighting first appeared in the city. Electricity slowly replaced gas as the decades passed, with Edison's customer base growing from a mere 7,000 in 1903 to nearly one million in 1950.*

◄ *This circa-1890 view of Woodward Avenue shows one of the 125-foot-high electric towers that once dominated the downtown skyline. The widely ridiculed towers were excellent for illuminating the sky, critics observed, but not the streets and sidewalks below.*

▾ Zachariah Chandler was an abolitionist, a prosperous merchant, Detroit's first "dry" mayor, and one of the fathers of the anti-slavery Republican Party. When he died in 1879, he was one of the city's wealthiest citizens and most accomplished politicians, having performed great service to the Union in the Lincoln and Grant administrations during and after the Civil War.

During this period two utilities that generations of Detroiters have taken for granted made their first appearances. The city's first "speaking telephone" was installed in 1877, and the following year a four-page phone book was issued listing all 124 subscribers. In 1886, the Edison Illuminating Company was organized in Detroit by 18 well-heeled backers. It would be many years before most homes had switched over from gas and kerosene lamps to electric lighting, though the city installed garishly painted electric towers in a controversial attempt to illuminate downtown streets. The 125-foot towers were too high to be of much use and were ugly to boot, but they stuck around for about 30 years before they were finally removed.

It was a decidedly quieter time, even as the population edged past 200,000 by 1890, then swelled to nearly 300,000 a decade later as immigrants from all over the world arrived to fill jobs in the shops and factories. There were no radios or televisions, no airplanes or pneumatic jackhammers. For women and children, making conversation on the front porch was the usual way of whiling away an evening, though the piano in the parlor also was a central gathering spot for family and neighbors.

Work was largely seasonal, which gave too many men too much time to mumble into their beer. The pull of the saloon, with its hearty camaraderie, nickel suds, and free lunch, was so strong that employers and landlords typically stipulated in their classified ads that prospects be "sober." They often were disappointed, adding fuel to the local temperance movement, which was fiercely resisted by the city's largest ethnic group, the Germans.

As a rule, families were large and life expectancies short. In 1900, the average Polish-American mother had five children and could expect to live to be 46. Disease, hard work, and poor diet took their toll. Theresa Konieczny, born in 1897 to parents who years earlier had left Poland to work in the stove plants, remembered that two of her eight siblings died in infancy. A third, her sister Lillian, died while giving birth to her ninth child. She was only 38.

"Domestic engineering" is a subject rarely mentioned in history books, probably because everyday life for housewives in Detroit, as elsewhere, was pure drudgery. Nearly all households had at least one live-in maid, usually a young immigrant girl who exchanged her labor for room, board, and possibly a dollar or two a week. At century's turn, few immigrant households could afford primitive

Sea Serpents in the Detroit River

During the summer of 1897, the *Detroit News–Tribune* got its readers in a panic by reporting a series of sea serpent sightings on the Great Lakes. After weighing all of the evidence provided by mariners and other witnesses, the paper concluded that "the existence of the sea serpents is clearly one of fact." In August a city official spotted an 87-foot-long beast, sporting antlers and a single eye, in the Detroit River. Before he could organize a posse, however, the creature had "made good its escape into the green waters of Lake Erie." Ten days later, a 17-foot serpent with a mouth as large as a coal stove "came to grief" at the foot of Joseph Campau. It was reportedly being stuffed for presentation to the Detroit Scientific Research Association when it mysteriously disappeared.

electrical appliances like irons and vacuum cleaners. Housework was one relentless, thankless cycle of baking, sewing, ironing, and drawing water (usually from an outside pump) and boiling copper tubs of it for bathing and cooking. Because most residential streets were unpaved and most floors uncarpeted, they also had to sweep the never-ending dust out of the house.

Detroit was not without its squalor. A ghetto of filthy, ramshackle housing and anything-goes "pesthouses" was firmly established on the lower east side, catering to the poor, the unemployed, the transient, and the depraved. There were plenty of each—enough to give the city's few policemen pause about entering the area. Some denizens were savvy enough to routinely volunteer themselves to the House of Correction, figuring it a "good place to winter."

On the cheap, unincorporated land outside city limits, immigrant workers and their families squeezed into tumbled down sheds erected next to the small factories

The Big Pileups

Were snowfalls in Detroit really that much more plentiful in great-grandma's day, or have they simply grown larger in memory? For whatever reason—meteorological or mythical—it's a fact that eight of the city's ten largest recorded snowfalls happened between 1875 and 1900, with the whopper occurring on April 6, 1886. That astonishing early spring storm dumped 24.5 inches of heavy wet snow on the city, shutting down nearly all public transportation and commerce. "Business is almost suspended at J.L. Hudson & Co.'s stores," reported one daily, "the whole force of clerks being ready to wait on a single customer."

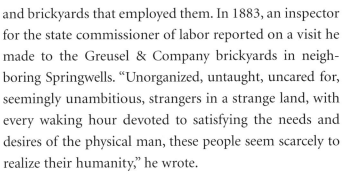

Detroit's record snowfall was removed from the business district in the back-breaking fashion of the day: shoveled by hand into horse-drawn wagons and then carted to the foot of Woodward, where it was dumped into the Detroit River. Municipal plows and scrapers also were employed, though it wouldn't be until the 1920s that these vehicles were motorized. Private citizens stuck inside their homes were left to their own devices. They could either "take the day off and grumble in mailless solitude," as one newspaper put it, or attempt to dig out of the surrounding snowbanks. Many hired laborers were provided by the Poor Commission, paying them 50 cents or so to struggle with a shovel.

While the blizzards of a century ago may have been more severe, they generally were less stressful. In fact, winter was considered the most dependable season of the year for travel. The muddy ruts that characterized warm-weather roads were gone, as streets often were rolled smooth after snowstorms, allowing frolickers to glide gracefully through the Currier & Ives landscape in their one-horse open sleighs.

▼ *Woodward in winter.*

and brickyards that employed them. In 1883, an inspector for the state commissioner of labor reported on a visit he made to the Greusel & Company brickyards in neighboring Springwells. "Unorganized, untaught, uncared for, seemingly unambitious, strangers in a strange land, with every waking hour devoted to satisfying the needs and desires of the physical man, these people seem scarcely to realize their humanity," he wrote.

Happily, this coarseness of life did not apply to the majority of Detroiters. By mid-century Woodward Avenue had replaced Jefferson as Detroit's main artery. The former toll road, which was named after the judge and runs more than 20 miles from the foot of the Detroit River to the city of Pontiac, was a grand avenue that included some of the city's most fashionable homes, though unimpeded commercial growth continued to push residents farther north of the city center. Victorian houses here were larger and more elaborate versions of those that were built in the middle-class neighborhoods, and all featured the same basic characteristics: peaks, turrets, leaded glass, and carved gingerbread.

The Whitney House, today a four-star restaurant, embodies this excessive style. The stone mansion at the northwest corner of Woodward and Canfield was built in 1893 by lumber baron David Whitney, then reputedly the richest man in town. The lavishly appointed "American palace" featured a third-story picture gallery, a basement billiard room, and a year-round conservatory. A few other preserved Victorian homes can be found today in Corktown and along Canfield, west of Second Street. As the city pushed farther out with the coming automobile boom, Victorian excess gave way to simpler, Craftsman-style

∧ Previous page: An interior view of the Whitney House.

∨ Below: The sumptuous mansion of Colonel Frank J. Hecker, who made his fortune manufacturing railroad cars, was representative of the elegance Woodward Avenue was famous for in the 19th century.

∨ Bottom: Piquette Avenue was typical of Detroit's neighborhoods at the turn of the last century, which featured block after block of single homes, usually painted white or green.

bungalows— "the home of the intelligent working man," as it was often described.

The part of Woodward north of the business district became known as Piety Hill because of the large number of stately churches built there. These included St. John's Episcopal, erected in 1861 at the corner of High Street and designed by the leading architects of the day, Albert Jordan and James Anderson. The Victorian gothic cathedral was funded almost entirely by shoe manufacturer Henry P. Baldwin and continues in use today. Two other notable houses of worship, First Presbyterian and Woodward Avenue Baptist Church, were built in the 1880s and served their congregations for more than a century.

Woodward Avenue contains a remnant of its namesake's largely abandoned plan. Grand Circus Park, a former swamp at the intersection of Adams and Woodward, was drained and in 1854 set aside by the city as a sylvan respite for city dwellers. One of the more eye-pleasing features of the park during the warm-weather months was watching the message, "In Detroit Life is Worth Living" blossom in its giant flower bed. Few disputed the boast as Detroit continued to grow in size and prestige, the city taking its place among the country's most important– and populated—urban centers.

Grand Circus Park also contains one of the city's most familiar landmarks, the statue of Hazen S. Pingree. In the spring of 2000, after decades of neglect, the city had it sandblasted clean with the opening of nearby Comerica Park. Probably not one in a thousand baseball fans walking past knows anything of the old fellow with the Van Dyke beard seated somewhat uneasily in his concrete chair. That's too bad, because Pingree, with whom this chapter concludes, represents the kind of grass-roots reformist zeal that has historically appealed to Detroiters.

Pingree was a Maine native who had come to Detroit after the Civil War to make his fortune manufacturing footwear. At the time, "boodle" was the time-honored grease of local and national political machines. During the 1890 mayoral election, several influential citizens, sick of corruption, begged Pingree to run on a reform platform.

"I'm too busy making shoes," was his response.

⋀ *The corner of Second and Canfield Avenues one winter morning, circa 1900.*

◄ *The ice fountain on Washington Boulevard was a favorite local landmark. Jets of water were allowed to play all winter, resulting in a mountain of ice that sometimes reached more than 30 feet high.*

◄ *Opposite page, lower right: Architects Albert Jordan and James Anderson were responsible for turning a house of worship into a work of art when they designed St. John's Episcopal in the 1860s.*

Fred Sanders stands with two employees in front of his sweet shop at 180 Woodward Avenue in the late 1890s. Sanders is widely credited with inventing the ice cream soda. Its popularity was spread by visitors who returned home and asked their confectioners to make the same drink, prompting sweet shop owners across the country to write to Sanders for his recipe. "The very simple thing of putting ice cream in soda water was quite a new thing then," he said in a 1907 interview, "and quite a few of them didn't believe it would work. My place used to be called 'that little soda place back there in Detroit.'"

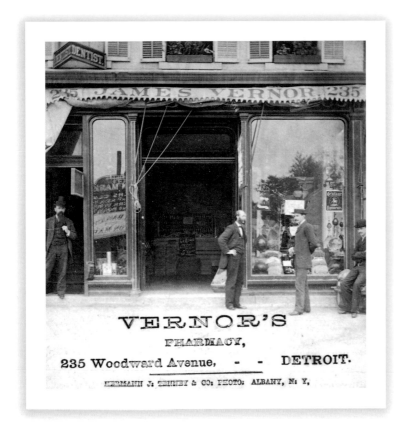

VERNOR'S
PHARMACY,
235 Woodward Avenue, - - DETROIT.
HERMANN J. TINNEY & CO. PHOTO. ALBANY, N. Y.

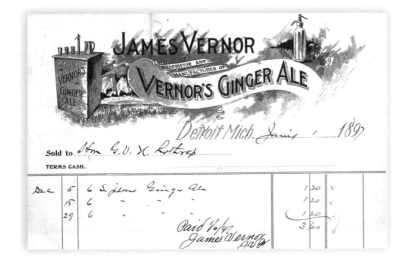

For many years, Detroit was home to the Vernor's gnome, a character as recognizable as the world famous ginger ale he promoted. People of a certain age remember the mythical dwarf dominating the 30-foot neon sign that stood outside the company's bottling plant on Woodward near Canfield. From 1954, when the company moved its operations from its longtime waterfront location into the former Convention Hall, until 1987, when the plant was bulldozed, the gnome poured a never-ending stream of bubbles from a giant bottle into a glass.

The best known beverage to ever come out of Detroit had its origins in an experimental concoction of ginger, vanilla, and 17 other ingredients that pharmacist James Vernor left to age inside an oak barrel as he went off to fight in the Civil War. Upon his return, Vernor discovered that he had created an elixir that was "distinctively different." He began serving his pale gold, nose-tingling tonic in 1866. Thirty years later, sales caused him to move his soft drink business into a plant at the foot of Woodward, where Cobo Hall now stands. It was near the Bob-Lo dock, giving generations of Detroiters a chance to sample two traditions on the same day.

Vernor's started using a gnome as an advertising gimmick in the early 1900s, the figure appearing on the bottles of ginger ale that customers increasingly bought for other household purposes. Not only could the drink quench one's thirst (especially when combined with ice cream to make a Boston Cooler), it could also calm upset stomachs and was a perfect ginger-based "sauce" with which to baste holiday hams and turkeys.

Unfortunately for the company's fortunes, ginger ale made James Vernor's heirs rich but dissolute members of high society, causing the family firm to go public in 1959. The stock was quickly oversubscribed, but a series of labor disputes and family squabbles quickly ate up the infusion of cash. In its centennial year of 1966, the financially crippled company was sold to its creditors. Three years later it was acquired by a Cincinnati food group. In 1975, United Brand bought a majority interest in the failing soft drink company. Powerful Detroit industrialist Max Fisher, a major United Brand stockholder, was instrumental in the deal. "I love Vernor's," he later explained. "I've always loved Vernor's."

Bit by bit, Vernor's traditional ties to the city were cut. By the early 1980s, the company had trimmed its workforce and soon afterward operations were moved out of state. Today the one-time Detroit institution is part of Texas-based Dr. Pepper/Seven Up, Inc., where it carries on as the oldest continuously made soft drink in the country.

Joseph L. Hudson

Mention J.L. Hudson to any adult Detroiter today and you are likely to trigger a flood of sepia-soaked memories, most revolving around the downtown store that was a fixture for generations. Sitting on dad's shoulders to watch the Thanksgiving Day parade . . . Gripping a sister's mittened hand on Christmastime visits to the Fantasy Forest . . . Arching one's neck to gaze at the world's largest flag.

Today, the man behind the retailing giant's corporate name is all but forgotten. But in his time Joseph Lowthian Hudson's stature was commensurate with the nine-foot-high rooftop letters that once towered over Woodward Avenue. When he succumbed to pneumonia in 1912 while on a trip to his native England, an entire community mourned his passing. "Joe Hudson is dead," eulogized one leading citizen. "Six of Detroit's biggest men will rattle around in his shoes."

Hudson did not come by his reputation easily. Early in his mercantile career, when he was operating a store in Ionia, Michigan, the eighth grade dropout was forced into bankruptcy by a severe national depression. It took him 15 years, but Hudson eventually paid back every creditor, with interest, even though the law did not require him to do so. "If you are only legally bound to be honest," he explained, "you are not very honest."

Hudson moved to Detroit in 1878, when he was 32. He helped a former employer, Christopher Mabley, make what was already the largest men's clothing store in the city even more successful. After the two had a falling-out, Hudson used his share of the profits to open a competing store on April 2, 1881. Six years later he moved into bigger quarters, the result of superior salesmanship and a rock-solid reputation for integrity. In September 1891, he opened his eight-story emporium at the corner of Gratiot and Farmer. Sales kept pace with Detroit's booming population, forcing Hudson to repeatedly expand his "Big Store" until it eventually covered an entire city block.

Hudson was a pleasant-looking, fastidious, teetotaling man who remained a bachelor for all of his 66 years. He directed his energies into his extended family, grooming four nephews to take over his growing chain of stores. He also donated enormous amounts of time and money to philanthropic endeavors.

His public image was impeccable. Detroiters recalled the failure of a bank of which he had been president. Although he was not responsible for its collapse, he promised to make good on every dollar lost, even if it "requires me to mortgage my future." It cost him $265,000, a staggering amount in 1894. But he recovered. So did Detroit.

Perhaps the most attractive of Hudson's many qualities was his unshakable belief in the community where he made his fortune.

"I always hold up my head when I speak of Detroit," he once said. "We sometimes hear people speaking slightingly of our city. I always resent it. There is not a better city anywhere."

➤ *Hudson's first store was on the ground floor of the Detroit Opera House.*

⋎ *Joseph Hudson was a civic booster whose influence was felt long after the downtown clothier died in 1912. The Hudson's band is pictured here during a recital on Belle Isle about 1890.*

⋀ Passenger steamships operated by the Detroit & Cleveland Navigation Company were part of the golden age of Great Lakes travel, an era that came to an end with the advent of faster forms of transportation.

➤ Right, top: The Detroit waterfront in the 1880s. The ship in the center is the India, built in Buffalo in 1871.

➤ Right, bottom: The Detroit Dry Dock Company, organized in 1877, was one of the most respected and prolific ship-builders on the Great Lakes, building hundreds of steel, iron and wooden hulled vessels. Before the shipyard closed in 1920, it had launched such ships as the Tashmoo, Samuel Mather and Sainte Marie.

➤ Opposite page: Waterworks Park opened in 1877 as the municipal waterworks pumping station. Officially known as Gladwin Park, the 72-acre plot offered citizens a pastoral retreat in an increasingly urbanized environment. The park's most famous feature was the floral clock that for years greeted visitors at the park entrance off East Jefferson Avenue.

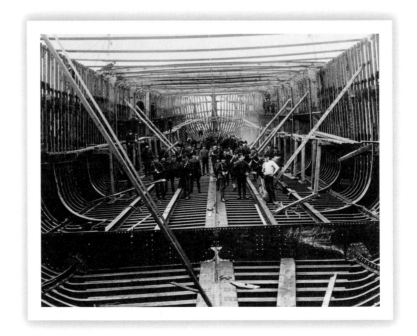

➤ *A view of downtown in 1901, Detroit's bicentennial year. Note the various forms of transportation—electric streetcars, horse-drawn carriages, bicycles—and the city worker (dressed in white) scooping up horse apples.*

▼ *Detroit, a leading center of stove manufacturing, boasted the largest cook stove in the world. The 15-ton facsimile of the Michigan Stove Company's popular "Garland" model was displayed in front of the company's factory on Jefferson from 1893 to 1965, when it was moved to the State Fairgrounds.*

Pingree's friends prevailed, however, and after a landslide win at the polls he set about becoming Detroit's first truly notable mayor. During his four terms the bombastic Republican successfully took on the utility and streetcar companies and other monopolies affecting the little guy. His battle with the private streetcar franchises was monumental, but in the end he prevailed. In 1895 the first municipal streetcars appeared, the three-cent fare undercutting the private lines' standard nickel fare.

The mayor was a tireless reformist. Whenever nerves threatened to get the better of him, he responded in typically maverick fashion: He pulled out the dried codfish he carried around in his coat and chewed on it as a tonic.

Pingree made his reputation during the severe national depression of 1893–94, when one-third of the local work force was idle. At a meeting of the city council, he suggested a plan that would allow starving families to grow vegetable gardens on vacant lots, both public and private. A member retorted: "Have the right people go to the homes of those who are destitute and if they have anything to sell, sell it, and don't add to the tax roll." At this, remembered a contemporary, "Mayor Pingree fairly blew up, as he always did when his sense of justice was outraged."

Pingree, an avid horseman, sold his prize mount at auction for $387 (about one-third of its real value) to raise money to buy seed and garden tools. Several citizens followed his lead, donating land and dollars to the cause. Ultimately, 945 families produced $14,000 worth of food on lots sprinkled around the city. Grateful gardeners planted signs in their gardens that read, "He who gives to others, gives to the Lord," and "The name of the man who originated this system will be handed down to posterity."

The innovative program thrust Detroit's mayor into the national spotlight and became a model for other cities.

Such acts endeared Pingree to working-class Detroiters, who voted for him time and again. John C. Lodge recalled an incident when the incumbent was running for his third term against a seemingly formidable opponent. "On the Saturday before election day I found him at the corner of Fort and Woodward looking at a torchlight parade," Lodge later wrote:

The marchers had torches made of small cans of kerosene, which they held aloft on a stick while marching. It looked like an impressive affair for our little city. Mr. Pingree looked at me and asked, "How many people are there in the parade?"

I said I didn't know, but that I would guess there might be 1,000. Then he said: "How many are there on the sidewalk?" and I answered, "Probably four or five times that number."

"Well," he said, "just remember what I am saying to you. Marsh [Marshall H. Godfrey, his opponent] has the parade. I have the sidewalk."

Thanks in part to Mayor Pingree, those sidewalks were extended well beyond the core city. Many people ridiculed the creation of Grand Boulevard as being too far out in the country, but Pingree not only heartily endorsed completing the

▼ Grand Circus Park contains a statue to Mayor Hazen S. Pingree, erected on Memorial Day, 1904.

unfinished project, he saw to it that the dirt artery was paved with asphalt—part of a road improvement program that made Detroit one of the best-paved cities in the country. Ultimately, the 200-foot-wide landscaped boulevard wrapped around the entire city for a distance of 12 miles and featured some of Detroit's finest residences. Initially thought to represent the absolute outer limit of Detroit's expansion, by the early 1900s the city's explosive growth resulted in subdivisions being built far beyond it.

Although Detroit's first "buzz wagons" appeared on his watch, Pingree wouldn't live to see the auto industry's impact on his fair city. Anxious to practice his liberal policies on a larger scale, he ran for governor in 1896. He was elected while mayor and held both jobs until the state Supreme Court ruled that he had to decide between them. In 1897 he reluctantly said goodbye to city hall.

"Potato Patch" Pingree, a populist built along the lines of Theodore Roosevelt, clearly was presidential material. But an untimely death from peritonitis while traveling in England in 1901 cut that particular dream short. His passing occurred just a month before Detroiters planned to celebrate the city's 200th birthday with re-enactments, river pageants, balls and a day-long floral parade—a

▲ *Mayor Pingree pitches a shovelful of dirt during the groundbreaking of Grand Boulevard in 1891. Among the reform mayor's accomplishments was replacing many miles of cedar-blocked streets with asphalt pavement.*

➤ *Grand Boulevard before the coming of the automobile.*

blowout that he surely would have reveled in. Instead, he was buried a few days prior to the bicentennial hoopla, with 20,000 members of civic and military organizations solemnly lining Woodward Avenue. Three years later, on Memorial Day, 1904, grateful citizens dedicated the statue of him in Grand Circus Park. The bronze tablet declares Hazen S. Pingree "the idol of the people," a sentiment undamaged by a century's worth of political cynicism and pigeon droppings.

The Jewel in the River

Midway between Canada and the United States in the narrows of the Detroit River sits Belle Isle, a 928-acre island that for over 120 years has served as an oasis for Metro Detroiters.

Throughout its rich history, the 2.5-mile-long island has hosted numerous events, from family picnics and school outings to Grand Prix auto racing and marathon bike races. For years, wealthy boaters at the Detroit Boat Club and the Detroit Yacht Club called Belle Isle their home port. To many, Detroit's "Central Park" is simply an idyllic place to walk, jog, fish, and watch iron ore freighters pass by on a warm summer day. However, Belle Isle was not always so inviting.

Although the Indians first called the island Mah-nah-be-zee, "The Swan," it later was renamed *Isle au Cochons*, or "Hog Island," by the French. At one time rattlesnakes overran the island and a number of hogs were released to destroy them. As commandant of Fort Pontchartrain, Cadillac declared the island a public commons as a refuge for livestock to protect them from rustlers and the "savages."

The island was later owned by the Macomb family and then by Barnabas Campau in 1817. Although it was private property, by the 1840s pleasure seekers and boaters were using it as a picnic grounds. Soon it was felt that the name Hog Island no longer befit its grandeur. At a July 4th picnic in 1845, several leading citizens renamed the island "Belle Isle" without

∧ / ➤ *America's most famous landscape architect, Frederick Law Olmstead (who designed New York's Central Park), was hired to design Belle Isle Park. Despite creative disagreements, what eventually emerged was a bucolic getaway featuring canals, tree-lined walks and a variety of attractions, including a zoo, aquarium, conservatory and casino.*

➤ *Opposite page: Detroiters wait to board one of the excursion steamers to Belle Isle, circa 1890.*

consulting the Campau family. Some claim the new name honored Isabella Cass, daughter of Lewis Cass, Michigan's foremost politician.

Under increasing pressure by a growing population clamoring for better park conditions, the city purchased Belle Isle from the Campau family for $200,000 in 1879. Within four years, America's greatest landscape architect, Frederick Law Olmstead—the designer of New York's Central Park—designed Belle Isle Park, replete with a canal system and a pedestrian and carriage street winding around the island. By 1908, Albert Kahn—influenced by the architecture of the World Columbian Exposition in Chicago—had designed the island's signature structures: the conservatory, casino, and aquarium. Several years later, nearly 300 acres of landfill were added at the island's western end to accommodate Scott Fountain, a gleaming white marble, terraced-step structure containing the bronze sculpture of James Scott, who had bequeathed $500,000 to the city for its construction.

A bridge connecting Jefferson Avenue to Belle Isle was built in 1889. It soon become famous not only for numerous suicide leaps, but also for one of magician Harry Houdini's greatest stunts. In November 1906, Houdini tied himself to a lifeline 113 feet long and, shackled with Detroit Police Department handcuffs, jumped from the Belle Isle Bridge's draw span into the freezing water. After an agonizing wait, Houdini freed himself and resurfaced, swimming to a lifeboat to the cheers of amazed onlookers and fans.

In 1915 the bridge was destroyed by fire and replaced by a temporary wooden structure. In 1923 the current art deco style bridge, later named after General Douglas MacArthur, was opened. A firestorm of another sort occurred on the bridge 20 years later. On Sunday, June 20, 1943, racial tensions came to a head when several brawls occurred between blacks and whites on the bridge and on the island, where thousands of Detroiters had gathered to find relief from the heat. False rumors spread quickly, including one that said white sailors had thrown a black woman and her baby from the bridge. The 1943 race riot lasted two days and resulted in 34 deaths, numerous injuries, and considerable property damage.

Today, Belle Isle is still considered Detroit's jewel on the river and is acknowledged as one of the most unique public parks in the country. Yet, with its structures showing nearly a century's wear and tear, the debate as to whether a user's fee should be charged to help pay for maintenance and improvements continues.

⋀ Generations of Detroiters have used Belle Isle as their retreat from the city, enjoying its baseball diamonds, bath houses, walking paths and picnic grounds. Here the Case family whimsically poses for the photographer with that staple of countless cookouts over the years—the hot dog.

◄ Opposite page: Strolling on Belle Isle in 1915.

➤ Pages 66-67: The Scott Fountain.

WHEELS FOR THE WORLD

As the birthplace of automotive giants General Motors, Ford, and Daimler-Chrysler, Detroit is justifiably known as the Motor City. It has never been subtle about letting the rest of the world know it. Where else can one find a three-story tire on the side of a freeway? Or a giant scoreboard that, like some proud electronic papa, announces each new car and truck as it's delivered off the assembly line?

The assembly line is the true nuts and bolts soul of Detroit. When Henry Ford introduced it at his Highland Park plant in the fall of 1913, it ushered in a revolution. Before then, cars had been built on sawhorses by craftsmen. The breaking down of assembly into simple repetitive tasks by unskilled laborers dropped the production time of a Model T chassis from nearly 13 hours to just 93 minutes.

Mass production not only created jobs for hundreds of thousands of workers, it brought the price of a new car into everyone's reach. By 1929 some 5.3 million vehicles were produced in the U.S. and 447,000 workers owed their living to the auto industry. Today those numbers have roughly tripled. Not bad for an industry that wasn't even listed in the 1900 census.

Detroit, a symbol of industrial might and a purveyor of middle class dreams, can be said to have entered the 20th century a few years earlier than the rest of the country. On the cold evening of March 6, 1896, a 32-year-old mechanical engineer named Charles Brady King took the tiller of his four-cylinder horseless carriage and took it for an experimental spin through the downtown streets—the first automobile ride in a city that would soon become famous for putting the world on wheels. "The apparatus seemed to work all right," reported the *Detroit Free Press*, "and it went at the rate of five or six miles an hour at an even rate of speed."

◄ *Charles Brady King at the tiller, 1896.*

Newsweek posed Henry and Clara Ford with their oldest grandson, Henry II, on its cover in 1946, the 50th anniversary of Ol' Henry's historic first drive in his quadricycle.

Participants and celebrants gather on Belle Isle before the beginning of the 1909 Glidden Tour, an annual endurance test whose starting point was Detroit's Pontchartrain Hotel. A reporter described the motorized procession as "the longest caravan of chugging automobiles ever gathered together in the history of the great 20th century industry, of which Detroit is the hub."

King was a man of many interests, but he lacked the single-minded drive that characterized others in the field and thus never became the household word that Ford and other auto pioneers did. One of these men, Ransom E. Olds, in 1899 built a three-story structure on Jefferson Avenue near the Belle Isle bridge to manufacture his gasoline-powered Oldsmobile. This was the first of Detroit's many car factories.

Olds offered his cars at $1,250 apiece, but sales were disappointing until he gambled on producing a cheaper one-cylinder runabout for $650. A fire on March 9, 1901, destroyed the Olds plant, but an employee managed to push the prototype to safety. Olds relocated to Lansing, where his curved-dash runabout became the country's first high-volume model and inspired a popular song, "In My Merry Oldsmobile."

"Automobubbling" was an adventure. The roads early motorists traveled on were dirt and thus nearly impassable in bad weather. Even under the best of conditions the rutted roads and rigid suspensions of the cars left motorists battered and bruised after a long drive. One young lady described an arduous seven-hour trip to Detroit in a Detroiter roadster: "Gee, I wouldn't go again in that. It's too jolly. I don't ever want to drive down there again in it. I had cramps & kidney trouble and a few more things from the jars."

As financially impractical and mechanically unreliable as the early cars were, everybody clamored to own one. Henry Ford did his best to accommodate them.

Ford, born on a Dearborn farm in 1863, was the night shift engineer at the Edison Illuminating Company when he test-drove his quadricycle on the rainy morning of June 4, 1896. "The darn thing ran!" exclaimed Ford, who never imagined the social and technological revolution that would follow. In 1899 Ford and several investors, including Mayor William Maybury, organized the Detroit

Automobile Company. By early 1900 a prototype was ready, but Ford quickly grew tired of his partners' interference and by the end of the year he quit. The company folded, having never put a car into production.

The automobile industry grew in fits and starts, with companies operating in several cities. In 1903, there were only 11,000 cars in the United States, but 1 million bicycles and 17 million horses. But the country was experiencing a rash of automotive wildcatting, with 57 firms starting up and another 27 failing that year. One of the success stories was the Ford Motor Company, principally capitalized by local coal merchant Alexander Malcomson. A two-story brick structure was erected on Mack Avenue, where workmen were paid $1.50 a day to build a two-cylinder model capable of reaching speeds of 30 miles per hour. It retailed for $850. Two years later the growing company expanded operations to a larger factory on Piquette Avenue at Beaubien.

The Model T's unsophisticated styling and utilitarian image made it the butt of countless jokes and cartoons, but the "Tin Lizzy" also was sturdy, practical, and inexpensive, traits that endeared it to the first generation of car-buying Americans.

Cars Named Detroit

What's in a name? Plenty, if you're a car company angling for a marketing edge. In the early years of the auto industry, many manufacturers assumed that no nameplate could pack more wallop among potential buyers than "Detroit," practically a synonym for the automobile. Between 1899 and 1924, at least 24 different vehicles carried the name. These included the Detroit-Dearborn, the Detroit-Oxford, the Oriental Detroit, the Wolverine Detroit, the Detroit Steam Car, the Abbott-Detroit, the Traveler-Detroit, and the Briggs Detroiter. Alas, many of the marques didn't survive past a year or two, though the Detroit Electric managed to stick around from 1907 to 1939, making it the longest-lasting electric car in history.

∧ *"Automobubbling" in a Detroit Electric.*

COPYRIGHT 1909 BY
PENINSULAR ENG. CO.

A Fatal First

Although automobiles first began puttering along Detroit's streets in 1896, it took six years before the fledgling Motor City recorded an auto-related fatality. The unfortunate first was a well-known retired businessman named George W. Bissell, who ironically liked nothing better than riding pell-mell on horseback or inside a carriage.

On the morning of September 2, 1902, the 81-year-old capitalist—who was said to have made and lost three separate fortunes in 19th-century Detroit—was guiding his spirited team of horses down Brooklyn Avenue, near the corner of Lysander Street, when an automobile "scorched" by. The horses became frightened and jumped to the side, causing one of the front wheels of the carriage to shoot off. Bissell was pitched headfirst into the pavement.

The accident occurred at about 9 o'clock. At 11:15 a.m. he was pronounced dead at Harper Hospital, the result of a skull fracture and internal injuries. The *Detroit Free Press* observed that, despite his advanced age, "Mr. Bissell was in splendid physical condition, due to the systematic course of training he followed, and he often remarked that unless he met with an accident, he would live to be 100 years of age. It is unfortunate that the exception he noted was the means of ending his life."

⋏ *The unlucky George Bissell.*

The Model T was offered in nine body styles, all built on the same chassis, but it wasn't until the early 1920s that buyers could order the car in anything but basic black. Not that most Ford customers were concerned with superficial facelifts. A big part of the reason for the car's success was the nationwide dealer and service system Ford established, a boon to travelers and rural customers.

Clearly, Ford had a better idea. At a time when a handcrafted automobile cost as much as the average workingman made in 10 years, he decided to such leave pricey vehicles to the "sports" and concentrated on producing a car ordinary folks could afford. That strategy wasn't unique to the hundreds of carmakers in business then. The Sears-Roebuck Company, for instance, offered a Sears Motor Car in its 1910 catalog for $395.

Ford's genius was in passing on to the consumer the savings he realized through improved mass production. Contrary to legend, Ford didn't invent the assembly line. Rather, he perfected it—first at his Highland Park plant, built on Woodward Avenue north of Detroit, then at the massive Rouge complex in Dearborn. As the time required to build a Model T continued to drop, so did its price. Between 1908 and 1924 the price of Ford's "family horse" shrank from $850 to $290. By World War I half of all cars in use were Model T's. Before Ford quit building them in 1927 more than 15 million of the beloved "flivvers" had rolled onto America's primitive, rutted roads.

One of the seminal events in Detroit's history was Ford's introduction of the five-dollar day on January 5, 1914. At the time, typical industry wages were 30 cents an hour, so Ford's announcement at a stroke more than doubled the prevailing minimum wage for auto workers. The news stunned the business world and made Detroit a mecca for unskilled laborers from overseas and around the country. Ten thousand applicants mobbed the employment office at the Highland Park plant the day after the announcement. Ford's largesse, applauded by social reformers and cursed by his competitors, was intended to cure the abnormally high turnover rate in his factory.

At the same time that he introduced the five-dollar day, he replaced the two nine-hour shifts at his Model T plant with three eight-hour shifts, meaning that the assembly line literally never stopped. A standard joke was that the beds of the many local boarding houses never had a chance to cool off, as one shift left for work just as another came to sleep.

The Highland Park plant was a place of mind-bending noise and furious activity.

Finding Work in the Motor City

IN EARLY 1914, 15-YEAR-OLD FRANK MARQUART AND HIS FATHER LEFT EAST PITTSBURGH, PENNSYLVANIA IMMEDIATELY UPON HEARING NEWS OF HENRY FORD'S "FIVE-DOLLAR DAY." MARQUART, A LIFELONG UNION ACTIVIST, LATER RECORDED HIS EXPERIENCES FOR THE ORAL HISTORY PROJECT OF WAYNE STATE UNIVERSITY'S LABOR ARCHIVES.

My family was typical of immigrant families of those days. I can't think of a single kid I knew then whose parents did not come from "the old country." And their fathers, like my father, supported their families by hard, unskilled or semiskilled labor, working either a 10-hour shift during the day or a 12-hour shift during the night. To foremen and higher supervisors in the mills the immigrants were all "hunkies," regardless of their nationality. . . .

My father hated his job as a common laborer in the chain mill and he hated me for not finding a steady job, and life became a living hell for me. Then came that memorable day in January 1914 when my father came home from work excitedly waving the *Pittsburgh Press* and shouting at us: "Look, in Detroit Henry Ford is paying five dollars a day to all his workers. I'm going to quit my job tomorrow and Frank and me will go to Detroit. We'll both get jobs at Ford's—why, we'll be making 10 dollars a day, think of it, 10 dollars a day!" Then he read aloud excerpts from the front-page story about the Flivver King philanthropist, who was revolutionizing wage scales in America. The more my father talked the more enthusiastic he became.

My mother, however, did not share the enthusiasm. "But how do you know you'll get work in Detroit?" she ventured. I don't recall all that was said but I do remember that her misgivings threw my old man into a rage. He accused her of not cooperating, of not lending moral support; he said she wanted to hold him back. "How to hell can we ever get ahead if you always pull back like that," he demanded, half in German and half in English. While he berated my mother, I picked up the *Press* and read the story for myself. I immediately sided with my father. With the thought of getting away from the hell-hole that was Braddock, of escaping the abuse of my father because I could not find work, of going to a big city—especially a city like Detroit where automobiles were made—I was all for pulling up stakes and heading for the Motor City as soon as possible. . . .

It was agreed that my father and I would go to Detroit, find work at five dollars a day, and send for the rest of the family later. Never, as long as I live, will I forget those days in Detroit in early January 1914! I can't recall how we found the boarding house run by Mrs. Hartlieb on the corner of Lycaste and Waterloo (now East Vernor), but I do recall how we rose early on the following morning, gulped down breakfast, and walked to Jefferson Avenue to take the Jefferson car to Woodward and then transfer to the car that was to take us to the Ford plant in Highland Park.

Nor will I ever forget the sight that greeted our eyes when we walked toward the Ford employment office. There were thousands of job seekers jam-packed in front of the gates. It was a bitterly cold morning and I had no overcoat, only a red sweater under a thin jacket. I don't know how long we stood in that crowd, but I became numb from cold. The crowd kept getting larger and larger and there were angry cries of "for Christ's sake, stop shoving" from men who were near the gates. Some of those men had been waiting there for hours; they were cold, ill-tempered, and in a snarling mood. Several times the company guards ordered the men to stand back and not push against the gates. But those near the gates were pushed by those behind them, who in turn were pushed by those behind them. Suddenly a shout went up—a shout that soon became a roaring chant: "Open the employment office, open the employment office!"

Whether the employment office was ever opened that morning I do not know; whether anyone was hired, I do not know, either. But I do know that a man shouted over a megaphone, "We are not hiring any more today; there's no use sticking around; we're not hiring today." An angry roar went up from the crowd: "You sonsabitches, keeping us here all this time and then telling us you ain't hiring, you bastards!" The crowd did not break up; it kept pushing toward the gates. With chattering teeth I suggested to my father that we ought to leave. He cursed me and shouted at me in German that he didn't bring me to Detroit so I could loaf like a bum.

Again the man came with the megaphone: "We ARE NOT hiring today. Go away; no use standing out there in the cold for nothing." And then the ominous warning: "If you don't stop pushing against these gates we're gonna use the firehoses."

I guess everybody thought that was an empty threat made to scare people away. It scared no one. The crowd showed no signs of being intimidated. In fact, it became more unruly. Someone yelled, "Let's crash the goddamn gates!" I can remember how the mood of the crowd suddenly changed; it became ugly, threatening. I heard a roar of approval as someone yelled: "We oughta take down the goddamn place brick by brick." There was shouting and cursing and confusion. Then from near the gates a cry was raised: "For God's sake the bastards are gonna turn the hoses on us!" Someone near me shouted: "Aw, that's bullshit, they wouldn't dare do a thing like that. . . ." He had hardly finished the sentence when the water came, the icy water that froze almost as soon as it landed on our clothing.

The hoses were turned at an angle and moved from side to side so that the spray hit all sections of the crowd. There was a wild scramble to get away; some people were pushed down and trampled. Several fist fights broke out when some workers shoved those ahead of us. My father cursed, in the way he always cursed when infuriated, his curses beginning in English and rising to a crescendo in German. But he was lucky; the water did not soak through his overcoat as it soaked through my jacket and sweater. By the time we were able to board a Woodward streetcar I was shivering from head to foot.

My father said it was a "Jew plot." A rabid anti-Semite long before Hitler arose to horrify the world, my father said Ford was a Jew and what we suffered that morning was the result of a "dirty Jew trick." When I suggested that "Ford" was not a Jewish name, he told me not to be stupid: "Don't you know Jews change their names for business reasons!"

Among the workers who quit their jobs at Westinghouse and went to Detroit to find work at higher wages was Otto Azinger, whom my father had known for years in Braddock. When we came to Detroit he was a production foreman in the Metal Products Company, a parts plant specializing in the manufacture of automobile axles for the Hudson Motor Company and other auto makers. Otto hired my father to operate a radial drill press, drilling axle shafts. At first he hated the work. He came home from work with his hands swollen and scarred from the hot chips encountered in the drilling. He talked nostalgically about the pleasant job he once had at Westinghouse; he rued the day he came to Detroit and roundly cursed Henry Ford. But what aggravated him most was that he had to work and I could not find a job.

Every day I made the factory rounds—Chalmers, Lozier, Continental Motor Company, Packard, Zenith Carburetor, and a host of small parts plants that have long since vanished from Detroit's east side. Everywhere I received the same answer: "No, we are not hiring today." The hiring agent of the Detroit Nut and Bolt Company told me: "Hell, kid, you're too skinny to run any of them machines we got in there."

Every evening when my father came home from work he asked me where I had looked for work; I told him, but he simply did not believe me: "You didn't look for work, you bummed around. Why to hell should you work when the old man's working? That's what you think, ain't it?" And so on and so on. He was too ignorant and brutal to understand that the worst thing a father can do to a boy is to crush his pride and self-respect. He made me feel that I couldn't find a job because of some fault within myself. Once one of the boarders told him at the supper table: "Don't blame the boy because he can't find work; today if you want to get a job, it's not what you know or how good you are—it's who you know." Then he added: "Isn't that how you got your job—through someone you know?" I gave my father a meaningful look. He didn't say anything.

And that was how I finally obtained my first job in Detroit—through someone my father knew, the employment manager of the Metal Products Company. . . . And so began my life as a factory hand, working "on the bench" filing castings and ring gears, grinding the burrs off nuts on a small power-driven emery wheel. Now that both my father and I had jobs, we sent for my mother, sister, and brother and rented a house on Fisher Avenue near Jefferson. In those days the Detroit River came all the way up to Jefferson Avenue in that area, and I can still remember the horse-drawn dump wagons unloading trash, little by little filling in the river and creating new land on which the Whittier Hotel, the River House, and other high-rise structures would eventually be erected. . . .

And so the months went by and I became increasingly conditioned to the ways of a young factory hand. I chummed around with factory workers of my age group—a "peer group," I guess the sociologists call it. After work we went home, ate supper, and met in a bar, usually Preemo's on Jefferson Avenue near the car barn (now a police station). Though a minor, I was tall and never got turned down by the bartender when I put my foot on the brass rail and ordered, "Gimme a beer." My ego always inflated when the bartender served me but refused one of my pals because he was shorter and looked younger. In the saloon, men gathered in groups and usually talked shop. Each tried to impress the others with how important his particular job was, how

much skill it required.

Saturday night was the big night. My pals and I met in Curley's Poolroom on Jefferson Avenue and shot several games of pool. Then we went downtown to take in a burlesque, either the Gaiety or the Cadillac. The Gaiety had a bar downstairs and during intermission we made a dash for the bar and ordered a hamburger with onion and a glass of beer. After the show we went to Champlain Street. How many Detroiters today know where Champlain Street was and what it was noted for in those far-off days? In our circle it was nicknamed "Joy Street." On a Saturday night you could see men forming lines at some of the houses on Champlain Street, with policemen on hand to keep order. Because of its red-light reputation the name of the street was changed to East Lafayette, after prostitution was outlawed during the First World War.

As time went on I discovered that I was working harder and harder for less and less money. We pieceworkers outsmarted ourselves; in the words of

Old Sam Johnson, the oldest worker in our department, "We cut our own throats." At first I was so naive that I actually believed the company would allow me to continue earning that high piecework pay. Then I found out why you couldn't win against the company. They re-timed one job after another. Then I had to work harder to earn my 20 to 25 dollars. The time-study man used a new system when timing a job. Instead of timing the worker, he took off his coat, rolled up his sleeves, worked furiously for 10 or 15 minutes, and set a time on the basis of his output. Once I told him: "You know damn well you couldn't keep up that pace all day long. How do you expect us to do it?" I remember his answer well: "Look Bud, if you get the rag out of your ass you can make out." And he walked away.

Λ *Two Ford workers inside their boarding house at 941 Russell Street, 1914.*

At its peak, 70,000 men worked there. In 1914, a magazine writer named Julian Street visited the glass-and-brick "Crystal Palace":

Of course there was order in that place; of course there was system—relentless system—terrible "efficiency"—but to my mind, unaccustomed to such things, the whole room, with its interminable aisles, its whirling shafts and wheels, its forest of roof-supporting posts and flapping, flying, leather belting, its endless rows of writhing machinery, its shrieking, hammering, and clatter, its smell of oil, its autumn haze of smoke, its savage-looking foreign population—to my mind it expressed but one thing, and that thing was delirium.

Fancy a jungle of wheels and belts and weird iron forms—of men, machinery and movement—add to it every kind of sound you can imagine: the sound of a million squirrels chirking, a million monkeys quarreling, a million lions roaring, a million pigs dying, a million elephants smashing through a forest of sheet iron, a million boys whistling on their fingers, a million others coughing with the whooping cough, a mil lion sinners groaning as they are dragged to hell—imagine all of this happening at the very edge of Niagara Falls, with the everlasting roar of the cataract as a perpetual background, and you may acquire a vague conception of that place.

As Model T after Model T rolled off the assembly line, the press burnished Ford's favorable image as a paternalistic captain of industry, someone for whom his workers' welfare was of paramount concern. His famous sociological department sought to educate and Americanize workers and their families, though it included such heavy-handed tactics as spying on and firing those employees whose lifestyle choices—drinking, gambling, whoring—were judged to be unsatisfactory.

This was an exciting time to be alive in Detroit, which by 1914 was the undisputed Motor City of the world. The mammoth electric sign atop the Detroit Opera House implored pedestrians to "Watch The Fords Go By." They also watched life as they had once known it rumble past.

Ford's assembly lines ushered in social upheaval on an unprecedented scale. In less than half of a lifetime, Detroit—a small, tightly knit, conservative community at the turn of the century—was made over into a sprawling, confusing, polyglot

▲ *Top: In 1904, a family was proudly pictured with its prized possession: a Cadillac designed by Henry Leyland (who insisted his invention be named after Detroit's founder and not himself).*

▲ *Above: For those who couldn't afford their own car, a popular option was being photographed behind a studio cutout. This gag photo was taken about 1910 inside the Woodward Avenue store of A.C. Dietsche.*

◄ *Opposite page: In 1924, photographers posed Henry Ford and his quadricycle with two famous offspring: his son Edsel and the 10 millionth Model T.*

CONGRESS AND WOODWARD
SUPENDED TYPE TRAFFIC CONTROL SIGNAL 3-100W 220VOLT R.L.C.
SERVICE (CITY HALL) 4-EACH RED GREEN AND AMBER LENS CONTROLLED
FROM TOWER AT WOODWARD AND MICHIGAN.

urban colossus. Fashionable residential districts such as Woodward and Cass avenues were irreversibly changed. Gas stations and dealerships sprang up while stately homes were sold and subdivided into boardinghouses.

"I am afraid that the old-time charm of Detroit has fled," Charles L. Freer, a longtime resident of upper Woodward Avenue, wrote a friend in 1911. "Smoke, dirt, noise and all the unfavorable features of a large manufacturing center are, by degrees, spreading over the entire old residential portion of our city."

Between 1900 and 1930 the city's population increased sixfold, to 1.6 million, making it the nation's fourth largest. Hamtramck and Highland Park, once somnolent communities of a few thousand souls, were transformed into factory boom towns and ultimately swallowed by Detroit. Throughout the core city and its outskirts, century-old shade trees were toppled, meadows were developed, and dirt streets were widened and paved over—all in a desperate attempt to keep pace with the demand for factories, housing, roadways, and parking space.

It's impossible to overstate the immense changes the automobile brought to everyday life. Introducing motorcars into already crowded city streets led to a new word— "traffic jam" (coined in 1910)—and a rising number of accidents and deaths. New forms of road regulations were regularly introduced, though motorists were slow to adopt many of them and police officers initially were reluctant to enforce them. Chaos reigned.

In 1917 the first "crow's nest" style signal tower appeared on Woodward Avenue, creating a highly visible (at least in daytime) symbol of authority with the power to single-handedly regulate traffic flow. Within a few years the signal towers were replaced by synchronized electrical systems, which proved to be far better traffic

▲ *In 1917, the first "crow's nest" signal tower appeared on Woodward, injecting an authoritative looking and highly visible presence into the chaos caused by the explosion of automobile traffic.*

◄ *Opposite page: William L. Potts, an employee of the Detroit Police Department, invented the modern four-way traffic signal using red, green and amber lights. Potts' creation debuted in 1920 at the intersection of Woodward and Fort. Shown is the traffic light installed at the intersection of Woodward and Congress two years later.*

⋏ As the automobile replaced the horse as the principal mode of transportation, businesses needed to change with the times or risk going out of business. The Anderson Electric Car Company, for example, switched from making wooden wheels for carriages to manufacturing electric vehicles.

devices. In 1920, the modern four-way traffic signal using red, green, and amber lights was created by William L. Potts, an employee of the Detroit Police Department. It debuted at the intersection of Woodward Avenue and Fort Street. As the number of vehicles on the roads continued to increase, smashups and fatalities grew exponentially. However, their numbers did begin to fall after the Detroit Automobile Club (today AAA Michigan) started installing more than 2,400 red and white stop signs at hazardous intersections in 1923.

Fuel was another problem. Early motorists depended on the direct delivery of gasoline from tank cars or sidled up to pumps installed inside barns and blacksmith shops. In 1910 the Central Oil Company built Detroit's first drive-in gas station with an island at the northeast corner of Fort and First Streets. A second station opened at Woodward and High Street (now Vernor). Soon gas stations were an integral part of America's landscape.

Not every motorist needed them. At one time there were nearly 40 manufacturers of electric vehicles in the country. Unlike internal combustion models, they required neither cranking nor shifting, making them ideal for women wishing to make a safe, clean crosstown jaunt. Even Henry Ford bought a Detroit Electric for his wife. But the easy availability of cheap gas and motorists' quest to explore America's hinterlands made the severe limitations of the electric cars' storage batteries even more apparent. By the end of the 1920s the once common sight of an electric car had almost turned into a novelty.

The automobile also was the catalyst of a sexual revolution. Previously, the best a couple could hope for on a date was the chance to steal a kiss on the front porch or while strolling along a park path. But now, to the horror of scandalized mothers and ministers, a motorcar not only enabled lovers to get miles away from parents' prying eyes, its detachable seats served as a mattress for copulation. The advent of enclosed car bodies and heaters allowed greater privacy and a comfortable place to make love when the weather was bad. Designers quickly caught on to the possibilities, designing front seats that folded out into the back.

As with any brand new industry, fortunes were made practically overnight. James Couzens, a bookkeeper who had invested $2,500 in Ford stock in 1903, cashed out in 1919 for $29 million. His sister's $100 investment grew to $355,000 in just a few years. Ford's only child, Edsel, shared in the bonanza. One memorable day in 1914, Ford strode into a Detroit bank, his son in tow.

"Bill," he announced to the banker, "I have a million dollars in gold here. This is Edsel's twenty-first birthday, and I want him to have it."

Visibly astonished, Edsel might have been forgiven for taking the rest of the day off to celebrate—or to recuperate. Instead, displaying his usual diligent, unassuming manner, the sole heir to the world's greatest private fortune went back to his factory office and spent his birthday working behind the desk. He did admit later, however, that he'd never made as many mistakes as he did that day.

After Ford bought out the last of the shareholders, Edsel was made president of the company in 1919. He was just 25 and his father 56. Although Edsel (who was referred to as "Mr. Edsel" by company executives to differentiate him from the other Mr. Ford) stayed in that position until his premature death of stomach cancer in 1943, everybody understood who really ran the show.

⋏ *The Edsel was intended to pay homage to Henry Ford's only child when it was launched in the fall of 1957, but the vehicle—a sales disaster—survives today as a metaphor for colossal failure.*

⋎ *Edsel Ford and family in 1939. From left: Edsel, his wife Josephine, and children Henry II, Benson, Josephine and William Clay.*

The Airship City

During the era of the Model T and Packard's Twin Six, the men turning Detroit into the hub of automobile production nearly made the Motor City the center of aviation as well. Local industrialists, their interest driven as much by boosterism as by commercial considerations, were early supporters. In the end, it was a shortage of capital—not enthusiasm or vision—that caused that particular dream to slip away.

Detroiters caught their first glimpse of an airplane on July 14, 1910, seven years after Orville Wright's historic flight at Kitty Hawk. Arch Hoxsey soared and swooped over the state fairgrounds in his biplane, prompting local postcard publishers to print scenes touting Detroit as "the airship city." Like many an early aviator, Hoxsey was destined to die in a crackup of his fragile craft. But the dangers didn't deter others from advocating the benefits of manned flight.

World War I was the real catalyst for Detroit's aviation boom. Howard Coffin, chief engineer of the Hudson Motor Company, chaired the War Department's aircraft board. Under his direction, Detroit automakers designed and built the 400-horsepower Liberty aircraft engine, as well as thousands of two-seat warplanes. Henry B. Joy, president of Packard, bought and leased to the army a large tract of land that is now Selfridge Field for use as a flying field. By war's end Detroit was angling to become the national leader in aviation, hosting the prestigious Pulitzer air races in 1922 and launching regularly scheduled flying boat service to Cleveland. Three years later, Henry Ford's famed trimotor "Tin Goose," designed by former Packard engineer William Stout, began hauling freight to Chicago and Cleveland. That same year, Ford's son Edsel donated $50,000 and a huge trophy for a 1,775-mile "reliability tour" that began and ended at the Ford Airport on Oakwood Avenue in Dearborn. The world's first airport hotel was built; it exists today as the Dearborn Inn.

Throughout the 1920s Detroit's newspapers were filled with the exploits of pilots and manufacturers like Stout, Eddie Stinson, the Buhl brothers, and Billy Brock and Ed Schlee, who stirred civic pride with their around-the-world flight in the *Pride of Detroit*. Edsel Ford became the principal underwriter of Admiral Richard Byrd's trailblazing polar flights. As a key member of the Detroit Aviation Society, he also helped sponsor an air exploration of the Arctic led by George Hubert Wilkins, an adventure shared by thousands of schoolchildren who had chipped in with their pennies. That 1926 expedition turned tragic when *Detroit News* reporter Palmer Hutchinson was killed by a whirling propeller.

Easily the most famous aviator with a Detroit connection was Charles Lindbergh, whose name normally isn't associated with the city. The fact

➤ Arch Hoxsey's historic flight at the Michigan State Fairgrounds, July 14, 1910. It was Detroiters' first look at an airplane over the city.

➤ Opposite page: August 11, 1927: As Henry Ford looks on, Charles Lindbergh adjusts his flying cap and waits to trade places with an old air mail friend, Herb Brooks, in the cockpit of Ford's single-seat "flivver" airplane.

DETROIT THE AIRSHIP CITY

remains, however, that Lindbergh was born in 1902 at an uncle's house at 258 West Forest, near what is now the Wayne State University campus. At the time of his solo flight across the Atlantic in 1927—the most celebrated individual feat of the century—his mother was teaching biology at Cass Technical High School and his great uncle, John C. Lodge, was mayor of Detroit.

Although he was raised principally in Minnesota and Washington, D.C., as a boy Lindbergh spent his summers with his mother's Detroit relatives, the Lands and the Lodges. It was at the homes of these two prominent, permissive, and mildly eccentric families that Lindbergh discovered the wonders of science, conducting experiments and perusing scientific journals inside their basement laboratories.

Legend has it that Lindbergh first approached John Lodge about finding local investors to bankroll his risky attempt to cross the ocean. The young barnstormer had $2,000 in a Detroit bank but needed five times that amount to have a plane built to his specifications. A little more foresight on the part of Uncle John—a lifelong advocate of walking who never understood the public's fascination with cars, much less those deathtraps called airplanes—and it might very well have been a craft called the *Spirit of Detroit*, not the *Spirit of St. Louis*, that carried the "Lone Eagle" from New York to Paris and universal fame.

Lindbergh returned in triumph to Detroit for three days in August 1927. He was greeted by 75,000 when he landed the Spirit of St. Louis at Ford Airport, then cheered by even more during a motorcade to and from Northwestern Field, where he gave a speech. The next day he took Henry and Edsel Ford for their first airplane ride, then took a spin himself in Ford's experimental single-seat "flivver" plane.

Lindbergh's Paris flight "created a boom in aviation," said Tim O'Callaghan of Northville, a Ford retiree who has produced a book and a film on Ford aviation. That year, the city's

⋏ The Detroit News *was a pioneer in the use of aviation for journalistic purposes. By the early 1930s it was employing an "autogiro"—a rotary-wing aircraft—to carry reporters and photographers to stories. The craft used a rotating rotor to lift off the ground and a propeller to move forward through the sky.*

➤ The Maiden Detroit, *designed by William Stout, was an all-metal aircraft that was a forerunner to the famous tri-motors built by Ford starting in the 1920s.*

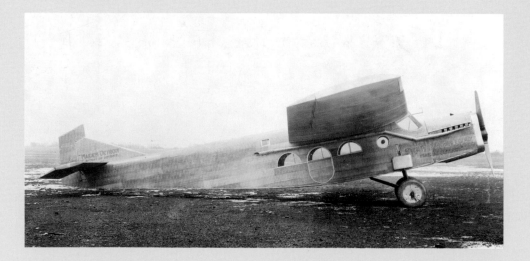

◄ Charles Lindbergh and his mother, a Detroit school-teacher, ride through the streets of the famous aviator's hometown during a 1927 parade celebrating his solo transatlantic flight.

▼ Detroit Municipal Airport, the city's first air field, opened in 1927 at Gratiot and Connor Avenues and quickly became the country's busiest commercial field.

first airport opened at Gratiot and Connor avenues; before long, Detroit Municipal Airport had supplanted Ford Airport as the country's busiest commercial field. (Within 20 years, however, it was too small to handle the larger jets, which instead used Willow Run Airport west of the city. Willow Run, in turn, was superseded by Wayne County Airport, which was expanded in the 1960s into Metropolitan Airport.)

In 1928, Lindbergh helped launch the first transcontinental air service, stocking the airline with the reliable 12-passenger Ford trimotors. Flush with money and know-how, by the end of the decade the Motor City was in position to do for the aviation industry what it had already done for automobiles. Ford, for one, envisioned a future where every home would have a garage and a hangar. The Fords' heavy involvement inspired other automakers to back aircraft activities. In 1929, Charles F. Kettering of General Motors helped organize the Detroit Aircraft Corporation, with an eye to consolidating various aviation companies into a GM of the sky.

The Great Depression changed all that practically overnight. "When automakers had to tighten their belts in the '30s, they decided to concentrate on what they knew best," said O'Callaghan. "And that was building cars."

Today, no single city can claim to be the center of aviation. But for a time, Detroit came as close as any.

The loyal and mild-mannered son labored uncomplainingly in the considerable shadow of his world-famous father. Edsel never gave a single press conference. Whenever reporters approached Edsel, he'd say, "See Father." They always did. If not good for a quote, Edsel was almost unmatched as a stylist, designing the Model A and such classics as the Lincoln Zephyr and Continental. He also quietly served as one of Detroit's major philanthropists.

With the notable exception of Edsel, Detroit's auto pioneers were a hard-boiled lot. Mechanics turned millionaires, they never got all of the grease out from under their fingernails. John Kelsey, who made his fortune building brake systems, continued to wash his socks in the sinks of luxury New York hotel rooms. The two-fisted Dodge brothers, Horace and John, served beer to their workers and occasionally shocked the silk-stocking set by urinating into potted plants.

➤ *Brothers Horace (left) and John Dodge were inseparable in life and death. Raised in poverty in Niles, Michigan, they made a fortune providing transmissions and engines for other automakers before striking out on their own in 1914.*

➤ *Of more than 200 nameplates being produced in 1910, including Lozier and a score of other Detroit-based manufacturers, only a handful survived the industry shakeout that followed.*

At the 1910 auto show, held at the riverfront Wayne Gardens, Hugh Chalmers, the 36-year-old president of the Chalmers Motor Company, warned of the proliferation of nameplates. Detroit alone was home to such nameplates as Lozier, Detroiter, Brush, Carnation, Everitt, Flanders, Paige, Owen, E.M.F., and Regal—none of which survived the 1920s. "I would not take too much stock in any new company," said Chalmers, whose own company was destined to fail, "because I believe the competition in the future is going to be keener by far than it has been in the past, and competition, of course, means the elimination of those who are unable to withstand it." Only four of the 202 different makes of cars being built around the world in 1910 are still in production today: Buick, Ford, Cadillac, and Oldsmobile.

But it was hard for men of means to resist entering the "automobile game." Millionaire Henry B. Joy, whose family's fortune had been made in the lumber and railroad businesses, opened the city's second car factory. In 1903 he and several local investors bought the rights to James W. Packard's gasoline car and moved production from Warren, Ohio to Detroit. Although he had a reputation as a bluenose, Joy was remembered by one contemporary as being "that rare but happy

▲ Henry B. Joy was responsible for opening the city's second auto manufacturing plant, the Packard factory, on a 40-acre site on East Grand Boulevard. Although the last Packard was built in 1958, the factory—one of the first to be made of reinforced concrete—still stands.

▶ A fleet of Packards, fresh off the factory floor, assemble for a test drive in 1905.

combination of a rich man's son with an eagerness to work, ambition in his own right, an aptitude for mechanics, democratic character, social position that made pretense absurd, a training in thrift despite his wealth, and a sense of humor." The solid and reliable Packards continued to be produced until 1958.

John Dodge and his younger brother Horace built engines for Ransom Olds and were the major parts supplier for Henry Ford before launching their own nameplate in 1914. "The Dodge brothers are the two best mechanics in Michigan," one industry publication claimed. "There is no operation in their own shop from drop forging to machining, from tool-making to micrometric measurement, that they can't do with their own hands."

The brothers had endured an impoverished upbringing in Niles, Michigan, but they became fabulously wealthy because of their early shares of Ford stock. Their original 1903 investment of $10,000 yielded a return of $32 million by the time Henry Ford bought back their shares in 1919. Crude and lacking social graces, the brothers were shunned by many members of polite society but admired by the rank and file. Upon their premature deaths in 1920 of influenza, 16 factory hands served as pallbearers at John Dodge's funeral, while Horace was eulogized as "a mechanic with the soul of a poet." The pair, inseparable in life, were buried next to each other in Detroit's Woodlawn Cemetery.

The Dodge Brothers' factory complex, Dodge Main, was built on a 30-acre site in rural Hamtramck in 1910 and featured a test track and hill climb adjacent to the manufacturing plant. Within a decade it employed 20,000 workers and produced 145,000 cars, making the Dodge nameplate one of the most popular in the country and transforming Hamtramck into an automotive boom town along the lines of Highland Park. Five years after the brothers' death, their widows sold the company to a New York investment firm for $146 million, which in turn sold it to Walter P. Chrysler.

Chrysler was a Kansas-born railroad machinist who, succumbing to the automobile bug, left an executive position with the American Locomotive Company in 1912 to overhaul the Buick division of General Motors. After leaving GM in 1920, Walter P. Chrysler similarly modernized the operations of the Maxwell Motor Company, which five years later became the Chrysler Corporation. In 1928 the

A A 1953 Corvette convertible and a 1956 DeSoto appealed to different segments of the car-buying public perhaps, but together they represented one immutable fact of American life during the 1950s: Detroit was indisputably the automobile capital of the world. But foreign carmakers like Honda and Volkswagen were already making inroads.

➤ Fins were in during the 1960s—a time of cheap gas, lax regulation, and high-powered "muscle cars." This model showed off the new Dodge Barracuda at the 1967 Detroit Auto Show.

company bought the Dodge Brothers and soon began manufacturing Plymouth and De Soto cars as well. By the time Chrysler retired as chairman of the board in 1935, his company was the second largest car producer in the world.

Unlike other giants of the auto industry, William C. (Billy) Durant was neither a tinkerer nor an engineer. The charming, energetic Flint native was, however, a superb salesman. In 1904 he reorganized the Buick Motor Company into a profitable concern. Four years later he consolidated 30 disparate automakers and suppliers into a corporation called General Motors. After financial reverses forced him to relinquish control to Eastern bankers in 1911, he teamed with Louis Chevrolet to build a new car under the Chevrolet name. Mechanical innovations like the self-starter and hydraulic brakes, coupled with sophisticated promotion, helped turn Chevrolet into the attractive low-cost alternative to the Model T. In 1928 Chevrolet surpassed Ford to become America's best-selling nameplate.

Time payments were another GM innovation and greatly increased the purchasing power of the growing middle class. A $495 Chevrolet touring car, for example, could be had for a mere $39 a month. America had long been a cash-and-carry economy, even with big-ticket purchases like automobiles, but GM's sales tactic helped erase the social stigma of being in debt.

Durant used his profits to buy up GM stock; in 1916 he regained control and was named president. Forced out again in 1920, he ultimately lost his $100 million personal fortune through failed business ventures and the stock market crash of 1929. In his old age he was reduced to running a bowling alley in Flint, and he died in a New York apartment in 1947. By then GM had become the greatest industrial empire in Detroit—and the world.

With its lopsided economy, dynamic Detroit grew in importance, esteem, and population. By 1930 it was challenging Philadelphia as the country's third largest city.

Exclaimed journalist Matthew Josephson in the February 1929 issue of *Outlook*:

Nowhere in the world can the trend of the new industrial cycle be perceived more clearly than in Detroit. In this sense it is the most modern city in the world, the city of tomorrow.

There is no past, there is no history. Neither traditions nor the accumulated hand-iwork of man's leisure time or deeply reflective moods obtrude upon the eye. There is primarily the wealth of mechanism and "turnover." One day, thousands and thousands of human beings turned themselves over and found that they were in the huge metropolis of Detroit.

⋁ It's too painful to recount the details of the Motor City's loss of market share over the last quarter-century—a tale of waste, short-sightedness, and wrenching socioeconomic changes. Far better to recall the spirit of the golden age of Detroit iron, an attitude that accounts for the phenomenal success of the "Dream Cruise" down Woodward Avenue each summer.

Homes of the Auto Barons

In the early years of the 20th century, when the auto industry was in full throttle and Detroit was a boomtown, several of the city's *nouveau riche* built American palaces that reflected their success and exquisite tastes. Although most of the grand estates were subsequently torn down and their acreage parceled for residential developments, Fairlane Manor, Meadow Brook Hall, the Fisher mansion, and the Edsel and Eleanor Ford home still exist.

While most auto tycoons relocated from stately homes in Highland Park, Indian Village, and the Boston-Edison neighborhood to more lavish estates in Grosse Pointe, Henry Ford built Fairlane in his hometown of Dearborn. Seeking privacy in a pastoral setting close to his business interests, in 1915 Ford and his wife, Clara, acquired 2,000 acres of land on the banks of the Rouge River. Their intention was to build a secluded mansion whose architecture and furnishings reflected their simple tastes.

Ford originally hired a Chicago firm to build a Prairie-style home, but a disagreement over contractors led to the hiring of William Van Tine of Pittsburgh, who significantly altered the original plans. As a result of Van Tine's modifications, Fairlane is a blend of Late English Gothic and Prairie style. Although the home was not as lavish as the typical lakefront Grosse Pointe mansion of the period, the landscaping designed by Jens Jensen— acres of woods filled with birds and wildlife—best represents the estate's beauty and the Fords' priorities. The estate included its own powerhouse, a laboratory, a man-made lake, and guest cottages, as well as a working farm built to scale for Ford's grandchildren.

On April 7, 1947, the 83-year-old tycoon died inside a damp and darkened Fairlane, on a night when the estate's powerhouse had been knocked out due to flooding. Today Fairlane is used as a conference center by the University of Michigan–Dearborn campus and is available for tours.

A decade after Ford's Fairlane was built, Matilda Dodge Wilson, the widow of auto magnate John Frances Dodge, built Meadow Brook Hall in Rochester. In 1907 Matilda Rausch had married her boss, John Dodge, who along with his brother Horace had left Ford to start their own auto company. Thirteen years later, the Dodge brothers died, leaving a multimillion-dollar inheritance to their widows.

Matilda and John Dodge were building a mansion in Grosse Pointe when he died of influenza at the age 56 in 1920. Five years later she married Alfred G. Wilson, a lumber broker. She soon abandoned construction of the Grosse Pointe mansion and instead spent $4 million of her inherited fortune to build an American castle on the grounds of the former Meadow Brook Farm, once used as a country cottage by the Dodges. Completed in 1929 after four years of construction, the Tudor revival–style Meadow Brook Hall features 14 chimneys, leaded Tiffany glass windows, and exquisite woodworking and furnishings. The breathtaking 100-room mansion resembles the English manor houses of the 16th and 17th centuries. Like Fairlane, Meadow Brook Hall is today owned by a university (Oakland University) and has found a second, useful life as a conference center.

Edsel Ford, the only child of Henry Ford and Clara Bryant, assumed the presidency of his father's company in 1919 at the age of 25, three years after his marriage to Eleanor Clay, the niece of department store magnate Joseph L. Hudson. After the birth of their fourth child in 1925, the couple began building their dream home at Gaukler Pointe in Grosse Pointe Shores. The property, purchased from the senior Ford, consisted of 125 acres with more than 3,000 feet of Lake St. Clair shoreline.

The Fords hired Albert Kahn to design their home and traveled with him to England's Cotswalds district to survey the architectural style they preferred. It took three years to build the $3 million, 60-room mansion, the family finally moving in during the Christmas season of 1929. The exterior of the home was covered with Briar Hill sandstone and the limestone roof was draped in planted moss to give it an established look. In true Cotswald style, the interior walls are of stone or English wood paneling from the 16th, 17th, and 18th centuries. Jens Jensen designed the grounds, which include a 132-foot-long swimming pool (constructed to look like a natural spring-fed pool) and a "Bird Island" nature preserve. The peninsula, created from a dredging operation, provided a protected cove for family boats.

After Edsel passed away inside the house in 1943, Eleanor Ford continued to live there until her own death 33 years later. During her lifetime she saw several Grosse Pointe estates fall to the wrecking ball, including Rose Terrace, an enormous mansion built in 1934 by Anna Thompson Dodge, the widow of Horace Dodge. Architectural historian W. Hawkins Ferry described Rose Terrace, torn down in 1971, as "unquestionably Grosse Pointe's most regal residence." During the estate's heyday, peacocks roamed the lawn and two servants worked full-time polishing the silverware.

➤ *Opposite page: Meadow Brook Hall*

THE MELTING POT

When it came to stew, Dinty Moore had nothing on Henry Ford. During the heyday of the Model T, the father of the $5-day required every non–English-speaking worker to enter an intensive 72-session "Americanization" program designed to teach language and social skills. Between 1914 and 1917, more than 14,000 factory hands participated in the program, which culminated in an elaborate commencement ceremony involving a model of an immigrant ship and a giant melting pot.

"Down the gangplank came the members of the class dressed in their national garbs," an observer wrote in 1916. After descending into the pot and disappearing, "the teachers began to stir the contents of the pot with long ladles."

The ingredients of an emerging metropolis were percolating inside. Hefty portions of Italians and Poles. A dash of Russians. A pinch of Lebanese. A sprinkling of Chaldeans. "Presently the pot began to boil over," the reporter continued, "and out came the men dressed in their best American clothes and waving American flags."

Human stew. Melting pot. Ethnic smorgasbord. According to Dave Poremba, manager of the Detroit Public Library's Burton Historical Collection, the old metaphors still apply.

"There's always been a remarkable ethnic and cultural diversity to this area," said Poremba, whose

◄ Immigrants arrive at the train station, about 1910.

Ford's melting pot ceremony.

own great-grandparents emigrated from Poland in the 1890s. "And it continues to this day."

Thankfully, assimilation does not mean homogenization. Over the years, the various nationalities that have made this region home have never completely abandoned the ways of the old country. Thus we have a thriving "Mexican Town" on the city's southwest side, the country's largest and most diverse Middle Eastern community in Dearborn, and a diminishing — but still distinctive — Polish presence in Hamtramck. In addition, concentrations of such disparate groups as Romanians and Filipinos have emerged in the city and the suburbs. All told, more than 80 ethnic groups are represented in the metro area.

Of course, there have always been tensions as various ethnic groups jockey for position on the socioeconomic ladder. Passions and prejudices occasionally bubble to the surface, and some stereotypes die hard. But overall, Metro Detroiters have been a commendably tolerant lot over the last three centuries. Ethnic differences have far more often been a source of pride rather than friction. During the Detroit Tigers' run to the 1968 world's championship, for example, baseball fans rallied around the cry, "Sock it to 'em, Tigers." Reflecting the cultural diversity of the area's fan base, the slogan appeared on bumper stickers in a multitude of languages, including Hungarian (*Verd neg oket Tigerish*), Yiddish (*Dalaing iss tze zay Tigers*) and Japanese (*Bonzai, Tigers*).

From its beginnings as a sparsely populated frontier settlement, Detroit had a pronounced multicultural look to it. Despite the efforts of authorities to discourage fraternization, the French freely mingled with Native Americans and blacks. The community soon had its share of mulatto offspring, distinctive by their yellow-hued skin. As Detroit passed into British and then American hands in the last decades of the 18th century, an unknown number of English, Scots, and Canadians immigrated. Encountering no language barrier, they blended in easily.

The first national groups to arrive were the Germans and Irish, who fled revolution and famine beginning in the 1830s. Large numbers continued to arrive through the 1870s. During this period many Irish settled in a vaguely defined area west of town

UNITED STATES OF AMERICA

DECLARATION OF INTENTION

(Invalid for all purposes seven years after the date hereof)

State of Michigan
County of Wayne
} ss:

In the _____ Circuit _____ Court

of __ Wayne County __

I, __ AlexanderKoscielny __, aged __ 21 __ years,

occupation __ Autoworker __, do declare on oath that my personal

description is: Color __ White __, complexion __ fair __, height __ 5 __ feet __ 8 __ inches,

weight __ 149 __ pounds, color of hair __ brown __, color of eyes __ brown __

other visible distinctive marks __ none __

I was born in __ Hohenzalzer Germany __

on the __ 11th __ day of __ Feby __, anno Domini 1 892 ; I now reside

at __ 1540 Campell av Detroit Mich __

(Give number, street, city or town, and State.)

I emigrated to the United States of America from __ Antwerp __

on the vessel __ Vaderland __ ; my last

(If the alien arrived otherwise than by vessel, the character of conveyance or name of transportation company should be given.)

foreign residence was __ Hohenzalzer Germany __

It is my bona fide intention to renounce forever all allegiance and fidelity to any foreign

prince, potentate, state, or sovereignty, and particularly to __ William 11 __

__ ~~############~~ German Emperor __, of whom I am now a subject;

I arrived at the port of __ New York __, in the

State of __ New York __, on or about the __ 19 __ day

of __ July __, anno Domini 1 903 ; I am not an anarchist; I am not a

polygamist nor a believer in the practice of polygamy; and it is my intention in good faith

to become a citizen of the United States of America and to permanently reside therein:

SO HELP ME GOD.

Alexander Koscielny
(Original signature of declarant.)

Subscribed and sworn to before me this __ 19 __

day of __ Sept __, anno Domini 191 3

__ Thos F Farrell __

Clerk of the __ Circuit __ Court.

By __ Field Marschner __, Deputy Clerk.

14—39

◄ / ⋎ *Alexander Koscielny was representative of the thousands of immigrants that poured into Detroit. Arriving as an 11-year-old immigrant, the German-born Pole built Model T's at Henry Ford's Highland Park plant before joining the army during World War I. After serving nearly six years in the cavalry, he spent the next 25 years as a Detroit firefighter.*

dubbed "Corktown" after County Cork. Thanks to the prevailing Roman Catholic French influence, Detroit's Irish didn't face nearly as much prejudice as their countrymen did in other American cities that were predominantly Protestant. Irish Catholics established the city's first English-speaking parish, Most Holy Trinity, in 1834, and built the current Gothic Revival structure on Porter Street in 1866.

Because of their lack of education, many Irish worked as laborers, domestics, saloonkeepers, policemen, streetcar conductors, and livery hands. They also made their mark in local politics. The offspring of these waves of "famine Irish" included Henry Ford and mayors Frank Murphy and Jerry Cavanagh, as well as scores of other politicians and judges. The annual St. Patrick's Day parade is the state's oldest continuing ethnic parade and causes the Tipperary Pub in Detroit to serve more than 150 pounds of Irish stew that day.

Detroit's Germans settled on the near east side, around Gratiot Avenue. Unlike the working class Irish, many were artisans and professionals. The Germans quickly put their stamp on the city, establishing such enduring institutions as the Harmonie Society (Michigan's oldest musical group) and placing several of their own in the mayor's office.

They also knew a thing or two about beer. When Colonel August Goebel opened his brewery in 1897, he became just the latest in a long line of German-American brewmeisters in Detroit. By 1900 there were 23 of them, including George Voight and Julius Stroh, each looking to slake the thirst of the city's growing population of "hyphenated Americans."

Today about one in four Metro Detroiters have some German blood in them. Their ranks include Margaret Wegener, a suburban Detroiter with fond memories of her grandfather. Anthony Wegener, a chemist in Germany, came to America in 1867 and three years later established A. Wegener & Sons Bottling Works on Riopelle, just off Gratiot.

"In 1885 my grandfather created a soft drink that he called 'Rock & Rye,'" Wegener recalled. "A liquor company that made a drink called 'Rye and Rock' sued, but lost when the court ruled that the two words were of such common usage that no company could have sole rights to them.

"In those days," she continued, "sarsaparilla, ginger ale, cream soda, and root

Detroit's Harmonie Society, organized in 1849 by German immigrants settling on the city's east side, is the oldest musical group in the state. Harmonie Hall was built in 1894 to house choral and concert activities.

➤ Opposite page: The Stroh Brewery Company, which employed 110 men at its Gratiot Avenue plant in 1900, was one of more than a score of breweries in operation at the time. Their names—Pfieffer, Goebel, Voight—and their east-side locations reflected the ethnicity and settlement pattern of the Germans, one of Detroit's largest immigrant groups.

beer, in addition to Rock & Rye, were popular drinks. The first deliveries were made by wheelbarrow, then by horse and wagon, and then by truck. A trip to Mount Clemens took all day.

"My father's older sister, Catherine, had some out-of-town visitors one time and wanted to take them around to see a little of Detroit. So she asked to use one of the horses. She was given the delivery horse, and it automatically stopped off at all the saloons along Gratiot Avenue!"

Detroit's foreign-born population was more than 156,000 in 1910—a figure that doubled within 10 years. In the numerous factories and ethnic neighborhoods, the symphony of dialects competed with the roar of machinery and the

"My godfather was in Detroit and wrote me that he had paper on the walls, shoes, meat every day, fresh bread, milk, water in the house, beer on the corner, soup, and plenty of money. From that time I was crazy to come." —*Immigrant to Detroit, 1905*

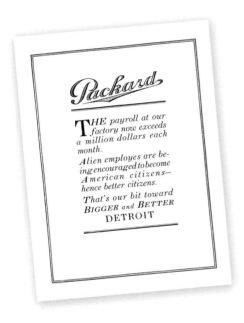

Packard

THE payroll at our factory now exceeds a million dollars each month.
Alien employes are being encouraged to become American citizens— hence better citizens.
That's our bit toward BIGGER and BETTER DETROIT

⌃ *Detroit's automakers actively recruited immigrants for their factories, helping to account for the 49 different nationalities represented in Ford's workforce in 1915.*

➤ *Opposite page: A sense of satisfaction and well-being can be gleaned from this portrait of Kattie and Wladyslaw Mudra, Polish immigrants who were photographed outside their small, neatly kept house on the city's west side.*

singsong of the street peddlers. Workers constantly suffered from the boom-or-bust vagaries of a one-industry town. Acute shortages of housing, health care, schools, and basic services plagued the city. But on the whole, life here was still better than it had been in Russia, Armenia, Lebanon, or Greece.

"My godfather was in Detroit and wrote me that he had paper on the walls, shoes, meat every day, fresh bread, milk, water in the house, beer on the corner, soup, and plenty of money," a wide-eyed immigrant recalled in 1905. "From that time I was crazy to come."

Life in this noisy, polyglot urban colossus often was bewildering, as Christopher Raab of Utica related. In the early 1910s, said Raab, his grandparents lived on Chene, near Gratiot. "Their neighborhood was a typical melting pot, consisting mostly of European and Mediterranean people trying to understand each other. While Grandfather was eager to assimilate, it was a fearful prospect for Grandmother; she simply did not know what was expected of her and found things confusing.

"Apparently, there were others like her. One night a drunk staggered into their bedroom, started undressing and told her, in German, to move over. She screamed, and my grandfather, also in bed, woke up.

"The next day the man, accompanied by his daughters, came by to apologize. He had mistaken his block for ours because the houses all looked the same."

Language instruction was the cornerstone of the local Americanization program, which began in earnest in 1915. Automakers like Ford and Packard, forced to post work signs in several languages inside their factories, joined forces with the Board of Education, which offered night classes to immigrants. The failure to understand English could lead to disaster, as Jim Pikalus, a Greek immigrant, learned on his first day of school at Crossman Elementary. "I couldn't speak English," he recalled. "My mother only spoke Greek and my father was working all

Detroit's Front Door

It was once the grand gateway to Detroit, and for many it was the first impression they had of the city. For 75 years, beginning in 1913, the Michigan Central Depot saw millions of people—from immigrants to presidents, war heroes to celebrities—pass through its doors. With 11 tracks and up to 43 trains a day pulling through the platforms, it was a city unto itself.

The massive Michigan Central Depot, which faces Michigan Avenue between 15th and 17th streets, was at one time the tallest railroad station in the world. It also was arguably the most elegant of its day. The base structure, which is Renaissance and Imperial Roman in style, contained the waiting room, ticket lobby, and concourses. Upon exiting their train and walking up a tunnel to the main waiting room, travelers stepped into an opulent setting of breathtaking beauty, with tiled marble floors, chandeliers, and Gustavino arched ceilings supported by marble columns measuring three stories high. Three gargantuan arched windows supplied natural light throughout. According to Birmingham architect Garnet Cousins, "A traveler was treated to a variety of experiences and the exciting contrast of classical, temple-like forms which led him ultimately to the utilitarian world of the train shed, track, baggage handling, passenger coaches, and steam engines."

Conceived by the same architects who designed New York's Grand Central Terminal, the 21-acre terminal and adjacent park was built by the Detroit River Tunnel Company for $15 million. In the process, hundreds of families were moved, with nearly 300 homes either destroyed or relocated. Catering to thousands of daily travelers and visitors, the station contained numerous facilities and amenities, including a shopping arcade, restaurant, and a reading room. For a few pennies, a traveler could even rent an individual bathtub. In addition to serving as a railroad terminal, the depot was originally intended to also serve as an office complex. However, only five floors of the attached 16-story office tower were ever completed with wall-partitioned offices and marble-faced corridors.

The era of train travel came to an end with the advent of the interstate freeway system and affordable air travel after World War II. By the late 1960s, only 18 trains and a few hundred passengers a day were using the Michigan Central Depot. By then, many of the facilities in the station were closing.

On January 5, 1988, Michigan Central Depot closed for good after a Chicago-bound train left the terminal. Since then the station has gone through several owners and become a gutted eyesore. Today the building attracts vagrants, vandals, graffiti artists, and frustrated preservationists who would like to see the building restored along the lines of other famous railroad stations across the country. There have been periodic discussions of converting the station into a world trade center, a casino, or a hotel/office complex, but to date no serious developer has surfaced. With its Roman architecture, the terminal has the appearance of an ancient ruin, an empty and idle reminder of a bygone era in transportation.

∧ / ➤ *Michigan Central Depot in its heyday. At its peak, the terminal was a hub of activity, with up to 43 trains picking up or disgorging thousands of travelers each day.*

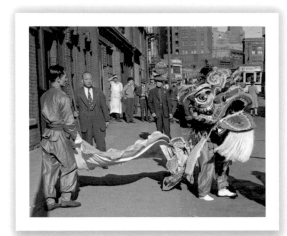

⋀ *Top: Chinese festivities in downtown Detroit, 1943.*

⋀ *Above: A Mexican fiesta in Detroit, 1939.*

the time at the restaurant, so I didn't learn any English. I went to school with my cousin that day, and he couldn't speak English, either.

"At some point during school, my cousin told me he had to go to the bathroom. I told him to ask the teacher. He said she didn't understand him and I knew she couldn't understand me, so eventually he wet his pants. We got kicked out of class, and when we got home we both got walloped."

Reflecting the civic zeal to aid the crushing number of immigrants, in 1919 several YMCA employees opened a small social service agency in a brick building at the corner of Adams and Witherell. From this grew the International Institute, which continues to offer English language, U.S. citizenship, and ethnic enrichment classes to residents and the foreign-born.

In an attempt to provide supervised recreation for the flood of children entering the school system, the city opened several facilities. The St. Clair Recreation Center was in its day commonly referred to as "the Rec," recalled Mary Mansour, who grew up near the place in the 1920s. The converted two-story frame house ran along Canfield between Fairview and Lemay. It was adjacent to a large playground equipped with a baseball diamond, slides, swings, monkey bars, and a sandbox.

"In our east side neighborhood, the Rec was the strongest influence on us, after God, parents, church, and school," said Mansour. "The Rec symbolized the American melting pot for us children, who were mainly the first generation of poor, immigrant parents. We learned to accept each other and to play together without ethnic discrimination, slurs, or fights."

Outdoor games were the order of the day at the Rec during the warm-weather months. In cold weather, children ice skated or took singing and folk dancing lessons indoors. They also rehearsed and staged skits pertaining to health, safety, and the holidays, said Mansour. "Christmas was the best of all. The Saturday before, Santa Claus spent the day in the Rec beside the tree that we had decorated with paper chains and cutouts. Santa gave candy or popcorn balls to each of us. During the years when our dads were laid off from Briggs and Ford, those were our only presents."

Detroit's largest immigrant group, the Poles, began arriving in the late 19th century, as labor agents hired them to work in the city's many stove manufacturing plants. Later, large numbers worked in the auto factories. Today, an estimated

800,000 people in the metro area have Polish roots.

Susan Tyszka, a retired teacher living in Sterling Heights, is one of them. Her great-grandfather, Edward Gajewski, was a tailor who came to Detroit in 1872 and helped found St. Albertus, the first Polish Catholic church in the city. Edward's son, Alexander, opened a tailor shop and married an energetic neighborhood girl, Mary Hinska. The experiences of the young couple, Tyszka's maternal grandparents, have always fascinated her.

"They also operated a confectionary shop at the front of their house on Chene Street," said Tyszka. "Besides offering candy, toys, and tobacco products, the shop had an area off to the side with a few tables and chairs where patrons could sit down and enjoy an ice cream treat. Every so often a candy butcher would come to the store and create fresh candy on the marble-topped table in the back room. An older cousin told me that our grandmother didn't like to leave her husband in charge of the shop too often because he gave away too much candy to children who wandered in."

▼ *Mass at St. Albertus, the first Polish Catholic church built in Detroit.*

A Alexander Gajewski, the son of Polish immigrants, poses inside his tailor shop in 1913.

➤ Opposite page: Mary Hinska Gajewski stands proudly behind the glass counter of the confectionary store she and her husband operated at the front of their Chene Street residence.

In those days before electronic entertainment, said Tyszka, each ethnic enclave had its own theater, an immense comfort to immigrants pining for the old country. Across the street from the Gajewskis' shop was the *Teatr Rozmaitosci*, a Polish-language theater that featured classic drama, melodrama, and musical variety shows.

"Just before the intermission, an usher from the theater would cross the street and fill a tray with ice cream cones from the store to sell to patrons during the break. A large wedding portrait of my grandfather was often used as set dressing at the theater if the script called for the portrait of a man to be on the wall. Since the portrait was covered in glass, the set designer could use chalk to whiten the hair or crayon to add a beard or eyeglasses if the script called for an older, dignified man.

"By the way," added Tyszka, "my grandmother baked, cooked, cleaned, did

Making Americans in "Little Poland"

THE COMMUNITY FUND WAS ONE OF MANY SOCIAL SERVICE ORGANIZATIONS ASSISTING THE FLOOD OF IMMIGRANTS TO DETROIT DURING THE EARLY 20TH CENTURY. IN 1922 A MEMBER OF THE FUND'S PUBLICITY DEPARTMENT, FAYE ELIZABETH SMITH, EXAMINED THE GENERATION GAP BETWEEN THE FOREIGN-BORN AND THEIR NEW WORLD OFFSPRING IN THE POLISH ENCLAVE OF HAMTRAMCK.

Jacob Street grinned slyly when Wanda Pulaski found a hat box on her door step Christmas Eve. The men slapped Stanislaus soundly on the back and the sheepish young Pole, filling up on congratulatory home brew, grew chesty with confidence. All Hamtramck waited to see Wanda at mass in the morning. The older women waxed reminiscent of their own courtship days in the old world. Stanislaus had rendered a free translation of an old Polish custom whereby the enamored swain of the rural Polish girl buys a gay kerchief for his love to wear on her head, and if she accepts it she accepts the donor, too.

Wanda, proud in her American education, wooed by a Pole lately from the old country who spoke no English, represented the younger generation, which glimpses American opportunity and new ideals engendered by a few years' education contact with new influences introduced by social services. The average Pole in Hamtramck knows as little—and cares less—about American customs and ideals as the average man and woman in Detroit knows of life in Hamtramck. If Wanda, whose deft fingers in the cigar factory had earned for her some measure of independence and advantage over the girls who had married when they were 16, capitulated to the old world Pole and wore the beguiling gilt bonnet to mass, little Poland had won another round in the bout with Americanization.

For the Polish girl there is no future outside the church and marriage. If she has any hopes of heaven she must either marry or go into the sisterhood. Such dance halls as the "Shimmy Center" do not foster religious aspirations, so the girls in Hamtramck for the most part marry. Love is not in any way necessary for such an arrangement; in fact, one social worker who has been close to a large club of girls for several years, and enjoyed their deepest confidences, declares that she has known of but one instance in which love was the impelling motive.

Marriage is an economic necessity for women. If the girl makes no choice for herself, her parents will make it for her, if she lingers long past 17. For this reason morals are lax and efforts to improve the living conditions of girls working in the factories have proven unavailing. The girls see nothing ahead of them but tedious days in the factory if they do not marry, and Polish men will not come to see them in carefully supervised homes with 10 o'clock closing hours and restrictions against smoking.

There is no affront intended nor any taken if the young Pole loosens the age-old repression of his race with a few fingers of "white mule" before he calls on his lady love in her home. What supervised dormitory could withstand the tumultuous passion of a dozen heaving accordions wailing with love songs?

Furthermore, wages are small and living costs are high in Hamtramck. Every family must eke out its income with revenue from boarders. They are a clannish people and timid except among their own. No Pole comes to this country without first finding where the Poles live in the city of his destination. Every house is subdivided and sublet, but sooner or later each man manages to buy a home which he in turn divides and rents.

Congestion is held accountable by the social service workers at the Tau Beta Community House for many of the evils which exist, but even though the Poles might all become sufficiently well off to live in single houses they must be taught to want the comforts and privacy of American homes before they will have them. Wanda grew up in a three-room home, where her mother and father lived with five children and four boarders. When prohibition came, a still and Stanislaus were added, each a necessity, the still to keep happiness in the family and Stanislaus to cover the expense.

Joseph Campau Avenue is lined with Polish shops which enjoy the whole trade of Hamtramck. Not one out of a hundred citizens of the village ever enter a Detroit store. They do not speak English and they find no one in the stores there who can understand their wants. Furthermore they resent the fact that Detroit displays so little interest in them. Many of the women have lived years in Hamtramck without coming into the city.

The shop windows are lettered in Polish and the clerks speak their language, but the stock and window displays soon cultivate a desire for American apparel. The shoes shown in the shops are smartly cut, there are many satin pumps and the ubiquitous galoshes, and the price tags are twins to those on Woodward Avenue.

The Polish woman who forsakes her kerchief wants a picture hat, laden with roses or feathers. Not only Wanda but her mother felt the persuasion of the tinsel toque from Stanislaus. There was the difference of three years' schooling in their viewpoints, however, and Wanda's mother exerted all her maternal influence to turn the tide in favor of the boarder.

In Hamtramck education fights a hard battle. The older people have never had any education, in many cases, and usually only a year in a rural Polish school. They begrudge the time the boys and girls spend in studies and take advantage of their early maturity to advance their age a few years so that they may go to work. Most of the children who are declared to be 14 are a year or two younger, and Wanda, like many others, had worked in a cigar factory since she was 12.

Earning her living meant only a bit more freedom, for her pay envelope must be turned over intact to her mother every Saturday night. However, she had the joy of picking out her clothes, with the certainty that her mother would buy them for her out of the money she turned in.

Life had been quite satisfactory under such conditions and she rather pitied the meagerness of her mother's life, so full of drudgery. She remembered her when she was younger and young married people had congregated in their kitchen to dance the old-world dances to her father's accordion. The night still rang with wild music of the mountain villages, but Wanda belonged to the newer generation who went to "Shimmy Center," the "S.C.," as the youth of Hamtramck call it, where the freedom of America is interpreted in jazz, "white mule," and license. Such dance halls have no supervision, and to offset the assault on the still primitive moral standards of the village,

social workers at the Tau Beta Community House have formed dancing clubs where the young people may dance under proper conditions.

These dances in the beautiful library of the Community House are made eminently desirable events to attend, and the young people flock there. They come in contact with the best in American life here rather than the worst. The girls are attracted to the sewing and cooking classes and books of romance from the library shelves lift love above the sordid realms of economic arrangement and elemental passions.

As the mothers of tomorrow they are learning to know life differently, and to Wanda and every other American-born Polish girl comes the decision to be made: shall she marry a native-born Pole who still lives by the old standards, who speaks no English and will disagree with her at every point, or demand one with education who may pass the civil service examination, perhaps, and even become a fireman?

Wanda wore that hat to mass on Christmas morning, but not until she had poured out her heart to the head resident of the community house. She had decided to take Stanislaus under her wing. Married life was for some purpose, she decided, and if she could bring her lover to see things through American eyes, she would have lived to some point. She wanted to sign up at once in the mothers' club and the cooking classes. Her name on the roll, she departed with shining eyes.

Stanislaus and Wanda were married on New Year's Eve with all the accoutrements of a fashionable American wedding and the stimulating lubricants of Little Poland. Wanda wore a veil and Stanislaus a slight slant. Jell-O, a giant ruby mountain, graced the supper table around which flowed rivers of home brew. The future of America trembled in the gelatinous confection over which Wanda presided. It was the first of her culinary accomplishments as a Polish-American wife, and Stanislaus in the corner gulping happily over the slippery stuff represented the first of her achievements in Americanization.

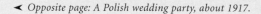

◄ *Opposite page: A Polish wedding party, about 1917.*

⋀ *A Polish girl's first holy communion in 1922.*

⋀ Top: The Weinman Settlement House, established by the League of Catholic Women of Detroit in 1908 at Larned and Orleans Streets, was one of several neighborhood centers designed to ease immigrants' transition from the Old World to the New. The children pictured here are the offspring of Italian and Middle Eastern immigrants.

⋀ Above: Francesco Petrella, an Italian immigrant, poses with his family and his first automobile in front of their rented home on Mount Elliott, circa 1917.

laundry, sewed, and raised five children while tending the store. I wish I had inherited her energy!"

Until World War I closed the floodgates to unlimited European immigration, automakers aggressively recruited workers overseas, with 18,028 hourly workers, representing 49 different nationalities, toiling in 1915 in Ford's Highland Park plant alone. By 1925, roughly half of the city's 1.2 million residents had been born outside of the United States, the largest percentage of any city in the country. Among them were 115,069 Poles, 49,427 Russians, and 42,457 Italians.

The latter group included the Boatins of Ravenna, Italy. Paul Boatin was 16 when his family came to Detroit in the spring of 1925. "My dad was an agitator against Mussolini," said Boatin, a retired autoworker living in Dearborn. "All night long the Fascists, the blackshirts with their skulls and crossed bones, would search for people to punish. I was there when they grabbed my dad and forced him to swallow machine oil, hoping to kill him."

The Boatins blended into the neighborhood of Italian immigrants forming at Oakwood Boulevard and Fort Street, an ethnic protectorate no different from the ones that have traditionally welcomed scores of nationalities. "We had stores and restaurants and newspapers, all operated by Italians. So for most intents and purposes, for the first few years I basically didn't have much contact with the outside world."

The first Belgians came to Detroit in large numbers in the late 19th century, settling on the northeast side and building Our Lady of Sorrows Church at Meldrum and Berlin. After 1914, refugees from the war-torn country helped grow the local Belgian community into the largest in the United States. Between 1900 and 1930, tens of thousands of Hungarians settled in a neighborhood known as Delray on the southwest side of town. During this period, a large number of Ukrainians also made Detroit their new home. Unlike other immigrant groups, however, they established no clearly defined ethnic colony. Instead, they tended to blend in with other eastern Europeans on the upper east side and in Hamtramck.

Perhaps no city-within-the-city produces more bittersweet memories than Black Bottom, the 60-square-block neighborhood on the near east side that was home to Detroit's burgeoning African-American population. At the turn of the century only one in 100 Detroiters was black. But then came the "Great Migration"

◄ *Belgian children fleeing their war-torn country arrive in Detroit in 1915. Many Belgians settled on the east side.*

▼ *This nameless subject had his portrait taken inside the Lincoln Studio at 560 Gratiot Avenue, one of the many small businesses owned and operated by blacks on the near east side.*

of southern Negroes, many of them impoverished sharecroppers, recruited to work in the factories during World War I. Like most northern industrial cities, the Motor City's complexion changed dramatically and irreversibly. The black population swelled from less than 6,000 in 1910 to nearly 500,000 a half-century later. Their number included five-term mayor Coleman Young, Motown Records founder Berry Gordy, and heavyweight boxing champion Joe Louis. Today, with three out of four residents claiming African-American ancestry, Detroit is the largest black-majority city in the country. It is hard to find a black Detroiter whose ancestry cannot be traced to Georgia, Alabama, Mississippi, or some other southern state.

The size and energy of the big city nearly overwhelmed Joe Louis, who came up from rural Alabama in 1926. "You can't imagine the impact that city had," he wrote in his autobiography. "I never saw so many people in one place, so many cars at one time; I had never even seen a trolley car before. There were other things I had never heard of—parks, libraries, brick schoolhouses, movie theaters. People dressed different, and then I realized that even with those brand-new overalls and country shoes, I wasn't dressed right. But one thing I knew, Detroit looked awfully good to me."

Paradise Valley, the neighborhood's famous business and entertainment strip, ran principally along Hastings Street. Here dandies, gamblers, and hustlers rubbed shoulders with peddlers, street-corner preachers, and ladies of the night. "Everyone was welcome in the Valley," observed one reporter, "whites as well as blacks, as long as they brought the right tolerance of human nature."

Scharrol Poole of Highland Park recalled streetcar rides in the 1940s to her grandmother's house on Hastings at Hendrie. "I loved to ride down Hastings, with all the aromas of the barbecue restaurants, laundries, shrimp shacks, and fish markets. The street was always alive with sights and sounds and stirring people; and to me, it was *the* place to go.

"My grandmother Sallie—everyone called her Big Mama—would take me to the movies: the Castle, on Hastings at Vernor, and the Willis, on Hastings at Willis. There would be a man selling hot peanuts and hot tamales day and night. It seemed he never went home. His hot roasted peanuts smelled like they floated from heaven, and his hot tamales were the most delicious ever!"

Paradise Valley was more than sizzle and snap and 'round-the-clock action. The district was filled with black-owned businesses of all types servicing a largely black clientele, a feature of everyday life that disappeared once residents scattered to other neighborhoods throughout the city. Former newsboy George D. Ramsey can conjure up at will the stores of Hastings Street, circa 1950: Stafford's Jewelry, Topps Grill, Mr. Louie Shoe Repair, Hazel and Carl's shrimp shack, Jackson's pool hall, and the Bee Dew Beauty School.

"The other block of Hastings that I delivered papers on had Del Smith's bar and restaurant," continued Ramsey, "Streeter's confectionary, where I got my first Boston cooler; two beauty shops; Mrs. Annabelle's record shop, where we shined shoes; Rex and Palace barber shops; and Dixon drugstore, where we could buy a nonalcoholic beer and hear those young boys that he had playing the harmonicas."

"Because of segregation, we were a close-knit community," said former Black

⋀ Top: Street peddlers were a common sight in Detroit's neighborhoods. This peddler was pictured resting his feet outside a near eastside store, about 1900.

⋀ Above: The Iroquois Club, photographed on Valentine's Day, 1910, was one of the African-American community's foremost social organizations.

➤ Opposite page: The Pittsburgh Inn on St. Antoine in 1920.

Bittersweet Justice

In an attempt to break out of the eastside ghetto that contained most of Detroit's blacks, in 1925 a doctor named Ossian Sweet paid $18,500 for a house at 2905 Garland, between Charlevoix and Navarre. His move into the otherwise white neighborhood touched off a killing, a pair of fiercely argued trials, and a landmark victory for the National Association for the Advancement of Colored People.

On the evening of September 9, 1925, several hundred whites gathered outside Sweet's tidy brick bungalow. This was the latest attempt in a bloody series of forcible evictions of black homeowners. Bottles, stones, slurs, and threats filled the air. Windows were broken. On this occasion, however, the object of the mob's wrath refused to be intimidated. As Sweet would later state, "I have to die a man or live a coward."

At some point during the commotion, shots rang out from inside the besieged house. One bystander fell wounded; another, a 33-year-old man shot in the stomach, dropped dead. As the mob swelled to perhaps 2,000 in the immediate aftermath of the shootings, police rushed in and arrested Sweet, his wife, his brother Henry, and eight other black adults. An arsenal of weapons and ammunition was found inside. All were charged with first-degree murder.

The resulting trials came at a time of tremendous racial tension in Detroit. The local Ku Klux Klan, their numbers swelled by the arrival of many white southern migrants to work in the auto plants, claimed 100,000 members. A cross had recently been burned at the foot of City Hall.

The NAACP, anxious to prove that the principle of a man's home being his castle applied to blacks as well as whites, hired legendary lawyer Clarence Darrow to lead the defense. Recorder's Court judge Frank Murphy, later to gain fame as Detroit's mayor and a Michigan governor during the 1930s, presided. The liberal-minded Murphy was aware of the implications of the case: "Throughout it all the question of how to secure a fair trial for the 11 colored defendants is constantly on my mind," he wrote. "Above all, I want them to know that they are in a court where the true ideal of justice is constantly sought. A white judge, white lawyers, and 12 white jury men are sit-

ting in judgement on 11 who are colored black. This alone is enough to make us fervent in our effort to do justice. . . ."

The jury heard 70 prosecution witnesses. Then Dr. Sweet, the only defendant to testify, took the stand. Murphy, in a critical ruling, determined that the defendant's state of mind was relevant. This allowed Sweet, the grandson of an Alabama slave, to describe a lifetime of racist encounters, all of which influenced his actions on the night of the shooting.

"When I opened the door and saw the mob," he testified, "I realized I was facing the same mob that had hounded my people through its entire history. In my mind I was pretty confident of what I was up against, with my back against the wall. I was filled with a peculiar fear, the kind no one could feel unless they had known the history of our race. I knew what mobs had done to my people before."

Darrow was equally eloquent in his three-hour summation. He spoke of race and religious prejudice as being "the two things that will take men and women and turn them into fiends. . . . You breathe prejudice in the air; you get it at your mother's knee; you get it up the street. You don't know how you got it or why. It comes as the sunlight comes, though you don't know from where."

After 12 white men deliberated 46 hours without agreeing on a verdict, Murphy declared a hung jury. The prosecution tried Henry Sweet, the only defendant to admit to firing a weapon, the following spring. But another brilliant summation by Darrow—this one lasting nearly eight hours—helped win an acquittal. After failing to get a conviction in two attempts, the prosecution decided not to retry Dr. Sweet or any of the remaining defendants. All were released from jail.

It turned out to be a bittersweet victory for Dr. Sweet. The house on Garland continued to be the scene of tragic happenings. His young daughter, his wife, and his brother Henry all died of tuberculosis in the years following the trials. He remarried twice; both marriages ended in divorce. He ran for various political offices on four occasions, losing each time. He moved from Garland in 1944, installing himself above a pharmacy that he operated. He gradually became a recluse. In 1958, the house he had fought so desperately to keep was lost to taxes. Two years later, the depressed doctor committed suicide.

According to Tom Jones, longtime director of the Historical Society of Michigan, the Sweet trials were "a milestone in civil rights jurisprudence. Here we have a black group literally under siege by a hostile mob, defending their safety. The fact that the argument was sufficient to persuade a jury not to convict them in the 1920s makes it a milestone."

But three quarters of a century later, there clearly remains work to be done. A 1999 University of Michigan study concluded that Detroit trailed only Atlanta and Cleveland as the most segregated of the country's 107 largest cities. Prejudice, like the house on Garland Street, still stands.

◄ *Opposite page: Ossian Sweet.*

▼ *Henry Sweet and his defense counsels, Julian Perry, Thomas Chawke and Clarence Darrow, pictured on May 17, 1926.*

"I KNOW ONE FINE IRISH CITIZEN BORN IN CORK TOWN WHOSE MOTHER AND FATHER WERE BORN IN DUBLIN. HE MARRIED AN EAST SIDE GERMAN GIRL WHOSE PARENTS WERE BORN IN MUNICH. ONE OF HIS TWO SONS MARRIED A FRENCH GIRL, ANOTHER MARRIED A BELGIAN AND HIS DAUGHTER MARRIED AN ITALIAN...THAT IS DETROIT AND THAT IS THE GREATER PART OF AMERICA." —*Malcolm Bingay,* Detroit Is My Own Home Town

∧ *Louis Perentesis, pictured with his wife in 1918, reportedly was the Greek community's first millionaire. Detroit's Greeks were notoriously entrepreneurial, disdaining factory jobs and instead opening candy stores, flower shops and restaurants.*

Bottom resident Torrence Alvin Cain. Nostalgia disguises the deadly downside to living inside this overcrowded ghetto. Tuberculosis and other communicable diseases spread like wildfire through the cramped flats and apartments, and infant mortality rates were sky-high. For years, deaths actually exceeded births in Black Bottom. Blacks finally began moving in large numbers into other parts of the city after illegal housing covenants were struck down in the 1940s. Eventually, most of Black Bottom was demolished to make way for the freeways and urban renewal projects. Forcibly evacuated residents called it "urban removal."

Not all immigrant groups succumbed to the siren call of the factory. Detroit's Greeks were notoriously entrepreneurial, disdaining the drudgery of the assembly line in favor of opening small restaurants, soda fountains, hat cleaners, shoeshine stands, grocery stores, flower shops and *kafeneion,* the intimate coffeehouses that were for generations the center of social and political activities. Demetrios Antonopoulas, for example, came over from Korinthos, washed dishes for a while, then in 1895 opened what is the oldest continually run Greek business in the city, the Hellas Cafe. Several of his countrymen worked as waiters, most hoping to save enough money to start their own business.

The census bureau counted a mere 884 foreign-born Greeks in the city in 1910. That figure included Theodore Gerasimos, who by 1907 was the Greek community's first millionaire, thanks to a successful wholesale candy, tobacco, and ice cream business. By 1920 the number of Detroit Greeks had increased fivefold. Most settled on Monroe and Macomb streets, in an area close to downtown inevitably dubbed "Greektown." They gradually displaced the German community there.

The four Constantine brothers—Peter, George, Michael, and Harry—were typical of the Greek immigrant experience. Arriving in the city in the early 1900s, they started out selling flowers from a pushcart. In 1912 they opened a flower shop in the lobby of the Majestic Building at Woodward and Michigan. "We left Greece because it was too small, with too many people and no opportunity," said Peter. "Here, I've known all of the judges, lawyers, and mayors. Mayor Philip Breitmeyer was the first mayor to step into my shop after I opened. He liked to wear a white carnation and I gave him one free every morning."

The brothers stayed there until the building was demolished in 1961, moving to the First National Building before finally selling the business in 1975. As an old man, Peter Constantine returned to his birthplace in the grape-growing region of southern Greece. "My heart wasn't in it once I got there," he admitted. "My life in Detroit is what mattered to me after so long."

Over time, the more affluent Greeks left Greektown for other parts of the city as the neighborhood became predominantly commercial, multi-ethnic, and poorer. Second-generation Greeks, the children of the immigrants who had settled the area, typically lived the American dream—going off to college, getting married, and then moving to suburbs like St. Clair Shores, Farmington, and Lincoln Park. By 1948 Greektown was considered expendable enough to be torn down to make room for a new judicial center; only a latent storm of protest saved Monroe Street businesses from the wrecking ball.

▲ *An early Greek funeral in Detroit, circa 1897.*

Greektown fell into decline for several years before staging a comeback in the mid 1960s. Local merchants organized, painting storefronts and installing colorful awnings. Diane Edgecomb, president of the Central Business Association, was instrumental in acquiring additional street lighting and delivering flower-filled olive barrels for sidewalks. She persuaded city officials to hold the annual Freedom Festival on Monroe, and a street fair made its debut in 1965, inspiring the annual series of ethnic festivals that are now a summer tradition downtown. Featuring Old World-style bakeries, heavy-duty belly dancing, and triumphant cries of "Opa!" as waiters light up plates of *saganaki* (flaming *kasseri* cheese), Greektown has since evolved into one of the city's most popular attractions for tourists and residents.

The sort of evolutionary migratory pattern displayed by Greek Detroiters has been repeated throughout the metropolitan area. For example, the core of the region's estimated 96,000 Jews, now concentrated in the southern part of Oakland County,

In 1906, the three Barbas brothers—John, Christos and Tom—opened a candy store at 33 Cadillac Square. Four years later, the Greek siblings moved into their own building at 17 Cadillac Square and commemorated the event with this photograph.

Opposite page: A belly dancer entertains several customers inside a Greektown restaurant in 1939.

is many miles and several decades removed from the Jewish neighborhood originally centered around Hastings Street. The Jewish pattern of movement can be traced through the gradual shifting of major businesses and congregations from Detroit to the suburbs. Shaarey Zadek moved to Southfield in 1962, followed by Temple Beth El to Bloomfield Hills in 1973 and Temple Israel to West Bloomfield seven years later.

A more startling transformation has taken place on the east side of Dearborn. Over the last 30 years, the influx of Middle Eastern immigrants—Yemeni, Iraqi, Palestinian, Lebanese—has steadily replaced the Italian and Polish families in much the same way that these eastern and southern Europeans replaced the Germans who originally settled the area in the 19th century.

Whether it's the call to prayer issued five times daily from the mosque or the

◄ Opposite page: Greektown remains one of Detroit's favorite tourist destinations.

◄ The Jaafar family, recent arrivals from war-torn Iraq, has dinner inside their Dearborn home in the summer of 2000.

▼ The Irish first came to Detroit in large numbers in the 1830s. Their offspring included J.J. Hayes, who operated this drugstore at 227 Porter, in the heart of the lower westside neighborhood known as Corktown.

nearly 200 Arab specialty shops, bakeries, and restaurants lining Warren Avenue, there is a definite Old World feel to Dearborn's "Arab Town." But to the credit of the community leaders who each summer organize the annual Arab International Festival, they are also interested in recognizing and celebrating the area's other cultures. That is why organizers intentionally inserted the word "international."

"We thought it was important that it have an international flavor—that it not just be for Arabic people," festival founder Ismael Ahmed told the press before the 2000 street fair, which drew 150,000 people. "From the very beginning, we incorporated things like African drummers and salsa bands and other kinds of cultures. . . . The barriers and the stereotypes fall away, especially if you have the ability to do things like this where people can come and comfortably enjoy each other's culture."

Father Mitchell Szarek is the Polish-born pastor of St. Cunegunda Catholic Church. The working class neighborhood, centered around McGraw and Lonyo on Detroit's southwest side, was "originally only Polish, settled in the 1920s by immigrants from Galicia in the southern part of Poland," he said. After half a century, many of the original parishioners died or moved away. The neighborhood has

since been replenished by immigrants from other countries. According to Fr. Szarek, the percentage of Hispanic families is now roughly 15 percent and growing. Romanians who left their home-land in the wake of the breakup of the Soviet Union represent an even larger number of households.

Similarly, the Corktown neighborhood a few miles east has had at least a dozen waves of immigration wash over it. As late as 1946, newspaperman Malcolm Bingay claimed that "offhand I do not know of a single Irish family now living in old Corktown. Holy Trinity of tender memories now has Mexicans and Maltese mostly as its communicants." Today, half of all marriages performed at Holy Trinity are Irish-Mexican, reflecting the growing bond between two seemingly disparate cultures. "There's a real affinity between the Irish and Mexicans," insisted Maria Elena Rodriguez, a community leader in Mexicantown. "We look at life similarly: very spiritual, very mystical."

No matter what tongue newcomers speak, no matter what religion they follow, they share the goal that has historically attracted immigrants to Detroit: the desire to carve out a new life in tolerant surroundings. Because of cultural differences and ethnic prejudices, they haven't always succeeded. But most Metro Detroiters, nearly all of whom can trace their ancestry back to some foreign land, are able to recognize in Fr. Szarek's heavily accented English a sentiment that translates well into any language.

"We must always be open to new changes," he said. "We have to recognize that all different cultures have dignity."

◄ *John Sciopu waves a flag during the 1981 swearing-in ceremony of new American citizens at Hart Plaza.*

Albert Kahn's Blueprint for Detroit

Nearly 60 years after Albert Kahn last pulled a jackknife out of his vest pocket and whittled the business end of a drafting pencil, his standing as one of history's great architects remains as solid and enduring as any of the more than 2,000 buildings he created during his lifetime.

Kahn, respected today as one of the fathers of modernism, is principally remembered as the man who built Henry Ford's factories. However, this sawed-off, bespectacled steam engine also was responsible for some of metro Detroit's most distinctive landmarks. They include such architectural gems as the Fisher Building, Police Headquarters, the Belle Isle Casino, General Motors Headquarters, the Detroit Athletic Club, and the Edsel and Eleanor Ford House.

Not that the modest old master got carried away with the "artsy" aspects of his classical masterpieces. "Architecture," he liked to say, "is 90 percent business and 10 percent art."

Kahn's emergence was complicated by the lack of a formal education and by his being Jewish in a virulently anti-Semitic world. "The prejudice was particularly strong in the auto industry," recalled his nephew, Bill Kahn. "It was very rare for a Jew to advance far."

As imposing as these obstacles were, however, it was a simple inability to distinguish between certain colors that threatened to put the brakes on his career before it had a chance to take off.

It was about 1885, and the teenaged Kahn was tracing and drafting at the office of Mason & Rice, one of Detroit's leading architectural firms. An associate suspected the apprentice was color blind—a fatal handicap for a fledgling architect—and marched him into the office of George Mason. The youngster, facing dismissal, was asked to identify the colors in an area rug.

Some colors came easier than others. Finally, he had to guess between green and brown. With his future hanging in the balance, he mentally flipped a coin and chose green.

"If I had guessed brown," Kahn later reflected, "I might be a butcher today."

Kahn was born in Germany in 1869. His father, an itinerant rabbi, soon left Westphalia for America. It wasn't until 1880 that 11-year-old Albert, the oldest of six children, shepherded the brood across the Atlantic to join their father in Baltimore. Four years later, the entire family moved to Detroit.

Albert demonstrated promise in art and music. "But his mother decided that being a concert pianist wouldn't do," recalled Kahn's daughter, Rosalie Kahn Butzel of Seattle. "There were not enough opportunities in the field. But he loved listening to classical music until the day he died."

Albert concentrated on his drawing, but was fired from his job as an office boy with the firm of John Scott & Co. Legend has it that the city's premier sculptor, Julius Melchers, found the boy crying on a downtown street corner and took him under his wing. It was Melchers who recommended him to Mason & Rice.

Narrowly surviving the rug color test, Kahn impressed his bosses with his dedication. "Every spare moment of the day and evening . . . Albert would spend reading our collection of architectural books," Mason remembered. "Hours meant nothing to him when he was absorbed in his work." When he was 18, the promising Kahn was given his first commission: designing the porch of the Grand Hotel on Mackinac Island.

In 1890 he had progressed to the point that he won a traveling scholarship to Europe from *American Architect* magazine. The prize required him to regularly submit drawings and an accompanying article for publication. His companion was artist Henry Bacon, the future designer of the Lincoln Memorial. Kahn, a wonderfully fast and accurate sketch artist, learned a great deal about drawing from Bacon, but nothing about writing. "Never mind the articles," his editor finally wired. "Send more sketches."

In 1896, the same year the first experimental automobiles appeared on Detroit's

▲ *The architect and his masterpiece: Albert Kahn at day and the Fisher Building at night.*

▼ *The 15-story General Motors Building was the auto giant's world headquarters for three-quarters of a century. Built in the 1920s, it boasted more than 1.3 million square feet of office space, making it the largest office complex in the world.*

cobblestone streets, Kahn married Ernestine Krolik. The petite University of Michigan graduate was "the power behind the throne," said Rosalie. "She was quiet, sophisticated, and graceful and ran a very good household. She was a great gardener and talented interior designer. She advised my father on color and design and fabric. They complemented each other wonderfully."

Albert had started his own firm with two partners the year before, so the newlyweds lived with Ernestine's parents until the business could get established. The company's first commission was Children's Hospital, followed by such varied jobs as a library for *Detroit News* founder James Scripps and a pneumatic hammer factory. By 1902, the firm had become Albert Kahn Associates and now included his brothers Julius and Louis.

"Uncle Albert was one of the first architects to recognize that an industrial building was worthy of a competent architect's work," said Bill Kahn, Louis's son and a retired engineer. "Prior to him, industrial assignments commonly were given to apprentices."

Kahn and the auto industry came of age together. In 1903 he became the architect for the Packard Motor Car Company. His tenth building for Packard, built in 1905, broke new ground. Previous factories had been dark, cramped mills with creaking, oil-soaked wooden floors. Kahn replaced the traditional fire hazard with a building made of reinforced concrete. It had wider floor space and featured loads of extra glass to allow more natural light and ventilation. Building No. 10 was so advanced it became a tourist destination.

Kahn's reputation soared after he hooked up with Henry Ford to design his most famous building, the Model T plant in Highland Park. Ford's vision was to have a moving assembly line create his cars from start to finish, and to have the entire production process housed under one roof. "I thought he was crazy," Kahn later admitted, but the resulting factory, opened in 1909, made possible the mass production of the American dream. By 1917, more than 700,000 Tin Lizzies were being assembled at the heavily glassed "Crystal Palace."

All told, Kahn was responsible for more than 1,000 Ford buildings, including the sprawling Rouge complex. His clients also included the Dodge brothers, Walter Chrysler, and the Soviet government (for whom he designed 521 factories during the 1930s). In addition, he designed many of the buildings on the University of Michigan campus.

Kahn was an Old World autocrat, always working in vest, shirt, and tie, and tolerating no challenges to his authority. Sheldon Marston spent the bulk of his professional life with Albert Kahn Associates, retiring in 1967 as the executive vice president. The 102-year-old Birmingham resident recalled "A.K." in his prime:

⋏ *The Fisher Building in 1929, one year after its opening. Were it not for the Great Depression, the 28-story Fisher would have been just the first of three planned towers.*

"I joined the firm in 1923 as an assistant superintendent of construction for the Michigan Stamping Plant on Mack Avenue," he said. "Mr. Kahn liked to put the responsibility on your shoulders. If you did your job, you were all right with him. If you didn't, you probably wouldn't last long."

There never was any doubt as to who was in charge, added Marston, who dared to correct his boss on a certain minor matter and got "a good bawling out" for his trouble.

Kahn's energy was legendary. Twelve- and fourteen-hour days were the norm. He was known to grab a catnap by stretching out his 5-foot-4-inch frame on a drafting table. Reenergized, he might decide to drive out to a job site—a dangerous proposition.

"He had a hard time distinguishing between red and green," said Bill Kahn, "which made it a little difficult driving in the city. He knew that red was on top and green was on the bottom. But if the lights were changing, he was in trouble." Added to this, "He was always in a hurry. Consequently, a lot of people in the office wouldn't get in the car if he was going to drive."

Albert and Ernestine had four children: Edgar, Lydia, Ruth, and Rosalie. Edgar shunned the family business. He captained the University of Michigan's hockey team and became a noted surgeon, accomplishments that his father took great pride in. The family lived in a mansion Kahn designed on Mack Avenue; today it's home to the Detroit Urban League.

"He was a strong disciplinarian when it was needed," said Rosalie, who remembered once accidentally melting some of her father's beloved opera records on a radiator. "He didn't spank us. His voice was all it took. It wasn't raised, just very firm."

The exactitude that marked his work could sometimes be exasperating in a domestic situation. When one of his children used the phrase, "that guy," Kahn issued an immediate reprimand. "'That guy?' We don't speak that way." On those occasions when Kahn did allow himself to relax, it typically was inside an opera house or museum on either side of the Atlantic. He also was a big baseball fan, enjoyed playing bridge with members of his extended family, and escaped the heat of the city at a five-bedroom summer house he built on Walnut Lake.

"For the most part, though," said Bill Kahn, "his life was his work."

Kahn always considered himself a Jew—an American Jew. He belonged to Temple Beth El (which he designed) and the exclusive Jewish club, the Phoenix Social Club, and gave generously to Jewish causes. But he was criticized in some quarters for not taking a more visible role in local Jewish affairs. Like most of Detroit's old-line German Jews, which as a group was more cultured and better educated than the Eastern European Jews who began arriving in the early 1900s, he favored assimilation over such ritualistic practices as bar mitzvahs and Passover seders.

⋏ / ➤ Albert Kahn's architectural masterpieces include the seven-story Detroit Athletic Club, which opened its doors in 1915 and immediately became the town's social center for the automotive set. The main dining room featured painstakingly painted frescoed ceiling beams while the equally elegant natatorium attracted major national swimming meets.

For all of his status and his desire to be Americanized, Kahn encountered anti-Semitism on a regular basis. He designed the prestigious Liggett School, but his daughters were shunned by sororities. The equally exclusive Detroit Athletic Club, opened in 1915, also was one of his creations. The club, normally off-limits to Jews, offered Kahn a token membership, but he quietly turned it down.

Henry Ford's infamous anti-Semitic ramblings in the *Dearborn Independent* "were a major strain on the relationship" between tycoon and architect, said Bill Kahn.

Displaying the same kind of hard-headed practicality that characterized his buildings, Kahn swallowed his bile and continued to build for Ford. "Let's be reasonable," his nephew said in defense. "You wouldn't turn down a commission for an entire firm because your nose was out of joint." Kahn's compromise was to not personally meet with Ford after the 1920s.

Kahn's last great project was for Ford. With America retooling to fight World War II, he built the massive Willow Run plant to produce the bombers that would ultimately turn the land of his birth into a nation of rubble.

Kahn's phenomenal pace ultimately caught up with him. He suffered a heart attack that confined him to bed for the last month of his life. He was a terrible patient, continuing to conduct business in his pajamas. On the morning of December 8, 1942, he phoned Rosalie to wish her a happy 30th birthday. An hour later he was dead.

"He really died with his boots on," is Rosalie's assessment of her father's remarkably productive 73 years. "He kept going all the time, all the way."

Albert Kahn Associates continues as one of the country's largest and most respected architectural firms, though none of today's 400 employees have any personal memories of the company's namesake. Even Bill Kahn admits that, after all these years, thoughts of Uncle Albert pop up infrequently.

"Principally it's when I go down to the Fisher Theatre, or I'm in Ann Arbor and I see buildings that I know were his personal favorites—the Clements Library or Hill Auditorium."

And exactly what is it that goes through his mind on these occasions? Kahn deliberated a few moments before answering.

"I'm thinking: 'I am very damn proud.'"

⋎ *Albert Kahn and company, with the steel skeleton of the General Motors Building rising behind them.*

➤ *Opposite page: Detail from the Fisher Building. Commissioned by the seven Fisher brothers (of "Body by Fisher" fame), it and the General Motors Building were intended to anchor a secondary business district west of downtown.*

WHEN DETROIT ROARED

On a winter day in Chicago in 1926, Detroiters John "Red" Cole and Thelma Gordon lost their chance to become America's Charleston champions when Thelma tragically lost her footing midway through the national finals. Newspapers gently noted that Thelma, who was sporting the traditional "flapper" look of short, bobbed hair and dropped-waist dress, "slipped" as she and Red frenetically shined the dance-hall floor with their happy feet.

"Actually," Cole admitted, "Thelma fell flat on her butt."

In any event, the fall proved fortuitous for the couple, who returned to Detroit with $100 in prize money and the genesis of a new dance craze, the Black Bottom.

"We staged exhibitions all around Detroit," recalled Cole. "We danced with the Sullivans, the brother and sister act from Grand Rapids that beat us out in Chicago. In the middle of a number, Thelma would take a pratfall. The Sullivans would stop dancing, point to Thelma and say, 'That's how we won it.' The crowd loved it."

Despite his advanced age, the sprightly Cole demonstrated the Charleston and the Black Bottom on the kitchen floor of his Dearborn home, conjuring up the mad energy of a vanished age with barely a puff.

"Oh, those were some days," he exclaimed, sitting back down. "Detroit in the 1920s—someone today wouldn't recognize it. There was no TV, and radio was boring as hell, so people

◄ *Arcadia Dance Hall.*

➤ *Thelma and Red.*

▼ *Bathing beauties on Belle Isle, 1920. The "modern" woman of the Roaring '20s rejected her mother's more traditional ways, raising the hemline of her skirts, bobbing her hair, smoking cigarettes and drinking.*

➤ *Opposite page: The Masonic Temple at Second and Temple Streets was completed in 1926 at a cost of $7 million. The ornate temple counts three ballrooms, a cathedral and a 4,400-seat performance hall among its 1,037 rooms.*

went to dance halls. Theaters like the Strand on Grand River and the Oriole Terrace on East Grand Boulevard were packed with people. Double features were only a quarter, and dance contests would go on at intermission. On Saturday nights, I'd get fancied up with gray spats and a felt fedora."

Although Detroit had the reputation as a wide-open town then, Cole contends the period was one of good humor, respect, and fellowship. "You opened doors for women, and if you found a drunk sitting under a street lamp, you put him in a cab and sent him home."

Cole showed his visitor a knee-high silver-plated loving cup that was presented to him January 26, 1926 at the Arcadia Ballroom on Woodward for being the best Charleston dancer in Michigan. "Those days," he said, idly fingering a tarnished handle, "it really was the Jazz Age."

Detroit was the lion of the industrial world in the 1920s, a time of gangsters, discarded corsets, bathtub gin, and widespread optimism. The city had reason to feel good about itself. It was producing most of the auto industry's 4 million vehicles and was in the midst of a construction boom consistent with its image as "Dynamic Detroit." During the decade such landmarks as the Detroit Institute of Arts, Fox Theatre, Olympia Stadium, City Airport, Fisher Building, Ambassador Bridge, Greenfield Village, and Union Produce Terminal were completed. Gleaming new skyscrapers hovered over the soot-stained, 19th century City Hall. The population was exploding, a million citizens making Detroit the country's fourth-largest city by 1920. The era's blend of energy and boosterism was evident everywhere one looked, from the Majestic Institute, which in 1923 inaugurated the national craze

Λ *November 15, 1929: The bridge is formally opened as Mrs. Charles P. McTague, representing Canada, and Mrs. J. L. Fozard, representing the United States, cut the white ribbons.*

Y *Spanning one and three-quarters miles between the United States and Canada, the Ambassador Bridge was the world's longest suspension bridge when completed in late 1929. The privately financed venture cost $23.5 million and did not turn a profit for bridge operators until 1944.*

of marathon dancing, to the Hudson store, which draped the world's largest flag on the side of its building. "We have the biggest of everything," boasted the 1925–26 edition of the city directory, "the tallest building, the biggest electric sign, the longest bridge, the most money. . . ." Unsurprisingly, the directory failed to mention the city's biggest claim to fame: the trafficking in illegal booze.

Prohibition is what put the roar in the Roaring '20s—and beyond. In 1929, the *New York Times* estimated that Detroit's illegal liquor trade was producing $215 million in profits annually, outstripping all other legal industries, including carmaking. Bootlegging became even more financially attractive in light of the Great Depression that followed Detroit's boom decade.

Michigan's own prohibition act, effective May 1, 1918, was followed by the 18th Amendment—national prohibition—on January 16, 1920. These acts prohibited the manufacturing or consumption of any beverage containing more than 0.5 percent alcohol. A mere two weeks before the United States went dry, Canada dropped its wartime prohibition act. The following day, customs officials remarked about the sudden demand for motorboat licenses.

With numerous natural hideaways and hundreds of shoreline homes and docks, the Detroit River was bootlegger heaven. Thousands of Canadians and Americans crisscrossed the watery strip in a variety of crafts, purchasing booze in Canada and stowing it under floorboards and inside false bottoms on the return trip. An estimated one quarter of Windsor's population was involved in bootlegging.

In response, an ersatz fleet of prohibition agents sailed forth to challenge these buccaneers of booze. Employing a motley collection of slow-moving vessels of

The Prince of Jazz

For two days in the spring of 1924, a harmonious disturbance filled the usually staid Detroit Athletic Club. Inside a closed and locked private dining room, Jean Goldkette's famous Graystone Orchestra was busy scratching into wax eight sides of such dance favorites as "Dinah" and "My Pretty Girl" for the Victor Recording Company.

Of course, under those conditions no one in the clubhouse could be expected to keep their feet still. As the club magazine described it, "Waiters foxtrotted to and from the kitchen, card players doubled and redoubled in jazz time, and the boys in the locker room shimmied as they dressed and undressed." The musical arrangements of Goldkette, the acknowledged "Prince of Jazz," had that effect on people.

In his dinner coat, boiled shirt, and Stay-Slick hair treatment, Goldkette more than personified the Jazz Age of post–World War I America—he helped create it. A shy, sophisticated man whose childhood goal had been to become a classical pianist, Goldkette discovered his real talent was in arranging and marketing. The result was that during the Roaring '20s one could hardly enter a Midwestern ballroom, hotel, or lakeside resort without encountering the unmistakable sounds of a Jean Goldkette band.

Goldkette was born in Greece in 1893 and raised in France and Russia, where he attended the exclusive Moscow Conservatory, then considered the finest music school in the world. He immigrated to Indiana as a teenager and got his big break a few years later leading a five-piece dance band that played weekends at the Detroit Athletic Club. In 1923, with the financial backing of several DAC members, the popular bandleader reorganized the failing Graystone Ballroom on Woodward into a profitable concern. His genius was not only in wedding the symphonic aspects of classical music to the popular tunes of the period, observed jazz historian Stan Kuwik, but in acquiring the best musicians available—including up-and-coming jazz greats Bix Beiderbecke, Joe Venuti, and Jimmy and Tommy Dorsey—to staff the various units that performed under the Goldkette aegis. "From Detroit," wrote Kuwik, "Goldkette ran what might be classified as an early conglomerate. . . . Together with his partner Charles Horvath, they were able to supply dance bands to clubs, hotels, and ballrooms."

At his peak, Goldkette served as musical director of the DAC and the luxury Book-Cadillac Hotel, recorded on the Victor label, operated a local music school, and had more than 20 bands operating under his name. But the Great Depression turned life sour for the tireless impresario. By 1933 he had disbanded all of the Goldkette bands and left Detroit, ultimately settling on the West Coast. He died of a heart attack in California in 1962. Although largely forgotten by then, knowledgeable jazz fans eulogized him as one of the true greats in the development of a uniquely American art form.

∧ *During the 1920s, Jean Goldkette's orchestra was the band to dance to.*

➤ *This speakeasy on East Columbia Street was one of an estimated 25,000 blind pigs operating in Detroit in 1930.*

⌄ *The Detroit-Windsor Tunnel cost $25 million to build. It opened November 3, 1930, almost exactly a year after the first vehicular traffic crossed the equally impressive Ambassador Bridge.*

dubious seaworthiness, it was in historian Larry Englemann's opinion "the wackiest navy that ever sailed," a fleet "without admirals or admiration." The chagrined press dubbed it the Prohibition Navy.

Undermanned and undisciplined, with a number of its crew on the take, the Prohibition Navy fought a losing, albeit entertaining, battle with its criminal counterparts. The Navy was as liable to shoot up an innocent pleasure craft as a legitimate rum runner, and ramming and sinking a suspected smuggler's boat was an accepted form of enforcement. Summer picnickers on Belle Isle were regular witnesses to these sea battles, as the waters became fouled with bloated bodies and the debris of smashed boats.

There were tremendous profits to be made in bootlegging. Nowhere were the riches to be reaped more evident than in the downriver communities, especially Ecorse, whose waterfront was known as Michigan's Barbary Coast.

Fishermen and dockworkers gave up their jobs to concentrate on smuggling, all with the blessings of the local police and judges. Citizens got angry with anyone who tampered with their good fortune. In 1923, for instance, Treasury agents were forced to fight off 2,000 irate neighbors after staging a raid in Ecorse. The agents were able to escape, but not before the mob tried three times to dynamite their escape route across a local bridge.

Red Cole was playing the clarinet and saxophone at the Polar Bear Cafe in Ecorse in 1923. "The Polar Bear was a supper club on Jefferson, right on the river," he recalled. "There was a group of bootleggers that used to deliver booze right at the dock under the club. You could hear their motors running. That's when we'd get a signal from someone in the back: 'Heat it up!' In other words, play louder." As Cole's band drowned out the sound of the engines, bootleggers unloaded another week's worth of whiskey for the customers.

But even Ecorse paled alongside Hamtramck's experience. "Hamtramck was the headquarters for bathtub gin," said Cole. "Highland Park and Dearborn were quiet, but if you wanted anything to drink, you went to Hamtramck. You were considered a real rounder if you knew that crowd."

In Hamtramck, which was populated by 80,000 hard-working Slovaks—70,000 of whom were immigrants in the 1920s—liquor was sold in candy stores, restaurants, pool halls, and at more than 400 "soft-drink" stands. Cars cruised up and down main streets, selling booze from backseat bars to thirsty factory workers. Exasperated, Governor Alexander Groesbeck sent in the state police to clean up the town. In just three months, police destroyed 75 stills, two back-alley breweries, and 20,000 gallons of moonshine.

Cooperation from city officials, however, was sadly lacking. The chief of police was arrested for public drunkenness, while Mayor Peter Jezewski, who had been elected on a law and order platform, was sentenced to two years in federal prison for violating the prohibition laws. Hamtramck's history,

➤ This young scofflaw was photographed by the Windsor Star *dressed in an outfit ingeniously designed to smuggle Canadian booze into Detroit.*

▼ Charles Hughes, entertainment coordinator at the swank Detroit Athletic Club, wasn't about to allow Prohibition to keep club patrons from having a good time. He regularly arranged to have shipments of quality liquor smuggled in, typically in cushioned crates or wardrobe trunks.

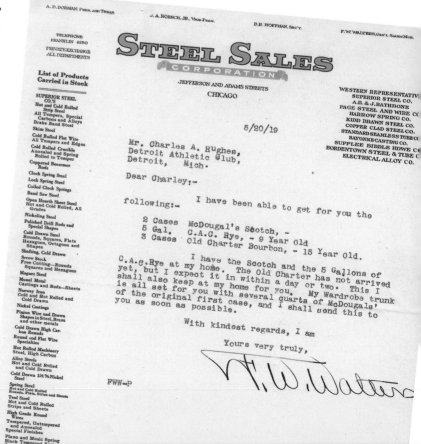

while exceptional, was not unique among southeastern Michigan communities. So much booze flowed between Detroit and Canada that the Detroit–Windsor Tunnel, opened in 1930, one year after the Ambassador Bridge, was dubbed the Detroit–Windsor Funnel.

Ordinary citizens thumbed their noses at Prohibition. Those who didn't frequent one of the city's estimated 25,000 blind pigs brewed their own concoctions. Countless private stills percolated peacefully inside closets, attics, basements, and garages.

Helen Sanecki, the third of six children born to Polish immigrants, grew up in an upper flat on 35th Street. A grocery store—a front for a blind pig—was on the ground floor.

"Boisterous voices, loud laughter, singing, and an occasional argument filtered through the walls and could be heard clearly upstairs," she remembered. Music from the player piano floated upward too. "Whether we wanted entertainment or not, we got it," she said. "By the time my baby brother learned to say, 'Mama,' he could also sing 'Over There.'"

➤ A Prohibition party at contractor Alfred Tenge's house on Hubbell Street, circa 1925, featured several familiar faces. Among them were New York Yankees slugger Babe Ruth, seated at center, and Detroit Tigers Harry Heilmann (No. 9 at far right, trying his best to shield his face from the camera) and Heinie Manush (No. 12, with lady's hand under his chin). All three were Hall-of-Fame outfielders—and drinkers.

➤ Prohibition forced many local breweries out of business. Stroh's survived by selling "near beer," ice cream products—and a malt syrup that was popular with home brewers.

Sanecki recalled another neighbor's operation. "Its unusual dispensing system was located in the kitchen sink—one faucet gave whiskey, while the other yielded beer."

Homebrewing was simple, cheap, and smelly. Parts for stills could be bought at the neighborhood hardware store, and ingredients were readily available at the grocer's. Stroh Brewery, for example, which was forced into making nonalcoholic products like ginger ale and ice cream to survive, also offered consumers hops-flavored malt syrup. Consumers used the syrup in brewing their own beer.

Homebrewing could also be lethal, said Sanecki, who remembered several men in the neighborhood dying gruesome deaths before it was discovered that the local bootlegger was using lye in her moonshine.

By the mid-1920s, Detroit's population had mushroomed to an estimated 1.2 million, and crime and vice grew accordingly. In 1925 the city had 232 murders, including seven police officers slain in the line of duty. Fifty-three bodies were pulled from the Detroit River. In 1926, the bloodiest year of the Roaring '20s, the city recorded 326 homicides. Many were gang-related and went unsolved. Trigger-happy police contributed to Detroit's national image as a frontier town. In a two-year span, 1927–28, they shot 204 people, 70 fatally. On the other side of the ledger, 8 policemen were shot to death and another 25 wounded during this period. Some Detroiters drove around with car stickers that pleaded "Don't shoot, I'm not a bootlegger."

Extortions and kidnappings became popular. One kidnap victim was seven-year-old Regina Latessa, who on the morning of June 10, 1924 was playing with a friend in the lot next to her parents' confectionary store at 3517 Russell Street when a sedan suddenly squealed to a halt. A man raced out, plucked Regina off a teeter-totter and shoved her into the backseat. There a teenaged girl held her down on the floor as the abductors sped off to a farm somewhere downriver. The kidnappers demanded $25,000 ransom for the little girl, "but it might as well have been $25 million," recalled the victim, now Regina Corsi.

"The reason the kidnapping received so much front-page publicity is because those things seldom happened to children. It was common for gangsters to do that to each other, but not children." Corsi was not harmed, but she believes today that her milk was drugged every night to keep her from escaping. While the newspapers and police pondered her fate, the girl's parents sought help from the head of the East Side Gang, Italian gangsters that had forged a foothold in various illegal activities, most notably bootlegging.

"It was very similar to *The Godfather* then," she said. "My mother got him to arrange my release." Eight days later, amid gunshots and squealing tires, Corsi was thrown out of the kidnappers' car on Michigan Avenue near downtown. Members of the police department's Black Hand Squad, organized to deal with the rash of extortions and kidnappings then plaguing Detroit's Italian community, rescued the girl.

"After that, my father started drinking heavily and my mother refused to let me out of her sight," said Corsi. "Even after I got married, it was always me, my hus-

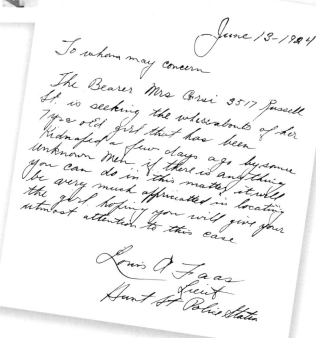

▲ *After her rescue from kidnappers, Gina Corsi posed with one of the detectives that helped secure her release.*

Battling the Rummies on the Detroit River

ENFORCING PROHIBITION WAS A DIFFICULT TASK IN EVERY AMERICAN CITY. BUT IN BORDER CITIES LIKE DETROIT, WHICH WAS A SHORT BOAT RIDE FROM CANADA, ENFORCEMENT PROVED NEXT TO IMPOSSIBLE. FIGHTING A GAME, IF LOSING, BATTLE, WITH THE "RUMMIES" ON THE DETROIT RIVER WERE MEN LIKE TED TAIPALUS, WHO SERVED FROM 1929 TO 1937 WITH THE U.S. CUSTOMS BORDER PATROL.

In Detroit the gangsters had control of everything. City policemen acted as lookouts for the rumrunners in exchange for a bottle. Private watchmen did the same. The U.S. Coast Guard, which was supposed to patrol Lake Erie, hardly ever made a seizure. The judges often would levy a small fine or perhaps suspend sentence entirely when a rummy came up for trial. The newspapers were against the law. The general public was totally down on it.

That was the background at the time a newspaper advertisement caught my attention one day in 1928, when I was working in the Upper Peninsula copper mines near Calumet. The ad was seeking out applicants for the U.S. Customs Border Patrol, just being organized to apprehend liquor smugglers in the Detroit area and elsewhere.

Although I had never completed high school, I qualified because of my three years' duty in the Marine Corps. I passed the required examination, and finally, on March 24, 1929, along with about 20 other men, I was sworn in as one of 154 new customs patrol inspectors appointed to the Detroit area.

After an orientation period, we were outfitted in dark whipcord uniforms which looked flashy—but were not very functional for high-speed chases on the Detroit River. With our leggings, leather puttees, and Western style

hats, we were often referred to as "Western Bandits" or "Seagoing Cowboys." But the hats often wound up in the water, and the light gray overcoats we had for cold-weather duty always got dirty. Later on we traded our leggings for straight trousers, the cowboy hat gave way to a uniform cap with grommet, and the heavy overcoat was replaced by a hip-length black leather coat.

Our vehicles at first were hardly top of the line, but we had a team of first-rate mechanics and carpenters to look after them. Our patrol cars were a hodgepodge consisting mostly of seizures. Most of them had been altered—the rear seats removed and the springs reinforced—by the previous owners to help carry heavy loads of liquor.

Our boats were open, motorized luggers, also claimed mostly through seizures. Gradually we purchased new speedboat hulls and big, 175-horse-power Kermath and Hall Scott motors. So bit by bit we got rid of the old boats. At first we auctioned them off, but we found out the rummies were buying them back. After that our policy was to destroy any boat seized twice by hoisting it up and smashing it against the dock. We threw the pieces into the river.

In the beginning I hardly knew what the Detroit River looked like in daylight hours—I worked the night shift for my first three months. As it turned out, that may have been the best time. The river was a cesspool. Detroit's sewers emptied into it, and the water was so dirty you couldn't see a foot below the surface. Big fat carp would gather at the sewer outlets to the river and feast on the odorous cornucopia, only to become meals themselves for fishermen. In the Depression people would eat almost anything.

The river also was clogged with trash from the boats we broke up, along with old timbers from dock work going on along the shore. And during the spring thaws there was the additional problem of corpses floating to the surface. The Detroit Police Harbormaster crew took care of most of the bodies, but we helped out. One day I had just finished taking a corpse to the dock when a ferry captain hailed me, pointing his finger. Sure enough, there was another body floating nearby.

There was plenty of activity on the Detroit River during Prohibition. Since Detroit was dry, lots of people went to Canada to get liquored up. In the early years, cars would line up on Atwater from Woodward to Riopelle on weekends to take the ferry over. Later they took the tunnel or the bridge, both of which I watched being built.

And then there were the rumrunners.

At first we patrolled two men to a boat or car, but later on we worked mostly by ourselves. Our base was located initially at the foot of Leibe and Atwater, but we soon moved to Orleans and Atwater, where we had a much larger slip for boat storage and more building and garage space. When we became fully organized, the Detroit base covered the river from Lake St. Clair to Wyandotte. The area was split up into eight beats, or patrols, plus bases at Marine City, the Clinton River, and Grosse Isle. With all this coverage, liquor was still being smuggled in.

The rummies had devised all sorts of tricks, and it took us a while to catch on to most of them. I remember one 30-foot cabin cruiser that would leave River Rouge just about every day with two men bound for Fighting Island across the Canadian border. Typically they would return after six or seven hours, sometimes with fish and sometimes not. I searched the boat many times, even pulling up the floorboard, and never found anything but bilge water. Finally some of our agents went to observe the "fishermen" in Canada, and, sure enough, they saw case after case of liquor being put on board. When the boat came back this time, we seized it, brought it to the base and searched it in the water. Still no liquor. We then hoisted the boat out of the water, noted the dimensions, and pumped the water out. The measurements did not jibe, and eventually we found a false bottom hiding 18 cases of liquor.

Then there was the old decoy trick, which didn't always work, either. Once we spotted two speedboats coming upstream on the Canadian side of the river. One kept darting toward the American side, trying to get the patrol to chase it. The other, obviously heavily loaded, began easing slowly toward our side. We finally went after them, and during the chase the two boats passed on either side of a 600-foot freighter in midstream. But when they cleared the freighter, they collided and the rum boat sank. The decoy boat managed to get almost to the Canadian side before it too began to sink. We rescued the operator of the rum boat and dropped him with his partners to argue about who was to blame for the collision.

The water was often a more dangerous adversary than the smugglers. There was sort of an informal understanding among all the rumrunners not to use firearms in their business. I never arrested a rummy who carried a weapon or had one in his boat or car. And most of them would rather run than fight.

We tried to exercise restraint with firearms, too. One time I was patrolling by car near a swampy area in Ecorse. This was a favorite spot for the rummies to bring in their loads, since it was behind a railroad roundhouse and out of sight of boat patrols. I left my partner in the car and went to look around.

⋀ *Authorities won this battle with "rummies," uncovering a winch used to help move submerged cases of booze across the mile-wide Detroit River.*

◄ *Opposite page: A load of captured booze.*

DETROIT TODAY IS THE WETTEST AND WIDEST OPEN TOWN IN THE COUNTRY AND HAS THE LARGEST PER CAPITA CONSUMPTION OF LIQUOR OF ALL THE CITIES IN THE UNITES STATES—NEW YORK INCLUDED. WHEN THE RIVER FREEZES, THE RUMRUNNERS CROSS THE ICE, TOWING TOBOGGANS BEHIND AUTOMOBILES OR HAVING MEN ON SKATES PUSH SLEDS. — Plain Talk *(March 1930)*

Suddenly I spotted a loaded speedboat coming in. The operator threw the boat into reverse, and I fired my revolver into the air a couple of times, ordering him back in. He started to obey, when from out of nowhere came about 10 rumrunners. They had me pretty well cornered, so I backed off. I wouldn't shoot anybody for a load of booze until it was in my possession and thus technically government property. When I got back to the patrol car, I asked my partner why he hadn't come to help. His answer: "Oh, I had to guard the car. I thought they might take it." He soon was transferred to the Immigration Service.

We made quite a number of good-sized seizures on the river. One was near Zug Island when we stopped a large boat loaded down with several hundred cases of beer, about 30 cases of liquor, and several barrels filled with beer. A week later we made an even bigger haul on Lake Erie when we overtook a lugger outfitted with a silent underwater exhaust. I forget the exact figures, but it was carrying more liquor than I'd ever seen.

We usually dumped any beer we seized into the river by the case. The liquor went to a dump on Detroit's eastside for disposal. Those were the seizures we made. Right from the beginning, however, it seemed that there were a lot of seizures we didn't make.

My first assignment was on a boat crewed by one of the old-timers and tied almost all the time to the State Street dock in Ecorse. Night after night I could hear motorboats running in the dark. We would untie the boat, go a few hundred feet toward the engine noise, see nothing, and return. I wondered how many loads were being smuggled past us as we sat tied to that dock. But the older inspector was in charge, and, being schooled in the Marine Corps to obey orders, I kept my mouth shut.

Then came the purge. Just about every old-timer was fired or sent to Leavenworth Prison for accepting bribes. That wasn't the end of it, however.

During the next few years, I had a different beat and a different partner each day. Most were good men, but the rummies had managed to "buy" some of them. The going rate was 25 cents per case of beer and $2.50 per bag of whiskey landed successfully under the eye of the crooked agent. When I became suspicious of one of my partners, I would drop him off at one end of the beat to patrol on foot while I took the boat to the other end and kept watch over the entire area with field glasses.

I remember one partner who would phone the rummies with directions on where to cross with their loads. I would see the rum boats from Canada ease over to his side of our beat. I'd gun the patrol boat over there, and he'd signal the boats to scram. His standard reply was that he hadn't seen anything because he'd been talking to a watchman.

I was never openly approached with a bribe until I made sergeant. One night I was parked alone at the foot of 12th Street when one of the big shot rum runners, a fellow named Toledo Slim whom I had known a long time, drove up. His offer: "I'll pay you $1,500 a week and I won't work on your shift. You just tell me when to bring my load in and where."

President Herbert Hoover had just cut our salary from $2,100 to $1,800 a year as part of an economy move, so the offer was a big temptation, needless to say. While I sat thinking, Slim said, "I'll raise that to $1,700 a week and more if things go right." I loved my wife and three children, but we were not starving and I had no desire to join my former colleagues in Leavenworth.

"No," I answered, "I don't want your money." At that time it was not against the law to offer a patrolman a bribe, so I never reported the incident.

Finally Prohibition was repealed, and that put a stop to the rumrunning. Most of our agents were scattered around the country, but we still maintained a token force to patrol the river, and I stayed on. Without the booze, we began seizing other products being smuggled over from Canada to more lucrative markets in Detroit: face powder, perfumes, bacon, and hams.

Then there were the onions. Selling for 5 cents a pound in Canada, onions began commanding up to 30 cents a pound in Detroit. So the one-time booze haulers went into the onion smuggling business, and it was our solemn duty to apprehend them and seize their cargo. You could tell what made up the bulk of our seizures every time you got a whiff of our base.

Maybe it wasn't just the onions, but somehow things weren't the same on the Border Patrol after the end of Prohibition.

➤ *This truck, loaded with barrels of illegal alcohol, didn't make it across the partially frozen Detroit River.*

band, and her. But I can't blame her. Even when she was dying, she insisted on staying in my room. She wanted to keep an eye on me until the end."

Far from solving the universal problem of drunkenness, Prohibition was responsible for the birth of modern organized crime. Nowhere was this more apparent than in Detroit. During these rat-a-tat-tat years, members of the infamous Purple Gang strode through town, dispensing bullets or $20 tips at will, depending on whom they were dealing with. Rival thugs feared them, law enforcement respected them, the community they preyed on loathed them, and those on the outside—reporters, show girls, and Grosse Pointe swells—were fascinated by them.

"The Purple Gang was a hard lot of guys, so tough they made Capone's play-mates look like a kindergarten class," jazz musician Milton "Mezz" Mezzrow once recalled. "Detroit's snooty set used to feel it was really living to talk to them hood-lums without getting their own brains blown out."

The Purple Gang was the true power of Detroit's underworld for only a short while, from the mid 1920s through the early 1930s. In their prime, however, the Purples were a force to be reckoned with. Generally preferring muscles to brainpower, they bullied their way into a variety of activities, including kidnapping, extortion, and labor racketeering. They controlled an extensive bootlegging empire, providing clients such as Al Capone with a steady supply of liquor from Canada. Above all, they were unblinking killers for hire who participated in scores of hits, including that quintessential gangland slaying, the St. Valentine's Day Massacre in 1929.

After several top Purples were sent to prison three years later for their roles in the Collingwood Massacre in Detroit, individual Purples continued to operate through the 1940s, although internecine warfare and the Italian mob combined to make them little more than a footnote in crime annals once Prohibition was repealed. Their reputation, however, had been secured, with references appearing in various television shows and theatrical films. The gang even popped up as a lyric in Elvis Presley's "Jailhouse Rock" ("the whole rhythm section was the Purple Gang").

To understand the Purple Gang, one has to understand the environ-ment that spawned them. Unlike today's urban gangs, they were not prod-ucts of crushing poverty, broken homes, or widespread economic despair.

▲ *The Purple Gang's reputation reached as far as Hollywood, which released a movie version of the mob's story in 1959. Robert Blake starred in his first feature film.*

◄ *Opposite page: The destruction of these bottles of cap-tured hooch represented just a drop in the ocean of booze either made or shipped into Detroit between 1918 and 1933, the city's "dry" period.*

Suspected Purple Gangster Abe Kaminski. "I never heard of an organization of businessmen where men with guns would come around and collect dues," one mystified judge said of the Purples' shaking down of merchants.

Most were raised in middle class households in the east side neighborhood around Hastings Street. Their parents were religiously conservative Eastern European immigrants who owned delicatessens and scrap yards or worked brutal hours at Dodge Main and Briggs Manufacturing.

The core of the group was several sets of brothers: Abe, Joe, Ray, and Izzy Bernstein; Harry and Phil Keywell; and Harry, Sam, and Lou Fleisher. Except for the much older Abe Bernstein, who was born in Russia in 1893, the boys grew up within several years of each other. Most of them attended Bishop Ungraded, a trade school on Winder Street. The playground was the site of daily card and crap games, where the impressionable youths picked up a few tricks and ran errands for older hoods. In the years following the First World War, these restless adolescents graduated from stealing fruit at Eastern Market to shaking down neighborhood merchants.

Exactly how this loosely organized band of budding gangsters acquired its name is open to conjecture. One theory is that a shopkeeper forced to pay them for "protection" described them as being "purple—like raw meat." Other versions have them being named after an early leader, Sam "Sammy Purple" Cohen, or by an imaginative member of the press. Whatever the origin, one thing about the Purples is clear: They might have outgrown the petty thievery and moved on to respectable professions if not for the advent of that great social experiment known as Prohibition.

Under the guidance of mentors Charlie Lighter and Henry Shorr (father of Mickey Shorr of appliance store fame), who ran the Oakland Sugar House on Oakland Avenue, gang members made and shipped their own brand of booze. But they found it more convenient to simply steal what other operators had taken the time and risk to haul across the Detroit River from Canada.

Few were better at it than Harry Fleisher, the unassuming, soft-spoken son of a scrap yard dealer. Born in 1903, he was admired as a man who "did his own

PURPLE GANG? AW, FERGIT IT. THIS PURPLE GANG STUFF MAKES ME SICK. THE PURPLE GANG, THE PURPLE GANG! ALL THE TIME THE PURPLE GANG! WHO GOT UP THAT NAME? EVERYBODY'S A PURPLE. IT'S THE BUNK! *— Izzy Bernstein, speaking from his jail cell in 1929.*

work." A favorite tactic was to break down the door of a garage suspected of housing a still and promise a vagrant $5 to transfer the booze to his truck. After the loading was finished, so was the loader: Passersby would eventually discover the bullet-riddled body in the alley. Like most Purples, Fleisher was arrested scores of times, for everything from murder and kidnapping to assault and drug possession.

Strictly speaking, card-carrying members of the Purple Gang never really existed. Certainly none of them ever referred to themselves as Purples. More than anything, the name was a media device, an attempt to impose order, logic, and organization on a wide range of illegal activities that often resisted all these. In May 1929, Joey Bernstein represented their interests at an Atlantic City meeting of sev-

∨ Police rounded up known and suspected members of the Purple Gang for this group shot, circa 1928. Authorities conjectured that before the gang fell apart in the 1930s, it had participated in an estimated 500 killings, including the infamous St. Valentine's Day massacre in Chicago.

The Rise and Fall of Jimmy Hoffa

In 1931, when the Kroger Company in Detroit hired a stocky, muscular teenager named James Riddle Hoffa to unload boxcars full of strawberries, lettuce, and carrots at 32 cents an hour, little did they know they were giving birth to one of this country's most powerful and controversial labor leaders.

Tired of the low pay and poor working conditions, 17-year-old Jimmy Hoffa convinced his fellow workers—later tagged "the strawberry boys"—to stop unloading a shipment of perishables, an action that eventually forced the grocer to bargain and remedy labor grievances. Within two years, Hoffa was elected president of Local 299 of the International Brotherhood of Teamsters. Twenty-five years later, Hoffa—whose critics say built his reputation and the union on brute force and payoffs—was awarded the presidency of the International Teamsters.

According to Ralph Orr, the longtime labor writer for the *Detroit Free Press*, Hoffa's crowning achievement was the National Freight Agreement, which standardized trucking rates throughout the country, especially for the long haulers. "The rank and file worshipped him because he got them good contracts and made working conditions so much better," said Orr.

Although Boss Hoffa's public image was that of a cantankerous, heavy-handed labor leader, he also was easily accessible to the rank and file and a tireless worker on their behalf, demonstrating an intelligent grasp of trucking economics. "He was a rough character, but a lot of people don't know that he was a devoted family man and had a soft side," said Orr. "When he was at Local 299, a guy came in and told Hoffa that he hocked his wedding ring so he could feed his family. Hoffa blew up. 'No man should ever take his wedding ring off!' He gave the guy $50 to get the ring out of hock and found him a job the next day. I liked him. He talked gruff but when you asked him a question you got a direct answer. He didn't horseshit around and that's the way he bargained. His word was his bond."

Hoffa was able to continually improve the Teamsters' wages and working conditions. But to the public, what gains he made were eclipsed by scandal and his eventual murder. Hoffa's number one enemy was Robert F. Kennedy, U.S. attorney general during the Kennedy administration. John F. Kennedy's younger brother doggedly pursued the Teamsters head, alleging that Hoffa built his empire on violence, fraud, and misuse of pension funds. Although Hoffa was acquitted in 1962 of taking a $1 million dollar kickback for labor peace, he was convicted two years later of bribing two of the jurors and a prospective juror. Several weeks later, Hoffa was convicted again, this time for mail fraud and misuse of $20 million in Teamsters funds. After spending five years in prison, his combined 13-year sentence was commuted by President Richard Nixon in 1971, with the condition that he was to abstain from union activity until 1980.

Hoffa's self-stated philosophy was, "If you get knocked down and kicked, you get up and kick back harder." It would eventually lead to his death. For the next four years, he appealed Nixon's condition while setting forth a strategy to unseat Teamsters President Frank Fitzsimmons, his hand-picked successor. Fitzsimmons had learned to like the job and did not want to relinquish it. Organized crime, having developed a cozy relationship with the Fitzsimmons regime, did not want Hoffa back, either.

During the summer of 1974, the power struggle between the two former friends became violent as a Hoffa supporter's boat exploded, another's barn was burned down, and a trustee of Hoffa's old Local 299 was blinded by a shotgun blast. Finally, the following June, Fitzsimmons's 46-year-old son, Richard, was sitting with friends at Nemo's bar near Tiger Stadium when his Lincoln Continental exploded in the street. The end for Hoffa was now just a month away.

On July 30, 1975, the 62-year-old Hoffa reportedly was waiting to be picked up in the parking lot of the Machus Red Fox restaurant on Telegraph in Bloomfield Township when he disappeared. He was allegedly to be taken to a meeting with Anthony "Tony Jack" Giacalone, a Detroit mobster, and New Jersey Teamsters boss Tony Provenzano, who also opposed Hoffa returning to power. The next day, Hoffa's 1974 Pontiac Grand Ville was found in the Machus parking lot. But his body was never found.

Although the FBI and many other crime experts believe Provenzano engineered Hoffa's murder, there was not sufficient corroborating evidence to bring charges against the alleged perpetrators. Provenzano died in December 1988 of a heart attack while serving 20 years for labor racketeering, taking whatever he knew of Hoffa's disappearance to the grave.

One of Hoffa's most capable biographers, Arthur A. Sloane, professor of labor relations at the University of Delaware, admitted that "organized labor continues to suffer from the connection in the minds of millions of the criminalized Hoffa to unionism." But when measured as a labor leader, Sloane wrote, "Jimmy Hoffa must be given the highest of marks. He infused a once chaotic industry with a great deal of stability and allowed it to prosper. Trucking was undoubtedly better off for there having been a Hoffa."

A Hoffa finally did regain control of the union. Twenty-three years after his father's death, Detroit attorney James P. Hoffa was elected president of the International Teamsters.

➤ *A beaming Jimmy Hoffa hands out pension checks to the rank and file. The mobbed-up Teamsters boss lived—and died—violently.*

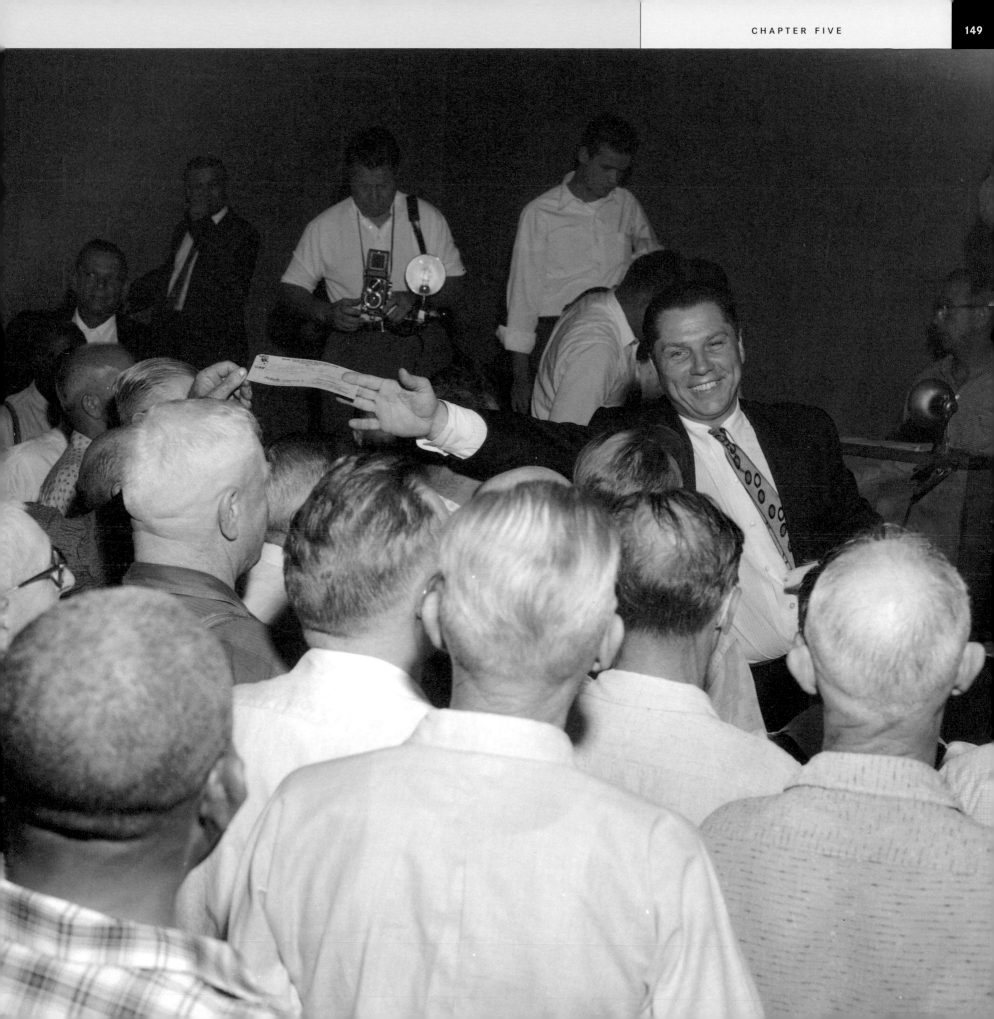

Purple Gangster Eddie Fletcher, a former boxer from New York, laces up the gloves of one of his fighters, welterweight Jackie Sherman, inside a Detroit gym in 1932. One year later, the criminal kingpin was found shot to death on a lonely Oakland County road.

eral crime groups, including New York's Dutch Schultz and Lucky Luciano. The attempt to carve out individual territory represented the first step toward organizing the American underworld—an irony that isn't lost on Paul Kavieff.

"The Purples were never structured like the Mafia families," explained Kavieff, author of a book on the Purples. "Certain groups might get together to pull a heist or a bombing, but they basically did their own thing most of the time. Which was the problem, in the end. It was hard keeping these guys in line for any length of time."

The Purples first made headlines in the fall of 1925, when a group of cleaning wholesalers, looking to fix the price of cleaning suits in the city, hired them for $1,000 a week to "convince" independent shops to join the association. Abe Bernstein, the acknowledged brains behind the muscle, orchestrated a long series of bombings, kidnappings, and murders. The level of violence in the four-year "cleaners and dryers war" appalled the wholesalers, who at one point tried to back out of their agreement. They had a change of heart after the association's leader, Sam Polakoff, was found shot to death inside his car on Dexter Boulevard.

The opportunities presented by Prohibition attracted countless out-of-town hoodlums, with major crime bosses or their representatives coming from St. Louis, Chicago, and other cities for a look-see at the country's main port of entry for booze. At a 1927 meeting inside the Book-Cadillac Hotel with Abe Bernstein and other local gang leaders, Al Capone was told in no uncertain terms to "stay the hell out of Detroit." Scarface liked the Purples' style enough to hire them to transport his favorite Canadian whiskey, Old Log Cabin, to Chicago.

Abe Axler and Eddie Fletcher—two "Yorkies," as the Purples called transplants from New York—arrived in Detroit about 1926. Fletcher, a one-time boxer, was a particularly natty dresser, typically sporting spats, diamond stickpin, a brightly colored silk suit and a wide-brimmed hat. Like Axler, who had spent time in Sing Sing, he could just as well have worn a hood and carried a scythe, for both are thought to have personally dispatched scores of men to that great roadhouse in the sky.

Inseparable pals, Axler and Fletcher pulled off the first tommy gun murders in Detroit. In early 1927, Axler and three other Purples rented a room at the Milaflores Apartment at 106 East Alexandrine for a meeting with three members of a visiting St. Louis gang, who had thoughts of installing a satellite operation in Detroit. It was a setup. The Detroit gangsters peppered the unsuspecting trio with powerful Thompson machine guns (which, remarkably, could be purchased off the shelf at hardware stores at the time). Police dug 110 bullets out of the floors and walls. As was the case with most gangland shootings, the Milaflores Massacre went unsolved.

Like other Purples, Fletcher and Axler also assisted in numerous freelance hits for payoffs that usually numbered several thousand dollars. They had a peripheral but important role in the most famous gangland slaying of them all. On February 14, 1929, seven members of Bugs Moran's gang were slaughtered inside a Chicago garage while waiting for a load of hijacked whiskey. Only one member of the hit team has ever been positively identified: Fred "Killer" Burke, an Adolf Hitler look-alike from St. Louis who did occasional work with the Purples. Axler and Fletcher are thought to have acted as lookouts for the massacre, which eliminated Capone's chief underworld rival.

The term "underworld" could be applied only loosely to the high-profile Purples. They were regularly seen about town—stirring coffee at Segal's Drug Store on 12th Street, shooting pool at Nick's on Cass Avenue, fanning the breeze with Tiger stars from their box seats at Navin Field, or taking steam at the Oakland Schvitz. The Cream of Michigan Restaurant on Grand River had so many known gangsters sitting around its tables, sipping barley soup and idly building igloos out of sugar cubes, the press dubbed the café the "Crime of Michigan."

At night they squired teenage showgirls around the city's countless speakeasies. They might spend the evening at Ruby Jones's Montmartre cabaret, where the diminutive singer would croon, "Big Bad Bill is Sweet William Now." Or at Morey's on Michigan Avenue, where a rendition of "My Yiddish Mama" was always good for a $5 tip from Ray Bernstein. However, all-night orgies at Oakland County road-houses or downtown opium dens were also part of the lifestyle for some Purples. Harry Millman, in particular, was known for his almost inhuman consumption of booze, cocaine, heroin, and women.

However, being in the Purples' wake sometimes meant crossing paths with a bullet. Mary Lou Neiger of Troy remembered growing up in the upper flat of a house at 1963 West Euclid. The flat's owner, a Jewish man she called "Mr. L," was a bondsman for the Purples. "Warm, motherly Mrs. L" had brothers and a cousin in the gang.

The Purples' notoriety continues to cause much consternation among older Detroit Jews, who prefer to remember positive role models from the period, such as Tigers slugger Hank Greenberg (who nearly broke Babe Ruth's single-season home run record) and Michigan quarterback Benny Friedman, whose passing skills popularized the forward pass.

"I was only four or so," said Neiger, "but I can remember sitting on a gangster's lap in the kitchen. He let me play with his gun." One day, little Mary Lou wandered farther than she was allowed.

"I was leaning against a telephone pole when this long black touring car drove slowly by. When it drove past about the third shop from the corner, they started shooting. I could hear gunfire and glass breaking." After Mr. L's bodyguard was found murdered in their trash can a little while later, Mary Lou's father decided to move the family to a safer location in Palmer Park.

For years, such wild-west shootouts drew close scrutiny only when innocent citizens happened to get caught in the crossfire. Philip Keywell and Morris Raider, for example, were sentenced to life for killing a teenage boy who happened to peek into a garage that the gang was using as a distillery.

This attitude was beginning to change by "Bloody July" of 1930, when a dozen gangsters were gunned down on city streets. That month citizens, finally fed up with years of lawlessness, recalled Mayor Charles Bowles in a special election. A few hours after the polls closed, popular radio commentator Jerry Buckley was shot to death in the lobby of the La Salle Hotel. Police rounded up the usual suspects, including several Purples, but no one was ever indicted for Buckley's murder, which insiders attributed to the broadcaster's double-cross of certain criminals friendly to Bowles.

The uproar should have persuaded Bernstein and company to lay low. Instead, on September 16, 1931, they pulled off a triple murder that effectively broke the gang's back. That day, Ray Bernstein, Harry Keywell, Harry Fleisher, and Irving Milberg invited three members of a group of bootleggers called the Third Avenue Navy to an apartment at the Collingwood Manor at the corner of 12th and Collingwood. The meeting was set up by a bookie named Solly Levine, a friend of Bernstein's who innocently assumed the talk was to be of the upcoming American Legion convention, which promised a windfall in liquor sales.

Instead, midway through the meeting a car in the alley started backfiring—a signal for the Purples to draw guns and pump 16 shots into their unarmed guests, who had incurred Bernstein's wrath by encroaching on his territory. As Levine and the Purples fled into the getaway car, a gun fell to the floor. His companions asked Levine to pick it up. Levine did, then realized that he had sealed his fate by putting

◄ *One of the victims of the Collingwood Massacre,*
a triple murder that shocked the city in 1931.

his fingerprints on one of the murder weapons.

Protected by a personal bodyguard of 12 policemen, the bookie agreed to testify against Bernstein, Keywell, and Milberg. All received life sentences. Harry Fleisher, who had disappeared after the shootings, showed up one year later (by which time he was being implicated in the Lindbergh baby kidnapping). Levine had long since fled, and without his testimony authorities had no choice but to let Fleisher go.

Repeal was right around the corner, and so was the end of the Purples' short reign. On April 10, 1933, Michigan became the first state to ratify the 21st Amendment, ending Prohibition. With their primary source of revenue gone, and with their leaders behind bars, individual Purples fell victim to the east side Italian mobs and to each other.

Jackie Sherman, a ham-and-egg boxer in the early '30s, remembered what happened to his manager, Eddie Fletcher. "Sure, I knew Eddie and Abe Axler were

killers," said the former welterweight. "But they were alright by me. He never had me lay down in a fight. He'd tell the tough guys around the gym, 'Leave the kid alone. He's a good kid.'"

One November night in 1933, Fletcher and Axler left a bar in Pontiac. A constable later found them inside their car on a gravel road near Telegraph and Quarton Roads. Each had been shot several times in the face. "Eddie and Abe were in the back seat," said Sherman. "They were holding each other's hands when the bullets hit them."

Henry Shorr, who was thought to be ready to testify against some remaining Purples, disappeared one day in 1935. No one was ever indicted, although Harry Fleisher had his car reupholstered two days after Shorr was reported missing.

Harry Millman met his end on Thanksgiving eve, 1937, at Boesky's Restaurant on 12th Street. (The owners were the parents of future Wall Street trader Ivan Boesky.) Two men emptied their pistols into the burly brawler, whose post-Prohibition career had consisted largely of shaking down whorehouses.

"The wops got him," a lady friend lamented.

Detroit's Mafia, led by Joe Moceri, Joe "Scarface" Bommarito, "Papa John" Priziola, "Black Bill" Tocco, and Joe Zerilli, quickly filled the vacuum left by the Purples' demise. A few Purples finished their lives in prison. Others were paroled and disappeared. Ray Bernstein died shortly after his release in 1964, proclaiming to the parole board that "crime does not pay."

Detroit's decade of rowdy prosperity was followed by a resounding and unexpected crash. In October 1929, the stock market nosedived, and the freewheeling days of the '20s skidded to a disastrous halt. By the following year, car production had been halved, and by 1932 two out of every five workers were out on the street. The Motor City, eulogized one national publication, was now sadly "out of gear." Better times would come, though nobody then was sure of it.

Over the years, reminders of Prohibition periodically resurface. On one such occasion, workmen building a new city dock at the foot of West Grand Boulevard stumbled across the remains of an old tugboat that sank in 1923 with a cargo of bootleg beer. The workers cracked open bottles of the aged brew and, under the midday sun, cheerfully drank to their unknown benefactors from Detroit's uproarious past.

▲ *The Purples and attorneys sit through another day of testimony in the Collingwood murder trial. Several Purples were convicted and received life sentences, effectively breaking the gang's back.*

◄ *Opposite page: Under the watchful eyes of machine gun-toting policemen, members of the Purple Gang are led into a police wagon after appearing at their murder trial.*

Detroit's Skyscraper Boom

The city's skyline changed dramatically between 1890 and 1929, a period that saw skyscrapers shoot out of the ground like so many dandelions. "Detroit is certainly a booming town," one fascinated newcomer from Indiana wrote his mother shortly after his arrival in 1916. "She is a pretty town and has some 20- and 24-story buildings and they reach way up in the sky."

The phenomenon of offices climbing into the clouds was the result of late 19th-century advances in elevators and structural steel. Detroit's first skyscraper, an 11-story masonry structure called the Hammond Building, opened at the southeast corner of Griswold and Fort Streets in 1890. Built at a cost of $750,000 by railcar tycoon George Hammond, it was especially awesome to recent immigrants, whose villages featured nothing higher than the local church spire. Even some of the more enlightened members of the community distrusted the claims of engineers and architects; they walked briskly through the skyscraper's shadow, unconvinced that a stiff breeze wouldn't cause the building to topple over. Thousands of others had no such misgivings, however, flocking to the roof for an unprecedented four-corner look-see at the surrounding countryside.

What they soon saw was another skyscraper forming on the horizon. Merchant king Christopher R. Mabley had one command when designing his own namesake building at the northwest corner of Michigan and Woodward: Make sure it was higher than the Hammond Building. At 14 stories, it was, though Mabley—like Hammond—died before his dream was completed. The new owners, unwilling to replace the initial "M" adorning the capstone and hundreds of doorknobs, decided to rename the Mabley Building the Majestic Building when it opened in 1896. The dueling skyscrapers enjoyed long lives. The Hammond Building was demolished in 1956, followed five years later by the Majestic.

Other tall buildings followed, keeping pace with Detroit's growing prosperity. In the years leading up to World War I, such notable structures as the Ford and the Dime buildings on Griswold, as well as the 19-story Whitney

Λ *The Hammond Building, opened in 1890, was Detroit's first skyscraper.*

Building overlooking Grand Circus Park, were erected. The greatest burst of construction came in the 1920s, when such downtown landmarks as the Book Tower, the Buhl Building, and the Union Trust (now Guardian) Building were erected and the Penobscot Building (originally 13 stories high when built in 1903) was expanded to 47 floors. Each reflected a certain enthusiasm. The Guardian, in particular, resists easy description: a 40-story, block-long tribute to Aztec, American Indian, exotic modern, and jazz age influences, fused with French, Dutch, and American arts and crafts.

Elsewhere in the city, the General Motors and Fisher buildings (the latter bankrolled by the seven Fisher brothers of "Body by Fisher" fame) were intended to be the twin anchors of a "second downtown" centered on Grand Boulevard. The New Center area never achieved the level of retail-commercial success originally envisioned for it. But the structures themselves, both designed by Albert Kahn, remain architectural marvels. The GM Building (whose 14th floor, home to the company's senior executives, was for years a synonym for the pinnacle of power in the auto industry) has brass and iron chandeliers hanging from neoclassical vaulted ceilings and more than four miles of marble lining its corridors. Intended to be the world's largest office complex, with nearly 30 acres of space, it originally featured a day hospital, two swimming pools, a 19-lane bowling alley, and a cafeteria that could accommodate 1,000 diners. The monumental Fisher Building, home to the Fisher Theatre, radio station WJR, and a variety of shops, is a riot of colorful frescoes, embossed bronze elevator doors, 40 types of marble, and assorted other "pagan splendors."

Collectively, these lavishly appointed buildings mirrored the sky's-the-limit optimism of an exploding metropolis, one that trailed only New York and Chicago in new construction during the 1920s.

The golden age of Detroit skyscrapers came to an abrupt end with the onset of the Depression. The incredibly ambitious plan to have the Fisher

◄ *A steelworker nonchalantly lights a cigarette atop the Stott Tower. In the background is the Book Tower.*

Building connected to an identical twin by a massive 60-floor tower was scrapped because of hard times. Other lofty projects were put on hold and then forgotten. In the years following, once stately buildings like the $14 million, 29-story Book–Cadillac (the world's tallest hotel when it opened on Washington Boulevard in 1924) fell into disuse and exist today as crumbling, gutted eyesores. Most of the office towers from the period, however, have managed to survive. Accommodations have been modernized and decades of grime have been sandblasted off their stone, brick, and terra cotta faces.

As people and businesses moved to the suburbs after World War II, so did a new generation of office buildings—gleaming glass boxes that have made communities like Troy, Southfield, and Novi the region's new centers of commerce. Some critics insist that, along with downtown's 73-story Renaissance Center—an uninspiring and uninviting cloud-tickler that was erected at a cost of $337 million in 1977—these recent additions to Metro Detroit's skyline lack the character of the old skyscrapers.

The newcomers are like "hospitals with little anonymous rooms off corridors," sniffed Josephine Fox Fink, who worked as a secretary inside the Penobscot Building for nearly 40 years. "There's no individuality. They're erector set buildings or glorified silos."

◄ *The Penobscot Building, originally 13 stories high when erected at the southwest corner of Michigan and Griswold in 1913, was expanded to 47 stories during the 1920s. The 557-foot-high building is topped with a red neon beacon that can be seen from 40 miles away.*

➤ *Opposite page: The interior of the Guardian Building today.*

LABOR PAINS

The call came early in the afternoon of March 8, 1937: *Shut her down!* With that, some 57,000 supporters of the United Auto Workers simultaneously threw down their tools and gloves and began barricading themselves inside Dodge Main and eight other Chrysler factories in Detroit.

Later, one sit-downer explained the workers' motivation. "We weren't for getting rich," said Bill Mileski, "because you never can get rich working. We wanted seniority, so the guy didn't have to be a kiss-ass to keep his job."

The massive Chrysler sit-down came on the heels of a successful sit-down strike against General Motors in Flint. The takeover of nine Chrysler plants (as well as two Hudson Motors factories) was a remarkable demonstration of solidarity and coordination—one that quickly inspired workers in other industries. Sit-down fever swept Detroit. Laundries, bakeries, drugstores, lumberyards, clothing stores, restaurants, and many more auto plants and parts factories were seized by workers. Employees at the Statler Hotel kicked out their managers and took over the 950-room building, prompting the owners of three other luxury hotels to send their guests packing and to lock their doors before they were taken over by copycat sit-downs. Roughly 130 businesses were occupied—some for a few hours, others for weeks. When police dared to move against some of the occupied sites, they were interfered with by sympathizers or battled tooth and nail by the sit-downers.

◄ *The spirit of 1937.*

ELECT
FRANK
MURPHY
MAYOR
UNEMPLOYMENT RELIEF
OLD AGE PENSION

➤ *On March 23, 1937, during the height of sit-down fever, a massive rally in Cadillac Square demonstrated union solidarity against the "raiding, slugging, and blackjacking [of] strikers and innocent bystanders." Two weeks later, Chrysler agreed to recognize the UAW as its workers' sole bargaining agent.*

To the editors of *Detroit Saturday Night*, the takeovers were pure anarchy: "If lawless men can seize an office, a factory, or a home and hold it unmolested for hours and days, they can seize it and hold it for months and years; and revolution is here. . . ." The business weekly joined many other business leaders, publishers, and politicians in calling on Governor Frank Murphy to send in the National Guard or the State Police to evict the squatters.

Murphy, a devout Catholic and self-described "independent progressive," had often been attacked for his pro-union sympathies while mayor of Detroit. His liberal leanings became even more pronounced once he took the governor's office in 1936. He was not against big business; he simply wanted employers to behave in a more humane manner. "We have got to realize that no one is secure until all are secure," he said, "that injustice to anyone is injustice to everyone." He refused to send in state troops—a decision that cost him his re-election.

"There is no doubt the sit-down is illegal," he admitted. "But laboring people justify the sit-down on the grounds that it is effective. They contend it is moral."

On March 23, 1937, a peaceful crowd of 100,000 rallied in Cadillac Square. "Your slaves have declared their own freedom!" thundered UAW president Homer Martin. Then within days, Chrysler capitulated, agreeing to recognize the union in exchange for a no-strike pledge.

More than six decades after Bill Mileski and his fellow sit-downers marched out of Dodge Main in triumph, band playing and flags waving, it has become fashionable in some circles to say that organized labor has lost its clout. Certainly it has lost members. Statistics show that industrial unions have been in decline for several years. In 1979, the UAW had more than 1.5 million active U.S. members. That number has since slipped to

"AMERICAN WORKMEN ARE SUBJECTED TO PERIL OF LIFE AND LIMB AS GREAT AS ANY SOLDIER IN TIME OF WAR." — *President Benjamin Harrison*

762,000, about half of whom are employed making cars or parts for the big three American automakers of GM, Ford, and Daimler-Chrysler. Although one in every five workers in Michigan belongs to a union (compared to one in eight nationally), Detroit's image as a union stronghold has taken a beating. To cite one recent example, organized labor could not prevent the embarrassing defeat of striking newspaper unions at the *Detroit News* and *Detroit Free Press*. As troubling as labor's future may seem at times, the gains made since the 1930s guarantee that workers will never have to return to the hostile and dangerous environment that once existed.

At the turn of the century a staggering 25,000 workers a year were being killed in industrial accidents. The carnage moved President Benjamin Harrison to declare, "American workmen are subjected to peril of life and limb as great as any soldier in time of war." A 40-year-old Detroiter named Fred Moss was one such victim. He was working at Baugh's Steam Forge on Clark Avenue one afternoon when he was thrown into the cogs of two mammoth wheels. "His right arm and side struck the wheels," the Tribune reported, "the arm being broken in a dozen places and torn to shreds and his body crushed into a shapeless mass, the right lung being forced out through the bottom of the abdomen." Moss was "considered a careful and competent man" by his employer, who was bound by custom—but not law—to pay for his funeral. This was small compensation to the victim's widow and six children, who were left to fend for themselves.

It didn't matter how they died or who was at fault, workers were as faceless and interchangeable as the cogs that turned Fred Moss into jelly. Moving belts and machinery made auto plants especially dangerous places to work. In 1917, for example, one in four Packard employees suffered an injury on the job. A safety campaign dramatically reduced the number of accidents, but in 1919, 10 percent of Packard workers still were hurt at work. For years the loss of fingers was the most common cause of permanent disability, especially among shaper hands and

⋀ *Joe Labadie, a printer by trade, an iconoclast by nature, and a national leader in the socialist movement, was an early working-class hero dubbed "the dean of Detroit's Bohemia" for his anarchist views. In 1879 he declared: "I believe that by force alone can be removed the societary wrongs which have fastened themselves upon the people. But first must come agitation, organization, intelligence, and then the demand!"*

◄ *Opposite page: Punch presses and moving belts and pulleys helped earn Detroit the nickname, "Eight Finger City."*

Some Mighty Good Fellows

Veteran *Detroit News* columnist Pete Waldmeir can recall his family receiving a package while growing up in a single-parent household in the 1930s. "I was kind of young when we got the Goodfellow package," he said, "but I can remember that it contained a ham and a turkey and a shoe coupon. After that my mother got on her feet and we didn't receive any more packages."

One of the city's oldest and most treasured charities began with James J. Brady, whose own impoverished childhood made him determined to help the city's poor. Brady had left his Corktown home when he was six and supported himself by shining shoes and selling papers on downtown street corners. As an adult, he was changed forever by a cartoon that appeared on the front page of the *Detroit Journal* in 1910. Titled "Forgotten," the Tom May illustration showed a child slumped over a table, empty stocking in hand. The despair of a youngster being forgotten on Christmas morning tugged at Brady's heart. In 1914, the year the self-taught bookkeeper was named collector of internal revenue for the Detroit region, he started the Forgotten Club, aimed at collecting dollars for a more benevolent purpose. Sixty former "newsies" took to the street corners, hawking a special edition that brought in more than $400.

Brady died in 1925, by which time his annual effort had grown into a successful drive known as the Old Newsboys Goodfellow Fund. In 1928, a bronze statue depicting Brady alongside a tattered youngster was erected on Belle Isle.

Over the years, thanks to the generosity of countless donors, many of whom willingly give large sums of money anonymously, several million dollars worth of foodstuffs, clothing, books, toys, and medical services have been purchased and distributed to the city's underprivileged children. Not a dime of the money raised each year has ever gone for expenses.

"I think Detroiters remember the old days when times were very tough," explained Waldmeir, one of the most prominent of the hundreds of volunteers who annually help the Goodfellows reach their goal of no child without a Christmas. "There have always been vast swings of the economic pendulum. Everyone has had hard times, from the top executives on down. I was born in the depression when soap, meat, and butter were rationed. Remembering those hard times motivates people in my generation. The Goodfellow goal is to get the next generation involved."

➤ *James J. Brady about 1916.*

◄ *The Goodfellow Fund was designed to help underprivileged children like this Detroit youngster, pictured in 1926.*

➤ *A Goodfellow's check list from 1930 shows that the family of Alfred Moss received a holiday package consisting of a ham, a bag of potatoes, 12 cans of tomatoes and several other food items to help make it through hard times.*

Alfred Moss   1930
                    2900 - 16th St
✓ 1 Bag Potatoes
✓ 1 Ham
✓ 1 Pork Shoulder
✓ 3 Pkgs. Lard
  5 Loaves Bread
✓ 2 Bags Flour
✓ 12 Cans Tomatoes
✓ 4 Pkgs. Coffee
✓ 2 Sacks Sugar
✓ 2 Cans Baking Powder
✓ 3 Cans Milk
✓ 4 Pkgs. Macaroni
✓ 2 "   Salt
✓ 1 "   Candy
✓ 15# - 1 Bag Beans
✓ 10# - 1 " Split Peas
✓ 4 Pkgs. Spaghetti

punch press operators. The toll of lost digits inspired writer Erskine Caldwell to dub Detroit "the eight-finger city."

Beyond the ubiquitous hazards of industrial employment were the low pay and uncertainty. "In those days the auto industry had its model-change layoff in late summer," recalled one tool grinder. "The workers referred to the layoff as their 'starvation vacation.' I don't know how the laid-off auto workers with families to support managed to live during those payless weeks. There was no unemployment compensation to tide them over until they returned to work. And when they did work they never earned more than enough to keep the family going from payday to payday." There also was no health insurance, no pensions, no sick days, and no seniority. Workers could be fired on a whim. In order to keep their jobs, many "volunteered" to spend an off day painting or roofing the foreman's house.

"For women," recalled Margaret Collingwood Nowak, a union organizer, "it meant dating the boss at his whim or accepting unwanted attentions. Refusal meant few assignments, sometimes a transfer to another department and less desirable job, or even being fired. Pay for women was always less than for men, even for the same job and the same amount of production. This served as a whip over the men, who, if they complained, were told this particular operation could be given to a woman for less pay. The union promised release from such indignities and injustices and gave workers a sense of worth."

Since the mid-19th century, workers in various industries had occasionally been able to organize for better pay and working conditions. The gains typically were short-lived. In the early years of the 20th century, the union-busting Employers' Association of Detroit was so effective in stifling workers that the Motor City became known far and wide as a capitalist's paradise. Ironically, Detroit's reputation as an open shop town was one of the major reasons it became the center of auto production.

The few unions that did exist often self-destructed. The Carriage, Wagon, and Automobile Workers Union was a case in point. The first automobiles were carefully hand-built by different teams of carpenters, upholsterers, and other craftsmen. They assembled several cars simultaneously, each working around a stationary chassis until the vehicle was completed. By the mid-1920s, auto manufacturing had become standardized throughout the industry, lowering the status and wages of

▲ *From cigar plants and candy factories to sewing rooms and auto plants, thousands of women worked outside of their homes at low-wage, light-assembly jobs to help provide for their families.*

➤ *An unemployed Detroiter advertises for a job in 1932, the depth of the Depression. By the following year, 25 percent of the country's workforce—13 million people—were out of work.*

skilled employees. The influx of unskilled workers, many of them immigrants and Southern blacks, antagonized the elitist, xenophobic craft unions. In 1926, William Logan resigned as president of the Carriage, Wagon, and Automobile Workers Union, saying: "Where once we had men to deal with who were skilled or semiskilled and who felt a certain degree of independence, we now have a large body of workers . . . who are specialists performing an operation over and over."

One of the robot-like specialists was Paul Boatin, an Italian immigrant who followed his father into the Rouge plant in 1925.

"The working conditions were dehumanizing," he remembered. "You couldn't talk to another worker—couldn't even say hello without getting fired. There was no laughing, no smoking. You had to get permission to get a drink of water or go to the toilet. You'd sit and eat your lunch by your machine because the servicemen wouldn't allow any groups."

Ford's Service Department had originally been created to provide plant security during World War I, when industrial saboteurs were a very real concern. By the early 1930s, however, Ford's top aide, a stumpy, tattooed ex-boxer named Harry Bennett, had built the department into the world's largest private security force: 3,000 plug-uglies recruited from local gyms, college football teams, and prisons. Stooges were everywhere.

"They were all rotten, no-good sons of bitches," said Al Bardelli, who, despite his advanced age, practically flew off the couch when asked about Bennett's goons. The Dearborn resident, who first entered the Rouge in 1927, remembered how armed servicemen used to follow him home, to the market, and to organizing meetings.

The reluctance to directly confront management over pay and working conditions doomed early attempts to gather all auto workers under one union banner—that is, until the socioeconomic pressures of the 1930s drove hungry workers to desperate measures.

As a one-industry town, Detroit's pain was especially acute during the Great Depression. Auto production plunged from 5.3 million vehicles in 1929 to a mere

The Man Who Murdered McKinley

The tumultuous socialist labor movement at the turn of the 20th century produced its share of misguided fanatics, including a young Detroiter named Leon Czolgosz. The former factory hand and budding anarchist hated all people of wealth and authority, rationalizing that their power came at the expense of the working class, many of whom shared his poor, Eastern European roots.

On the afternoon of September 6, 1901, Czolgosz (pronounced ZOL-gus) stood in line inside the Temple of Music at the Pan-American Exposition in Buffalo, waiting to shake the hand of President William McKinley. A handkerchief was wrapped around his right hand, concealing a .32-caliber revolver. At 4:07 p.m., as McKinley took Czolgosz's extended left hand, the assassin pressed the hidden pistol against the president's vest. Two muffled shots followed.

Thousands of Detroiters had taken advantage of discounted railway and steamship fares to visit the exhibition. One of them, C.J. Emmons, was standing a few feet behind Czolgosz when the shooting occurred.

"For a few seconds, there wasn't a sound," he told reporters. "Then a man shouted, 'Great God! He's shot. They've shot him!' Women screamed and the men were shouting and cursing. I never saw such punching and screaming in my life."

While policemen wrestled the gunman to the floor, then whisked him away in the same horse-drawn cab that had brought his victim to the hall, McKinley was rushed to a small hospital on the exposition grounds. Emergency surgery to repair a severe stomach wound followed. At first it seemed that the president would recover. But gangrene set in, and eight days later McKinley joined Abraham Lincoln and James Buchanan on the sad roll of assassinated U.S. presidents. Vice-president Theodore Roosevelt was sworn in as chief executive.

Some insisted that they knew Czolgosz was headed for a bad end. He had been born 28 years earlier in Detroit and his family lived at 135 Benton Street. The *Detroit Free Press* interviewed one of the assassin's former neighbors, who remembered the young Czolgosz as "a terror to manage," a child who "gave evidence of a perverted nature."

Czolgosz left Detroit when he was 16, eventually settling on the family farm outside Cleveland that he had helped purchase with his wages at a wire factory. He retired there after suffering a breakdown of some type, spending his days making pottery and reading anarchist literature. Czolgosz, who had been living in a Buffalo boardinghouse in the weeks prior to the shooting, was a proponent of free love but opposed just about everything else, including marriage, organized religion, voting, and the judicial system. "I killed President McKinley because I done my duty," he explained in his only written statement to police. "I didn't believe one man should have so much service and another man should have none." Czolgosz evidently acted on his own; no accomplices were ever found. In fact, his murderous act was roundly denounced by anarchist groups across the country.

Czolgosz barely escaped being lynched by an enraged mob after the shooting, but he was to pay for his crime soon enough. Freely admitting his guilt, and with no defense witnesses called in the two-day trial that followed, the assassin was quickly convicted and sentenced to die. He was electrocuted on October 29, 1901, maintaining to the end that the popular, good-natured McKinley was "the enemy of the good people—the good working people."

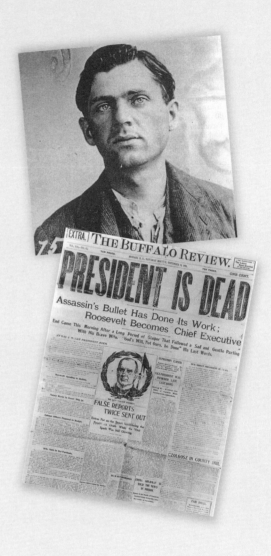

⋏ Top: The International Alliance of Bill Posters of U.S. and Canada participated in the 1916 Labor Day parade in this flower-bedecked truck.

⋏ Above: United Auto Workers Local 600 amused spectators by staging an impromptu sit-down during this Labor Day march.

Workers on the March

Over the years, Detroit's Labor Day parade has mirrored the ups and downs of organized labor. The first sparsely attended rallies were held at night in the 1880s because of employers' refusal to allow their workers time off to demonstrate their solidarity. Pinkerton spies often marched along, identifying troublemakers, who could be fired the next morning.

In 1886 the first daytime parade was organized by the Detroit Council of Trades and the Knights of Labor. That year an estimated 12,000 workers—four times the size of the previous year's crowd—defiantly marched down Jefferson Avenue in what was essentially a one-day general strike. Spotted in the three-mile-long procession was a banner reading: "Divided We Can Beg, United We Can Demand."

Labor Day became a legal state holiday in 1893 and a national holiday the following year, helping to create a tradition of a workers' parade on the first Monday of September. However, the parade was cancelled in 1917 because of World War I. Due to wholesale anti-union sentiment, it wasn't reinstituted until 20 years later, by which time Detroit had shifted from an open-shop town to a union stronghold. Recognizing this, such Democratic candidates as Harry Truman, John F. Kennedy, and Lyndon Johnson used the parade's climax in Cadillac Square as the platform from which to launch their fall presidential campaigns.

Curiously, the contentious split-up of the AFL-CIO resulted in two separate parades from 1938 to 1947. The American Federation of Labor would march in the morning, along with the Teamsters and the construction trades, while in the afternoon the more militant Congress of Industrial Organizations would march with the United Auto Workers.

At its height the Labor Day parade drew an estimated 250,000 people to lower Woodward Avenue. As union members grew more prosperous and complacent in the postwar years, the annual show of force began to shrink in size. Younger workers, disconnected from the struggles of their fathers and uncles, preferred a day at the lake to a day of marching and speeches. The apathy, coupled with the fears and friction that followed in the wake of the 1967 riot, caused that year's parade to be cancelled.

However, the same forces that have traditionally brought laborers together caused unions to revive the tradition in 1981, at a time when the city and the auto industry were grappling with seismic economic changes. Subsequent parades have numbered between 50,000 and 100,000 marchers, with the size usually dependent on the state of the local economy.

1.3 million two years later, creating unprecedented social anguish and upheaval. Jobs vanished, savings were wiped out, banks closed, and families were tossed out on the street by unforgiving landlords. Helene Weiss Urbach's middle-class parents were forced to move the family from the high-rent district of Dexter Boulevard to more affordable housing on the northern outskirts of the city. The Depression "taught me about survival, how to make do, or even do without" the material goods that future generations would take for granted, she said. "It was a time when every penny counted."

Janice Sofran, an Oakland County resident, grew up listening to her grandfather's stories about making a go of it during hard times.

"His memories of the Depression cause me to reflect upon the stark realities of making something from nothing," she said. "Necessity often brings out one's improvisational abilities and creativity. My grandmother would bleach flour sacks in the sun so that she could use the cloth for dresses for herself and my mother. The children would follow the railroad tracks to pick up bits of coal that had fallen from the coal car for the furnace at home.

"My grandfather saved everything. His collection included balls of string, rubber bands, paper foil, and shopping bags. Nothing was thrown away."

For many, the loss of a job represented a loss of dignity and an overpowering sense of personal failure for being unable to provide for the family. "It seems to me I have lost all my ability as a responsible man," an unemployed worker who refused welfare wrote Mayor Frank Murphy. "It seems to me I have some shortcomings somewhere." Those autoworkers lucky enough to continue working saw their average weekly wages drop from $35 in 1928 to $20 in 1932.

In the winter of 1931–32, three-quarters of the Rouge workforce was unemployed. On the afternoon of March 7, 1932, about 3,000 desperate men staged a "hunger march" on the Rouge. They were met by an army of servicemen and police, who opened fire. Bardelli, one of the fortunate few to still be working, returned home to find friends frantically tallying the score. "Bennett's men killed five marchers and wounded 20 or so others," said Bardelli. Ford remained the toughest nut to crack, even as conditions improved under President Franklin D. Roosevelt. Among the New Deal legislation was the Wagner Act, which gave workers the legal right to organize on the job.

In the spring of 1937, organized labor was on a roll. Successful sit-down strikes

▲ *A charitable outgrowth of the Great Depression was the soup kitchen started by Father Solanus Casey at the St. Bonaventure Monastery on Mount Elliott—a "temporary" relief effort that continues on the site to this day. The Capuchin priest (standing at far left) was declared venerable by the Catholic church and is poised to become the first American-born male canonized a saint.*

▼ *The "Hunger March Massacre" made headlines in 1932 when 3,000 Ford workers and their supporters demanded jobs and got bullets instead.*

V / ➤ May 26, 1937, the "Battle of the Overpass": As UAW organizers, including Walter Reuther (center) and Richard Frankensteen (right), passed out leaflets outside the Rouge plant, several Ford servicemen approached them. The beating that followed was recorded by several photographers, whose images in newspapers and magazines across the country helped turn public opinion against Henry Ford and his henchman, Harry Bennett.

had helped the UAW forge historic contracts with Chrysler and General Motors. Smaller carmakers and other industries fell in line. Henry Ford, however, vowed that he would close his plants before negotiating with a union. He openly thumbed his nose at the Wagner Act.

One day that May, several UAW organizers, including Walter Reuther and Dick Frankensteen, climbed the Miller Road overpass outside Gate 4 of the Rouge plant. Their announced intention was to hand out leaflets urging workers to join the union. As they smiled and lined up for some pictures, a cadre of servicemen suddenly moved in.

Bill May was a young reporter for the International News Service. Now retired and living in North Muskegon, he is one of the few surviving eyewitnesses to what was to become a seminal moment in the history of the company and of the labor movement, "the Battle of the Overpass."

"They had their targets all picked out—that was obvious," he recalled. "I had

Radio Days

One day in 1902, Tom Clark, a young Detroit inventor with an interest in wireless telegraphy, told *Detroit News* publisher James E. Scripps, "The time will come when you will sit in your home and be entertained by music played thousands of miles away." This seemed a bold prediction, considering that all entertainment in those days was experienced live.

But on the evening of August 20, 1920 the *Detroit News* made radio history when Harold Trumbo, a local Edison employee, placed a turntable next to a transmitting set in a corner of the city room. An estimated 100 ham radio operators heard the crackly sounds of "Roses of Picardy," the music amplified by an office boy holding a cardboard megaphone up to the phonograph speaker. This primitive program, organized by Clark and William J. Scripps, the publisher's son and successor on the masthead, was the world's first scheduled commercial broadcast. This made transmitting station 8MK the world's first commercial station.

▲ *On August 31, 1920, the* Detroit News' *8MK became the world's first commercial radio station, broadcasting election results over what was then known as "wireless telegraph." A few months later the station changed its call letters to WWJ.*

Eleven days after its debut, 8MK broadcast the results of the state, congressional, and county primaries, marking the first time that a paper had used a radiophone to broadcast news. The sending of the election results, the *News* reported, "was fraught with romance and must go down in the history of man's conquest of the elements as a gigantic step in his progress. In the four hours that the apparatus was hissing and whirring its messages into space, few realized that a dream and a prediction had come true. The news of the world was being given forth through this invisible trumpet to the waiting crowds in an unseen marketplace. With the perfection of aerials and amplifiers, the not too distant future may see the installation of regular news service."

The *News* soon changed its call letters to WWJ. (The first letter was mandated by the federal government; the second two letters were the initials of Scripps's son.) Early programming included such fare as a local musician plunking his ukulele, but by 1927 WWJ was broadcasting baseball games from Navin Field, with Ty Tyson doing the play-by-play.

Detroit claimed another radio "first" when the Detroit Police Department unveiled the world's first radio-equipped car, a Ford, in 1921.

"Radioland" grew exponentially over the next decade. Station WXYZ began broadcasting popular radio serials like *The Lone Ranger, Sergeant Preston of the Yukon, and The Green Hornet* from the top floors of the Maccabees Building at Woodward and Putnam. Helene Weiss Urbach, who grew up in northwest Detroit, recalled the era as a time of wonderment. "The radio, as I remember it in the early 1930s, was a magic box that told of adventures of derring-do by masked men and all manner of heroes," she said.

The most famous radio hero of them all was *The Lone Ranger*, a collaborative creation of WXYZ executives George W. Trendle and James Jewell and Buffalo scriptwriter Fran Striker. The adventures of the mysterious masked man, along with his loyal Indian companion Tonto, and their great white horse Silver (in the beginning, the two men improbably rode the same horse together), immediately captivated listeners when *The Lone Ranger* first aired in January 1933. That spring, during a promotional giveaway featuring a genuine Lone Ranger toy gun, WXYZ received 24,500 letters in less than a week.

There was a succession of Lone Rangers before the station settled on Earl Graser, a short-statured Wayne State University student. "He had mild blue eyes, fair skin and was inclined to be chubby," recalled longtime WXYZ broadcaster

Dick Osgood. "Born in Canada, he had never been west of Michigan, couldn't ride a horse, and shot a gun only once in his life." These weren't considered detriments until the show's overwhelming popularity made personal appearances mandatory. Brace Beemer, a tall, chiseled broadcaster whom a station executive discovered reading poetry over the air in Indianapolis was hired to meet the Lone Ranger's public.

When Graser was killed in an auto accident in 1941, Beemer took over the role of what *Time* magazine described as "the most adored character ever to be created on the U.S. air." By now the show was being heard on 155 stations. The title character was an institution, sending toy lariats, six-shooters, and 10-gallon hats to hundreds of thousands of commissioned little Rangers across the country.

With the postwar boom in television, the popularity of live radio drama faded. After more than 21 years of broadcasts from the Maccabees Building, the rights to the Lone Ranger character were sold to a television production company for $3 million, at the time the highest price ever paid for a radio property. The last live radio broadcast of the show was September 3, 1954. All of the performers knew it was the end of an era.

"When the show was over," recalled Osgood, "there was a sudden emptiness. Some went to the Van Dyke Club and got drunk. Others went to their homes, still feeling vaguely that something impossible had happened. All concealed their foreboding. One, as he snuggled into bed that night, thought, 'Oh God, let me sleep tonight and not worry. Something will turn up. Sleep, Lone Ranger, sleep.'"

Toby David, best known as the longtime children's TV show host, Cap'n Jolly, was one of Detroit's radio pioneers. In the 1930s he teamed with Joe Gentile (later the public address announcer at Tiger Stadium) on *Happy Joe and the Early Morning Frolic*, a popular show broadcast over CKLW. David's experiences give a flavor of the early days of radio in the city.

"I gave up a good job at Chrysler," he remembered, "good enough, in Depression Detroit, to provide me with a good car and fairly comfortable living. A couple of weeks went by while I learned to handle the equipment in

the studio—microphones, sound effects, and whatnot. Things were going along fine. There was one thing missing, though. A paycheck!"

Two weeks after starting on CKLW on May 1, 1935, David had seen none of the station's money. Admittedly, the issue of getting paid had not come up in the initial conversation with owner Ted Campeau. "I just assumed that they would pay me well. After all, this was the BIG TIME, and I was the co-star of a popular morning show at a 50,000-watt commercial station."

Finally, David went to the office manager and asked him when he would get paid.

"What pay?" was the response. "There is no pay."

David couldn't believe his ears. He approached Campeau. "What's this 'no pay' business?" he demanded. "I left a good job at Chrysler to come here and I haven't received a single cent."

"Well," said Campeau, "I thought you were just interested in getting into radio."

"I still couldn't believe what I was hearing," David said. "But I held my temper, and eventually we came to terms—Campeau's—which came to five dollars a week. I have never met anyone who made less in any business."

David's contributions to the show were a wide range of voices and dialects, plus some zany gimmicks.

"The gimmick that brought the greatest response from the early morning audience was a character we named Shirley," he said. "Shirley was so naive that she would let herself be thrown down the elevator shaft. The sound effect for this—Shirley tumbling from side to side as she hurtled toward the ground—was an old cymbal which I had found around the studio and filled with bits of metal. I would throw this down a stairwell and, screaming in a high falsetto voice, follow it down the stairs. The listeners loved it. Their letters and phone calls asking us to throw Shirley down the elevator shaft were ample proof that there was a fun-loving, if not too caring, audience out there.

"Adding to the mayhem of this show was a gambit Joe and I would pull off now and then. With a frying pan

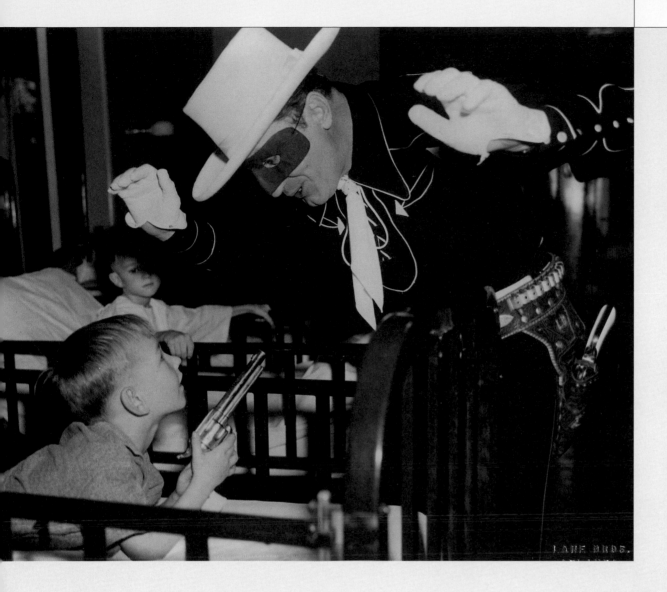

LANE BROS.

⤷ Opposite page, center: During the 1920s and '30s, popular Detroit News *columnist and poet Anne Campbell was one of many print journalists who crossed over to the new medium of radio.*

◄ A hospitalized youngster gets the drop on the Lone Ranger, a radio legend who hung his hat at the Maccabees Building on Woodward.

and a mallet, Joe would simulate the sound of banging me on the head. We got a great many calls for that stunt because, I think, I wailed so mercifully each time I was struck on the head. Anything to keep listeners awake and tuned in went in those days."

The show was a commercial success that was the envy of the other Detroit area stations, continued David. "Advertisers had to wait to get on it; and they got their money's worth not only in goods sold but in air time as well. Often those ad-lib commercials that Joe and I invented would run three minutes—far beyond the 60 seconds the advertiser paid for."

One particularly happy advertiser was Conn's Clothes, a men's store catering to the working class with suits in the $16.60 to $32.50 range. "Whether a male Detroiter shopped there or not, if he was at all aware of what was going on around him, he knew the Conn's Clothes jingle," said David:

Wear it, tear it, compare it, don't spare it
And if it isn't the best buy you ever made
Bring it back and get your money back.

"Everyone in Detroit knew that slogan."

Proof of that came nearly 40 years later when the old radio hand, now retired and living in Arizona, was introduced at a Lions Club meeting in Sun City. As he rose to acknowledge the introduction, 15 men in the audience, all obviously former Detroiters, rose as one and began to sing the Conn's Clothes jingle.

"And they knew all the words, too," he said.

⌄ / ➤ *Scenes from the sitdown strikes that paralyzed Detroit in 1937: sitdowners try to get comfortable on sewing tables turned into makeshift beds while musically inclined Dodge workers play tunes to boost morale.*

my eyes glued on Frankensteen, probably because I knew him best. They pulled his jacket up around his head and started letting him have it in the gut. Meanwhile, Reuther was on the ground. He was a small guy and he wasn't putting up too much resistance. They got Frankensteen up on the rail, as if they were going to drop him off the overpass onto the sidewalk below. I distinctly remember one of the fellas who were doing the beating say, 'No, don't do that, we'll kill the guy.' So they started booting him down the steps. It was all over in about five minutes."

Actually, the uproar had just begun. Bennett explained with a straight face that the beatings had been administered not by servicemen, but by workers who didn't want a union. He felt safe with this fiction, knowing that the company had been absolved of all blame in the "hunger march massacre" five years earlier, and thinking that in any case his thugs had seized all of the cameras recording the attack.

However, a couple of photographers had managed to flee the scene. The damning evidence of Ford's violent opposition to the law appeared on the pages of newspapers and national magazines. Once a hero to the working class, the man behind the five-dollar day was now exposed as perhaps its most ardent enemy.

Despite the swing in public opinion against Ford, and a National Labor

Relations Board ruling that the company was in violation of the Wagner Act, Ford continued to resist organization attempts for four more chaotic years. The UAW stepped up its efforts inside and outside the plant. Ford, ignoring the advice of Edsel, relied on Bennett's servicemen to identify, intimidate, and fire union leaders.

Working conditions remained unbearable. Bardelli recalled the infamous "Ford speedup," which stretched a man's ability to keep up with the moving parts to inhuman levels. "I'd come home so tired and irritated I'd take it out on my wife and my kids," he said, curling his gnarled hand into a fist. "What I really wanted to do was beat the shit out of Bennett. That's what we all wanted to do."

Despite Bennett's strong-arm tactics, the UAW continued to sign up more men. On April 1, 1941, eight workers were fired for union activities, prompting a climactic strike. Tens of thousands of pickets were wrapped like a giant boa constrictor around the plant, their cars parked three and four deep down every street. Nobody could get into the plant. Bardelli, then a picket captain, joyfully remembered workers picking up a car containing a half-dozen servicemen and turning it back in the direction from which it came. *This* was solidarity.

Edsel, who had been ill and was trying to regain his health in Florida, flew to Detroit to argue his case. He was weak, thin, and pale, and perhaps for this reason his father finally caved in to his plea to accommodate the workers. Over the objections of Bennett, Ford agreed to allow an NLRB election, which in his delusionary state he believed would result in his workers rejecting a union. However, only 2.5 percent of the Rouge's 80,000 workers voted that way. The rest demanded the right to collective bargaining.

Ford, once the paterfamilias of auto workers, was crushed. He refused to sign a formal agreement, yelling that he would close the plant if he had to.

An unlikely friend of labor stepped in at this crucial moment. The prospect of renewed picket line violence caused Clara Ford to finally confront her husband. If Henry would not recognize the union and put an end to the years of suffering experienced not only by the rank and file, but by their own son, she would sell her share of Ford stock and leave him.

Now 78 and showing signs of senility, Ford surprised everybody by suddenly capitulating. He instructed Bennett to negotiate a historic contract with the UAW

➤ / ⅄ *The social and economic unrest of the '30s spawned various demagogues and crackpot organizations. Father Charles Coughlin, pastor of the Shrine of the Little Flower in Royal Oak, became a national figure through his radio attacks on Jews, especially President Roosevelt, who he blamed for the Depression. More insidious were members of the Black Legion, modeled after the Ku Klux Klan. The paramilitary group was active in auto plants and was suspicious of anyone who wasn't white and Protestant. The Legion commited several killings and bombings until a high-profile murder trial in 1936 sent several top leaders to prison for life.*

"YOU'D BE SITTING IN THE OFFICE ANY MARCH DAY OF 1937 AND THE PHONE WOULD RING. AND THE VOICE AT THE END WOULD SAY, 'MY NAME IS MARY JONES, AND I'M A SODA CLERK AT LIGGETT'S. WE'VE THROWN THE MANAGER OUT AND WE'VE GOT THE KEYS. WHAT DO WE DO NOW?'" — *Myra Komaroff Wolfgang, Hotel and Restaurant Employees, describing "sit down fever."*

that was even more favorable than the ones it had signed with GM and Chrysler. "Never underestimate the power of a woman," Ford told an associate.

It all came too late to help Edsel, who was diagnosed with stomach cancer. He died on May 26, 1943, exactly six years to the day that Bennett had so brutally enforced his father's will on the Miller Road overpass. By then, one of those bloodied that day had become one of the rising stars of organized labor.

Walter Reuther, a West Virginia native who as a teenager had been fired from his first job as a tool and die maker for organizing a protest against Sunday work, founded and served as president of UAW Local 174. He directed a 113-day strike against General Motors that ended in March 1946 with workers winning significant pay increases and improvements in working conditions.

Reuther next took on his old nemesis, Ford, where he had once worked for two years before being fired for union activities. The key issue now was pensions. He emphasized the disparity between auto executives, who enjoyed generous retirement packages, and the pensionless rank and file, who grimly joked that they were "too old to work and too young to die."

"If you make $258 an hour," the fiery Reuther argued, "they give you a pension. If you make $1.65 an hour, they say, 'You don't need it, you're not entitled to it, and we are not going to give it to you.'"

Reuther picked his target well. Ford had an aging workforce and a more enlightened management now that Henry Ford II, Edsel's oldest son, had swept the company of Bennett and his cronies. "Young Henry" took over in 1945 and was anxious to test his philosophy of "human engineering," where workers and bosses strove to meet common goals.

The historic 1947 agreement was the first time an automaker had provided a

◄ *Opposite page: Members of the rank and file found it profitable to associate Henry Ford with Hitler, who in the past had openly expressed his admiration for the auto tycoon.*

▼ *The enforcer: Service chief Harry Bennett was the man who administered Ford's heavy-handed labor policies.*

Detroit's Cigar Industry: Up in Smoke

In her old age, Josephine Bielawski liked to shock strangers by announcing, "I used to be a stripper." She would then wait a heartbeat or two before explaining with a laugh, "My job was to operate a machine that stripped tobacco from the stem."

Bielawski's little joke reflected how far Detroit's once prominent tobacco industry has slipped in the public memory. There was a time when the sidewalks were alive with hundreds of young women in long, white aprons hurrying to work at the city's many cigar factories. For some 80 years, local companies such as Essex, Webster-Eisenlohr, and Mazur-Cressman provided millions of the proverbial 5-cent cigars. But those days have disappeared like smoke on the wind.

Detroit's first cigar manufacturing factory opened sometime in the 1850s, its cutting machinery powered by a blind horse that spent its life endlessly circling a capstan in the basement. Initially, seed farms provided homegrown tobacco, but rail and canal connections with Kentucky soon brought in superior leaves. By the early 1900s, cigar factories had popped up in the Junction-Michigan section of the city's west side and along Grandy Avenue on the near east side.

Bielawski was the youngest of eight children born to Polish immigrants. Her father died in 1912, when she was three years old. When she donned her apron as a teenager, she was following in the footsteps of two generations of unskilled Polish women who accepted the cigar plants as a distasteful but traditional way of contributing to the family income.

"I made 25 cents an hour," she remembered. "Each week I gave my whole paycheck to my mother."

Bielawski worked 12 years at various cigar factories in Poletown. The industry had its own jargon. Workers who placed tobacco leaves in bunches

◄ Opposite page: Employees of the San Telmo Cigar Factory, circa 1912.

◄ A sitdowner is hauled away by police during a strike at the Bernard Schwartz cigar factory on March 20, 1937. Thirty women employees, some of whom had battled police with heavy wooden cigar molds, were arrested in the melee.

were known as "bunchmakers," while those who shaped the tobacco into cigars were called "rollers."

By the 1930s many factories had installed giant cigar making machines. Four women worked each machine, including a "feeder," who fed it a constant supply of tobacco.

"You can always tell the cigar workers that are feeders because their faces are all marked from the tobacco dust," a worker once told the *Detroit News.* "You don't stay pretty long if you work one of those machines."

In terms of working conditions, the women working 60 hours a week at the tables and machines had little on the blind horse in the basement.

"It was hot and it was noisy," said Bielawski, normally not one to complain. Tobacco dust clogged noses. Workers couldn't open windows because the air would dry the stock. Instead, humidifiers ran continuously, turning the factories into damp, smelly sweatshops that produced nearly as many head and throat colds as they did cigars. Those who were paid piece-rates avoided going to the lavatory for fear of losing several cigars. And there were always the unwelcome advances of the foremen to contend with. Those who resisted were apt to be fired.

The cigar bosses had always dismissed their female employees as docile,

so they were stunned when activists seized and shut down a succession of cigar factories in February 1937. Soon more than 2,000 women occupied five Poletown plants. What followed were some of the longest and hardest-fought sit-down strikes of the decade.

Company goons and the police physically removed some of the strikers. Inside one factory, women battled an army of policemen by belting them with heavy wooden cigar molds while supporters in the streets hurled rocks and snowballs. Eventually the protection and support of the United Auto Workers and Governor Frank Murphy forced employers to recognize the union. The women negotiated a 20 percent raise and a 40-hour week. Before long, 5,500 boxes of union-labeled cigars were coming out of Detroit each month.

Bielawski never left Poletown. When asked, she would proudly display a silver five-year pin given to her by her last employer, the General Cigar Company, manufacturer of White Owl cigars. Then she would tell you that General Cigar, close on the heels of other cigar companies, fled the city in favor of the South, where labor was cheap and disorganized. By World War II, all of Detroit's cigar plants were closed. Most eventually were razed. All that lingers today is the memory of an occasional stripper, persistent as the smell of a 5-cent cigar.

In 1946, Walter Reuther defeated R.J. Thompson in a hotly contested election for the presidency of the United Auto Workers. He would remain head of the UAW until his untimely death in a 1970 airplane crash.

retirement plan for its workers. "It's a good thing for us old-timers," said one veteran of the assembly line. "Now I can get a little piece of land and have a nice little farm." Said another: "You got a little bit of human dignity."

Dignity was the operative word in Reuther's life and work. "There is no greater calling than to serve your fellow man," he said. "There is no greater contribution than to help the weak. There is no greater satisfaction than to do it well."

Like many of his contemporaries in the labor movement, Reuther had once been a socialist, but as he and the UAW matured he rid the union of leftists. Although he personally led a very austere lifestyle, proudly serving as the nation's lowest-paid union president, he was relentless in boosting the living standards of autoworkers, and, by extension, those of all American workers.

During the 1950s and 1960s, contract negotiations often resulted in long and painful strikes. But with America's postwar economy booming, automakers—flush with profits—always caved in to Reuther's demands. As a result, U.S. autoworkers became the best-paid industrial workers in history, with a range of benefits that would have staggered Ransom Olds or the Dodge brothers. These included vacations, health care insurance, cost-of-living adjustments, and supplemental unemployment benefits. Reuther's liberal agenda frightened some. George Romney of the Automobile Manufacturers' Association called him "the most dangerous man in Detroit" for his ability to effect social change without appearing like a revolutionary.

Reuther served as president of the international union from 1946 until his death in a small plane crash in 1970. During that time he built the UAW into a progressive, corruption-free organization that concerned itself with a broad range of social issues, especially civil rights.

"Who's Walter Reuther?" one black man asked another during a freedom march in the South during the 1960s.

"Who's Walter Reuther?" was the incredulous response. "He's the white Martin Luther King."

▼ *Two giants of the civil rights movement, Walter Reuther and Martin Luther King, are joined by tens of thousands of supporters in the 1963 march down Woodward Avenue.*

Dignity for the Worker

DOUG FRASER BECAME THE SIXTH INTERNATIONAL PRESIDENT OF THE UNITED AUTO WORKERS IN 1977, A POSITION HE HELD UNTIL HIS RETIREMENT IN 1983. THE MAN OFTEN CALLED "THE LABOR LEADER EVERYONE RESPECTS," FRASER WORKED THE LINE IN THE 1930S AND '40S AND WAS A LOCAL PRESIDENT BY AGE 27 BEFORE CONTINUING HIS QUICK RISE THROUGH THE UNION'S RANKS. IN ADDITION TO HIS EXTENSIVE PUBLIC SERVICE, FRASER IS A PROFESSOR OF LABOR STUDIES AT WAYNE STATE UNIVERSITY.

Too many unions are just unions. The UAW has always been more involved in the community than other unions. Walter Reuther said, "You can't make progress at the expense of the community." That's really the big difference between a union and a labor movement. The UAW is a movement, and it is about social change, being concerned about the local community, the country, and the world.

My family came to Detroit from Glasgow, Scotland, in 1922 when I was six after my father found a job at the Studebaker plant on Fort Street. We first lived in the area of Porter Street and Vernor Highway and later moved during the Depression to 4953 Daniels, five blocks west of Livernois near McGraw. It was a wonderful Polish neighborhood with a lot of autoworkers, but by my mid teens we were in the depths of the Depression. The unemployment rate must have been about 75 percent.

People don't realize the frustration of people who are ready, willing, and able to work, but can't find jobs to support their families. My dad was such a proud man. The devastating fact is that you lose your sense of dignity. We survived those years, though. We used to grow onions in our backyard, and I would go to the Tastee or Wonderbread plant and buy two- or three-day-old bread. My ma used to take the bread, soak it, and mix it with the onions. When you're hungry it sure tastes good.

There were a lot of utility shutoffs and evictions in our area. We got evicted from our home once. I can still remember lying in bed and hearing my mom crying. I suppose my first social action was when I moved the furniture back into the house from the curb. It was just a temporary victory because, of course, the landlord had it moved out again.

I never regretted living through the Depression because it formed my views on many social issues. I tell young people today that if there is one lesson in life, never, never, never forget where you came from.

I dropped out of Chadsey High School at 17 without a job. It was silly, and I shouldn't have done it. I was bored and restless. There was too much going on, and I used to go to different political rallies. My parents were wonderful, but they never talked to me about college. They were used to a rigid Scottish class system, where if your dad was a factory worker, you became one too. There was no pressure about going to college because that idea didn't even enter your mind.

I really belonged to the union movement before I went to work. My dad had been the secretary of his union in Glasgow and there was a lot of conversation about unions in our house between my dad and his friends.

One of my first jobs was getting paid a dollar a day knocking on doors, telling people the man peddling food was in the neighborhood. When I was 18, I got a job at Bryant Motor Sales on Warren near Rouge Park. The owner was Henry Ford's brother-in-law. There was a Ford salesroom in the front and a machine shop in the back. At that time it was the best job I had. In those days you just gave the money over to your parents. After two weeks, I tried to get a co-worker to join a union. It turned out to be Bryant's nephew. That was the end of the job.

After that I went to Everhart Heating Company for 32 cents an hour, insulating hot water heaters, which was a miserable job. At that place, they had a glassed-in lavatory in the middle of the plant so the bosses could keep an eye on the workers. I ended up getting fired there, too, for trying to start a union.

I first started work at the DeSoto plant on December 8, 1936. You always remember your seniority date. I was in the stamping plant, which was relatively clean.

The basic ill of all those factories was the authoritarian form of governance, where the foreman was the supreme boss. You couldn't complain, dissent, or argue, despite the conditions. A lot of people have asked me, "What is the greatest accomplishment of the UAW? Was it the benefits, pension, health care?" You know what it was? It was bringing the workers dignity. Giving them a voice where they could express concern. In the first auto contracts the wages were pretty good. It wasn't about wages or really even the working conditions. It was about dignity for the worker.

➤ *With flags flying and a band playing, sitdowners march triumphantly out of Dodge Main, ending their 17-day strike in March 1937.*

In March of 1937 I participated in the sit-down strike at our plant, right after the Flint sit-down strike. We got recognition. In '38 we were challenged with National Labor Relations Board elections, but we won our plant and nearly all Chrysler plants by 85 or 90 percent.

However, in 1938, one of the most traumatic events I ever experienced was being laid off for 11 months. It was terrible. When I was UAW president in 1982, probably the worst year since '38, people used to write me pointing out that maybe I didn't understand their problems being laid off. I used to write back to them and say, oh yes, I understand their problem, because it had been such a traumatic experience for me. Even when you go back, there's a rumor every day of lay offs, which hung over your head.

Another difficult experience was the 104-day-old Chrysler strike in 1950. By that time I was on the Chrysler staff working closely with Walter Reuther in negotiations. We were simply asking for an actuarially sound pension plan. It was the only issue. At the end of the three-month strike, the company finally settled. The ballroom downstairs at the hotel was set up for the press and photographers. Walter Reuther said to us, "This was an unnecessary strike, with a lot of suffering to the workers and their families. Why should we shake hands with those bastards?"

So we didn't. Maybe it was petty, but it sure felt good. It's the only time I know of Reuther not shaking hands after a settlement.

Reuther hired me as an administrative assistant soon after that strike. I held that position with him for the next eight years before becoming a regional director.

When I became president after Leonard Woodcock, 1977, 1978, and 1979 were pretty good years. One of the best years ever was '79, with UAW dues-paying membership at 1,517,000—the highest in history. Then in 1981, the devastation started from a combination of things, from the economy to imports.

I didn't think you could win the fight on import restrictions. Mike Mansfield was the ambassador to Japan, and he asked me to come to Japan to ask Japanese auto companies to invest in America. My slogan was you ought to put your capital where your sales are and create jobs. I raised a lot of hell. They were not used to frank and blunt talk. I told them about the Germans being responsible with their Volkswagen plant in Pennsylvania. What really persuaded them was when we starting advocating content legislation. I think that frightened them, and they made decisions to come here. After that it was to their advantage because it was cheaper to produce here than in Japan.

The absolute worst was 1982. There were more layoffs than ever before. Chrysler was on the verge of bankruptcy and Ford was worse off than anybody knew. Their international operations held them up. GM was also in difficulty. The companies were really pressing us. When we went to the table we made concessions with both Ford and GM. The Ford workers realized their problem and the negotiations were not that difficult. GM was more difficult, but we got the contract ratified.

Chrysler was particularly bad. We went to the bargaining table three times in 13 months, each agreement worse than the last. You know, you can go to the well too often. With the loan guarantee legislation, Congress and the loan guarantee board demanded concessions. I pitched "equality of sacrifice" like Reuther had done during World War II, when he gave the no-strike pledge. It was very difficult. You had some workers saying I was selling out. But it was a question of persuasion and we didn't persuade everybody. One of the satisfactions I have now is that over the last six years, the Chrysler workers have now received about $36,000 in profit sharing. Everywhere I go, workers tell me, "Thank God you did what you did." Even the guys who opposed it agreed. We ultimately convinced the workers that you couldn't survive unless the company survives. Helping to save thousands of those jobs at Chrysler is my proudest accomplishment.

I met with President Jimmy Carter initially. Lee Iacocca wasn't the folk hero yet. He worked the Republican side of the street. We had Carter, Senator Don Reigle, and Governor Jim Blanchard. When Iacocca sent an autographed copy of his book he wrote, "This wouldn't be possible without you" or something like that. Lee Iacocca did not save Chrysler Corporation. The Chrysler workers saved the company. It's undeniable.

It was a very painful period. I was getting it from both ends and I took a lot of abuse, but that is the price of leadership. Reporters asked me, "Doug, how do you sleep at night?" I said, "I sleep like a baby. I go to sleep, I wake up crying, go back to sleep, wake up crying, and go back to sleep again."

I do not need public accolades. I get a lot of satisfaction going to different locals and being introduced as the guy who saved Chrysler.

Another historic breakthrough occurred in 1980 when our bargaining committee asked for union representation on the Chrysler board of directors. I was eventually elected to the board and served until 1984, but only under our condition that the proxy statement made it clear to stockholders that I would serve as a representative of the Chrysler workers. I insisted that my annual $15,000 stipend for serving be sent to Wayne State University as a scholarship endowment for Chrysler workers and their children. Chrysler matched the money.

I always felt that any labor leader can make a contribution to a corporate board because they bring a different life experience and can open some eyes. You make them think, as I did when I objected to salaries and bonuses. Hopefully, you can modify their behavior. We were the first to have union representation on a corporate board. Now the steel industry has it, as do companies like International Harvester.

You know, the labor movement really created the middle class in Detroit and across this country. And I'm not just talking about union members. Non-union workers and salaried employees would not have the benefits and wages they have today without the work of the labor movement. I would agree that society as a whole has not shown an appropriate amount of appreciation for the sacrifices made by the unions.

Unfortunately, we have folks I call "hitchhikers." They get all the benefits of the union, but then when we try to organize, they turn their backs on us. We organized numerous units of Chrysler salaried workers in 1982. That same year at GM, salaried employees received a wage cut. We tried to organize them, but lost about 2 to 1 after Roger Smith wrote a letter stating he would restore the wage cut. In a post mortem, we imagined two white-collar employees talking and one says, "What if the company tries to cut our salaries again?" And the other guy says, "We'll just call the UAW."

◄ *Opposite page: As president of the UAW, Doug Fraser (center) helped convince Washington that it was in the public's best interest to save Chrysler Corporation. "Helping to save thousands of those jobs at Chrysler is my proudest accomplishment," said Fraser.*

CULTURAL AFFAIRS

Shortly after 3 o'clock on a muggy Sunday afternoon, 60 members of the Detroit Symphony Orchestra snapped their instruments to attention and, with a wave of the conductor's baton, began to play Rossini's *Semiramide Overture*. The notes floated up and away, rebounding like perfectly placed bank shots off the high ceiling and narrow walls before returning to fill the hall with a rich, vibrant sound.

"Everything I'd heard about Orchestra Hall was true," recalled Paul Ganson, a bassoonist who was performing there for the first time. "The acoustics indeed were marvelous—as good as the best halls in the world."

If the sound suggested Europe's greatest concert halls, the setting resembled the final days of the *Führerbunker*. The doors were missing, there were holes in the ceiling, and plaster dusted several charred and disemboweled seats. Although the appreciative audience gave the performers a standing ovation, true curtain calls were impossible. There was no curtain.

"It looked like a bombed-out building in Berlin in World War II," said Ganson, who later listened to a tape of the performance. Above the strains of *Beethoven's Piano Concerto No. 3 in C Minor*, the unmistakable sound of cooing pigeons could be heard.

Despite its rough edges, that benefit concert in the spring of 1971 helped kick off a

◄ *Orchestra Hall in the 1920s.*

➤ *Ossip Gabrilowitsch.*

grass roots "Save Orchestra Hall" movement that prevented the crumbling land-mark on Woodward from being torn down. Thirty years and some $7 million in donations later, the DSO is firmly and happily ensconced inside one of the country's most elegant and acoustically perfect classical music venues. Moreover, plans are under way to build a $125 million addition called Opera Place, a per-forming arts complex that will help revitalize the surrounding neighborhood.

Detroiters have always displayed an interest in culture, their pursuits ranging from the highbrow to the livelier arts. Artists of various mediums, whether they're partial to blue collars or wing collars, continue to find inspiration in their sur-roundings. Joyce Carol Oates, for one, found Detroit to be a valuable resource for her writings. "If we had never come to the city of Detroit," the prolific novelist said, "I would have been a writer . . . but Detroit, my 'great' subject, made me the person I am, consequently the writer I am—for better or worse."

During the Great Depression, Mexican artist Diego Rivera took the smoke-stack image of Detroit and squeezed the soot out of it. Rivera, one of the leaders of the Mexican muralist movement and a known Marxist, eagerly accepted a $22,000 commission from Edsel Ford to create a mural in the courtyard of the Detroit Institute of Arts. The result, the massive and controversial *Detroit Industry*, is the city's best known work of art.

"They had a mutual interest in art, engineering, and design," explained Linda Downs, former curator of education at the museum. "Rivera was fascinated with the Rouge complex. Edsel opened up the plant completely to him."

Rivera's commission came on the heels of the 1932 "hunger march massacre." His political sympathies became obvious as work progressed through the mural's unveiling in March 1933. In the panels, the unsmiling workers are straining at their tasks, watched over by the omnipresent servicemen. Many civic and religious leaders howled over the murals' supposedly irreligious and anti-capitalist themes. Nonetheless, Ford courageously stilled the cries for whitewash and arranged classes

◄ / ▲ *Diego Rivera labors over his masterpiece, "Detroit Industry." The Mexican artist later called the controversial frescoes—which were savagely attacked when unveiled in March 1933—his greatest work.*

"DETROIT IS NO STRANGER TO THE ILLS THAT PLAGUE THE HUMAN CONDITION, WHICH MAY BE WHY ARTISTS FIND IT TO BE SUCH A VALUABLE RESOURCE FOR THEIR IMAGES." — *Dolores Slowinski*, New Art Examiner

^ *The city's original art museum on Jefferson Avenue was replaced by the Detroit Institute of Arts, which opened in 1927 on Woodward, across the street from the Main Library.*

for visitors to be educated in Rivera's work. Although the enlightened industrialist had not intended it, the uproar underscored art's greatest asset: the ability to stir emotion and discussion.

Detroit's art scene stretches back many generations. During the 19th century several famous artists emerged from the city, including Alvah Bradish, Julius Rolshoven, John Mix Stanley, and Gari Melchers (son of the well-known sculptor Julius Melchers). Art appreciation, however, was largely restricted to those select few who could afford to buy and display their acquisitions. That began to change in 1888, when a $100,000 public subscription helped local art patrons open the Detroit Museum of Art. The core of the museum's collection was donated by *Detroit News* founder and publisher James E. Scripps. The original sandstone building at Jefferson and Hastings was replaced in 1927 by the Detroit Institute of Arts, which sits on Woodward across from the main branch of the Public Library. Wings added in 1966 and 1971 were made of dark granite walls so as not to compete with the white-marble Italian Renaissance main building. Notwithstanding the support of Edsel Ford and other major benefactors, like most of the city's cultural institutions the DIA has endured chronic financial problems over the years. Nonetheless, with more than 100 galleries showcasing works by Rembrandt, Renoir, van Gogh, and other world-famous artists, the DIA is consistently ranked as one of the top five art museums in the country.

Detroit's most controversial and unusual tourist attraction is an ever-evolving outdoor exhibit known as the Heidelberg Project, built on several properties on Heidelberg Street near Gratiot, where its artist, Tyree Guyton, was raised.

In an effort to wake up the city about his neglected and drug-infested eastside neighborhood, which deteriorated following the 1967 riot, Guyton transformed the surrounding landscape into his own urban theme park, employing thousands of discarded objects and large colorful polka dots.

Everything from tires, toilets, and toys to shoes, appliances, and bicycles was painted and installed on trees, houses, telephone poles, and vacant lots and turned into political statements like the Polka Dot Tree, the Tire House, the Lost and Found House, and the Babydoll House. The latter was covered with hundreds of broken and naked dolls, which the artist claimed represented child abuse and prostitution. Similarly, a tree covered with old shoes dangling from its branches evoked thoughts of lynchings. Even if visitors don't always quite get the message, they nonetheless are amazed at the volume of colorful items and the obvious passion behind the effort.

The Heidelberg Project inspires both admiration and derision. To some people it is a collection of junk, while to others it is a cutting-edge form of urban art. Although Guyton has received a variety of awards from civic groups and the arts community, he has ended up in court battling nuisance complaints and has seen his project partially bulldozed by the city.

Guyton was one of ten children raised in poverty by a single mother. Twelve years old at the time of the '67 riot, he discovered that art could effect change. His late grandfather, Sam Mackey, a housepainter, inspired him. "When I was eight years old," recalled Guyton, "he stuck a paint brush in my hand. I felt as if I was holding a magic wand." Guyton later took art courses at the Center for Creative Studies, Wayne County Community College, and Marygrove College. It was Mackey, along with Guyton's wife at the time, Karen Smith, who helped the artist start the Heidelberg Project in the 1980s.

Love it or hate it, Guyton's ghetto gallery has not only drawn busloads of visitors to the area, it has also created a most unique neighborhood watch program. After four drug raids at one Heidelberg crack house, Guyton painted it with bright pink, blue, yellow, and white polka dots and attached a baby doll and a bright blue inner tube on the roof. "Now all day long people drive by and stop to stare at the place," he said. "Believe me, in front of an audience like that, nobody's going to sell crack out of that house anymore."

Twice during the 1990s parts of the controversial project were torn down as eyesores, first on Mayor Coleman Young's insistence in 1991, and then in 1999

⋏ *Julius Melchers fled Germany in 1848 and by 1885 had established himself as Detroit's preeminent sculptor and artist. Among his works were the sculptures of Cadillac and three other early French explorers that he carved for old City Hall. His son, Gari Melchers, became even more prominent in art circles, gaining international fame as a portraitist and painting several of the murals on the walls of the Main Library.*

The polka-dotted world of Tyree Guyton.

through the efforts of the Archer administration. After the first partial demolition, Mackey told his grandson, "You can't stop regardless of what people might say. You gotta do it."

Despite the setbacks, Guyton and an army of children in the Heidelberg neighborhood continue to rebuild. Their spirits are buoyed by supporters, who stay connected to the project through national news reports, the Internet community, and Nicole Cattell's award-winning HBO documentary, *Come Unto Me: The Faces of Tyree Guyton.* The artist believes his "living canvas" has opened the children's world by exposing them to numerous worldwide visitors, and by allowing them to "express their feelings through art" and to "take pride" in their handiwork.

In addition to the internationally famous Heidelberg Project, Guyton's paintings and sculptures have been exhibited at several galleries, including the Detroit Institute of Arts. He has also lectured and displayed his work at Harvard University, a world away from the polka-dotted blight of Heidelberg Street.

Drama also has been a consistent feature of the city's life. Although neither the French nor the British cared much for theater—there was drama enough, perhaps, in their everyday struggles in the wilderness—under American rule Detroiters started finding some time for theatrical arts. They began staging productions in 1816, with a warehouse, a barn, and City Hall successively serving as playhouses. The city's first theaters opened in 1834; soon a block-long theatrical

The Poet of the Plain People

It was always fashionable in literary and intellectual circles to ridicule Eddie Guest. Dorothy Parker, for one, once claimed in print: "I'd rather flunk my Wasserman test than read a poem by Eddie Guest." But the ordinary person cared nothing for the nose-in-the-air opinions of critics. To them the widely read poet of the *Detroit Free Press* was a treasure, someone who addressed their hopes and concerns with good, simple faith and unflagging optimism.

"My English teacher almost ordered us to hate that guy because he didn't like Eddie's poetry," a new hire at the *Free Press* once exclaimed. "How can anybody hate Eddie Guest! He's the finest man I ever met, and I only wish that English prof knew half as much about life and literature as Eddie does."

Edgar Albert Guest was born in England in 1881 and came to America 10 years later. He dropped out of school when he was 13 and took a job with the *Free Press*, advancing from copyboy to police reporter. Along the way he began composing weekly verses, a feature that soon evolved into the daily "Breakfast Table Chat." Guest wrote the popular column until his death in 1959. He always insisted that he had but two loves in his life: his wife, Nellie, and the newspaper.

Guest never elevated his folksy, inspirational doggerel to the status of poetry, but readers didn't know or care enough to make the distinction. His first verse appeared on December 11, 1898; more than 15,000 would follow over the next six decades. He self-published his first book of verse in 1909, a run that amounted to only 800 copies. But his popularity quickly grew to the point that a 1916 volume, *A Heap o' Livin'*, eventually sold more than 1 million copies. At his peak Guest was syndicated in 300 newspapers around the country.

According to one admirer, "No one told Detroit's story or sang her song as well" as Guest. This was particularly true in a poem entitled "They Earned the Right":

I knew Ket and Knudsen, Keller, Zeder and Breer.
I knew Henry Ford back yonder as a lightplant engineer.
I'm a knew-em'-when companion who frequently recalls
That none of those big brothers were too proud for overalls.
All the Fishers, all the leaders, all the motor pioneers
Worked at molds or lathes or benches at the start of their careers.
Chrysler, Keller, Nash and others whom I could but now won't name
Had no high-falutin' notion ease and softness led to fame.
They had work to do and did it. Did it bravely, did it right,
Never thinking it important that their collars should be white.
Never counted hours of labor, never wished their tasks to cease,
And for years their two companions were those brothers, dirt and grease.
Boy, this verse is fact, not fiction. All the fellows I have named
Worked for years for wages and were never once ashamed.
Dirt and grease were their companions, better friends than linen white;
Better friends than ease and softness, golf or dancing every night.
Now in evening clothes you see them in the nation's banquet halls.
But they earned the right to be there, years ago, in overalls.

⋁ Loved by the public and ridiculed by critics, Free Press writer Edgar Guest spent more than 60 years with the paper. At one time, more than 300 newspapers across the country published his simple verse, including the classic that begins: "It takes a heap o' living to make a house a home...."

▲ *Elmore "Dutch" Leonard, born in Louisiana and raised in Detroit, first began writing fiction while working as a copywriter at a local ad agency. His first novel,* The Bounty Hunters, *was published in 1953 when he was 28; dozens more have followed, including* Fifty Two Pickup, Freaky Deaky *and* Get Shorty. *Many of his books are set in Detroit. "People ask me, especially in Hollywood, why do you live in Detroit when you can live anywhere you want?" Leonard told a reporter. "I say because I know all the streets now and I'm too old to learn them someplace else."*

district materialized on Jefferson, between Brush and Randolph. A century and a half later, Detroiters flock to world-class venues like the Fox Theatre—star of the rejuvenated Woodward Avenue theater district—and the Fisher Theatre, which under Joey Nederlander has become one of the country's premier showcases for major Broadway shows.

Scores of accomplished actors and actresses first faced the cameras and floodlights in their native Detroit. Tony Award–winning Lily Tomlin, educated at Cass Tech and Wayne State University, became an icon through her portrayal of Ernestine the telephone operator on the 1960s TV hit, *Rowan & Martin's Laugh-In*. The equally beloved Gilda Radner achieved cult status on *Saturday Night Live* during the 1980s before tragically succumbing to ovarian cancer. A pair of Oscar winners, the manic Robin Williams and the stoic George C. Scott, boasted local roots. Williams, son of a Ford executive, credits his improvisational genius to being a "juvenile pain in the ass" while attending Detroit Country Day school. Scott, best known for his big-screen performance as General George S. Patton, graduated from Redford High School in 1945 and worked in local theater before hitting it big in Hollywood.

Other familiar names in the credits include Ellen Burstyn (awarded best actress for her role in *Alice Doesn't Live Here Anymore*), Plymouth's Tom Hulce (star of the 1984 movie, *Amadeus*), Dearborn's Chad Everett, Della Reese, Tom Sizemore, and actor-comedians Dave Coulier and David Alan Grier. The most honored Detroiter is Julie Harris, who was born in 1925 and grew up in Grosse Pointe Park. Harris has received two Emmys, a Grammy, and a record five Tony Awards for her work on stage and on the screen. Notables on the other side of the camera include director Francis Ford Coppola and producer Sam Raimi. Coppola, whose middle name honored his father's longtime boss, Henry Ford, won multiple Oscars for *The Godfather* movies. Raimi, a Royal Oak native, achieved permanent cult status with his 1983 low-budget horror flick, *The Evil Dead*.

By 1900 "legitimate" theater was competing with vaudeville and motion pictures. Over the years, Detroit has seen thousands of playhouses, movie theaters, and vaudeville and burlesque

Orpheum The
Detroit.

◄ *In the years before radio and television made staying at home an entertainment option, Detroiters flocked to theaters. The Family Theatre, pictured here in 1910, was one of dozens of amusement houses then in operation, offering customers live vaudeville acts and a new phenomenon, moving pictures.*

▼ *Tim Allen, born Timothy Allen Dick in Denver in 1953, grew up in suburban Detroit. During the 1990s, the stand-up comic gained an incredible popular following by playing a grunting, tool-obsessed character named Tim "Tool Man" Taylor on the hit TV show,* Home Improvement.

houses come and go. They've run the gamut from garish downtown movie palaces to cozy neighborhood theaters.

The Orpheum was one of the city's grandest vaudeville houses. It was built in 1914 by Edward D. Stair, the dynamic publisher of the *Detroit Free Press*, who made a fortune in the theater business. At one time he held controlling interest in 158 theaters across the country. According to one reporter, Stair inculcated "lessons of economy, sobriety, and diligence where formerly there was discord, drunkenness, and follies."

The Lyceum, at Randolph and Champlain streets, housed road companies of popular Broadway productions. The 2,385-seat theater also was home to the city's first permanent stock company, one that produced stage and screen actress Mary

➤ The State Theatre in its heyday featured such acts as the four Marx Brothers. The theater on Woodward Avenue was one of several performance houses designed by local architect Charles Howard Crane, who also designed the Fox Theatre and Orchestra Hall.

⤙ Harry Houdini, despite suffering from a high fever, played the last performance of his legendary career at Detroit's Garrick Theatre on Sunday night, October 24, 1926. The following day he was operated on for a ruptured appendix at Grace Hospital. The magician died there on Halloween night.

Boland. The Garrick, located on Griswold north of Michigan Avenue, was owned by the Shubert brothers of New York. It staged many top acts before it was razed in 1928, including the final performance of magician Harry Houdini, who died inside Grace Hospital on Halloween, 1926, after a blow to his stomach ruptured his appendix which led to peritonitis.

The first viewing of a motion picture in the city was in 1896, when Detroiters watched *The Great Train Robbery* at the Wonderland. The 200-seat Casino, which opened at Monroe and Farmer streets in 1905, was the first theater devoted exclusively to showing moving pictures.

At its peak, bustling Monroe Street had a dozen venues offering entertainment for a dime. Among the most noteworthy houses were the National Theatre, designed by Albert Kahn and opened in 1911, and the

⋏ *The interior of the Fisher Theatre. The 2,089-seat theater was originally 3,500 seats when it opened in 1928. Since being managed by the Nederlander family starting in 1961, the theater inside the Fisher Building has been home to many big Broadway shows.*

◄ *For decades the Shubert-Lafayette, started by New York's Shubert brothers and later operated by the Nederlanders, was one of downtown's most prominent theaters.*

Palace, designed by C. Howard Crane and opened three years later. The bulb-studded signage was as gaudy as some of the acts, with declarations of "Continuous Vaudeville" and "Big Time Acts" lighting up the night. While the Palace closed in 1928, the National remained open until the early 1970s. Despite a vigorous preservation effort, the historic Monroe Block—home to half a century of vaudeville, burlesque, and motion pictures—was demolished by the city in 1990.

Countless performers and patrons have marveled over the cavernous, exotic Fox Theatre since it opened during the height of the Roaring '20s. The landmark downtown venue is outsized and outlandish—and thus it is a perfect reflection of the unbridled optimism of the period when it was built.

During the 1920s, with radio in its infancy and television still a generation away, Detroiters flocked to downtown theaters like the Capitol on Broadway and the State on Woodward to enjoy live entertainment. These theaters, along with Orchestra Hall, shared a common designer—Charles Howard Crane, a Detroit architect and one-time disciple of Albert Kahn. In 1926, Crane was enlisted by William Fox of the 20th Century Fox movie studio to design a theater that would showcase the most recent entertainment phenomenon: talking movies. It would be the first theater in the country to have a built-in sound system engineered specifically for "talkies."

What Crane delivered was a shrine equal to any Hollywood fantasy, one guaranteed to inspire awe in the generations of Detroiters to come. "I was always struck by the winding staircases," said Veronica White, who regularly attended Saturday matinees with her mother in the 1950s. "I had a vivid imagination, and it would always run wild inside there."

Small wonder. The Battle of Gettysburg could have been booked in the Fox, whose lobby alone was 65 feet wide, 125 feet long, and stood six stories high. Sixteen red faux marble columns, topped with jewels, rose like sentries before the main auditorium. Stone lions guarded the main staircase. A 13-foot, two-ton stained glass chandelier hung ostentatiously over the main floor, while carved elephants, Buddhas, serpents, and peacocks jumped out from the walls. A 3,000-pound carpet covered 3,600 square feet of floor. Construction took 18 months. At a time when autoworkers were living comfortably on $6 a day, the final price tag

➤ / ▼ *The Fox Theatre helped usher in the era of talking movies when it opened in 1928. The 5,042-seat theater cost $6.4 million to build and several more millions to restore in the 1980s. Today it is the anchor of the revived theater district and one of the top-grossing entertainment venues in America.*

for the 5,042-seat Fox was a stupendous $6.4 million. Only New York's Radio City Music Hall was bigger.

The grand opening was Friday night, September 21, 1928. At 8:30, the 60-piece house band was slowly lifted out of the orchestra pit on an elevator and struck up "The Star Spangled Banner." The last notes were smothered by thunderous applause from the 5,000 invited guests, who then settled in to view, oddly enough, a silent feature, *Street Angel*, starring Charles Farrell and Janet Gaynor.

"The Fox had opulence," said Fred Hamway of Southgate, recalling his Saturday trips downtown during the 1930s. "I remember those gold and marble lavatories. Geez, you'd go down there and feel like you were in a castle." In its early years, the Fox was known for not sparing any expense. It had its own orchestra, a dance troupe, and a choir, as well as a pair of giant Wurlitzer organs.

Hamway recalled a stage show accompanying the George Raft and Carole Lombard movie, *Bolero.* "There were ten dancers on pedestals, dressed in gold tights. The audience thought they were statues. At one point in the movie, though, these statues suddenly started dancing very slowly, very sensuously. It was wonderful."

A little more than a year after the Fox's opening, Detroit and the rest of the country slid into the Great Depression. While financial difficulties afflicted the Fox chain, the movie business as a whole flourished. Although 40 percent of Detroit's workforce was idle in 1932, more than half of the population was going to the movies at least once a week. For a quarter admission (a dime for children), moviegoers could temporarily escape their woes.

The Fox chain was sold in 1933. Three years later, the new owners went bankrupt. Union Guardian Trust Company, which held the mortgage, foreclosed on the property. A succession of owners kept the Fox open and profitable through the

∧ *The Fox Theatre in 1929. Its marquee proclaimed the Fox the "Showplace of the Nation," a designation few people, then or now, would dispute.*

1940s. Kay Kyser's College of Musical Knowledge attracted 61,000 "students" in three days, while such acts as Benny Goodman, Louie Armstrong, Sarah Vaughan, Sally Rand, Kate Smith, and Jack Benny also helped pack the seats. During World War II, the theater grossed $75,000 a week by offering a steady stream of movies and newsreels to audiences hungry for diversion and war information. "You'd dress up to go downtown," said Hamway. "It was a ritual. For 50 cents, you'd see a movie, and then there'd be some live acts. I remember seeing Red Skelton doing his Freddie the Freeloader routine years before he did it on TV. Afterwards, you'd take your girl out for spaghetti or ribs. That was the big thing then."

The 1950s saw the beginning of lean times for the Fox. Detroiters followed the freeways out to suburbia, abandoning downtown. The advent of television killed many live acts and gave moviegoers another reason to stay home at night. By the end of the decade the Fox was playing to audiences of only a few hundred people.

Berry Gordy's Motown Revue, featuring homegrown talent like Smokey Robinson, the Temptations, and the Supremes, became a Christmas tradition at the Fox in the early 1960s. "Our performers were young—the majority under 21—and they wanted to be home for Christmas," explained Gordy's sister, Esther Edwards. "There were four or five shows a day for 10 days from Christmas to New Year's."

Through the 1970s, the marquee continued to trumpet the Fox as "The Most Magnificent Temple of Amusement in the World." Over the years, though, the number of bookings gradually deteriorated with the neighborhood. Aside from a promoter occasionally staging a big-name act like John Cougar Mellencamp or U2, the theater that used to light up Woodward sat unused, its activity confined to plaster falling in the dark.

The Fox management changed hands several times before pizza magnate Mike Ilitch closed a deal in October 1987 to purchase the Fox, Palms Theatre, and Hughes & Hatcher buildings from developer Chuck Forbes and the City of Detroit. The ensuing $36 million restoration began the following January. That November, the fabulous Fox reopened in all of its original grandeur, with headliner Frank Sinatra jump-starting Ilitch's still ongoing attempt to revive the Woodward Avenue theater district and downtown nightlife.

Since then, the theater has become the country's top-grossing entertainment

▼ *Kentucky-born Harriette Arnow infused her novels with characters and situations true to her Appalachian roots, including her best-known work,* The Dollmaker. *Published to great critical acclaim in 1954 and later made into a successful television movie,* The Dollmaker *was based in part on Arnow's own experiences as a transplanted and slightly bewildered Kentuckian living in a Detroit housing project during World War II. Arnow lived in Ann Arbor Township until her death in 1986.*

^ *The best remembered of Detroit's many opera houses was located on Campus Martius, east of Woodward. The original Detroit Opera House was built in 1868, burned down in 1897, but was quickly rebuilt and stood until being razed in 1963.*

➤ *Opposite page: The old Grand Circus Theatre on Broadway was given a multi-million-dollar facelift and reopened in 1996 as the new Detroit Opera House.*

venue several times, making good the boast that once graced its marquee: "Showplace of the Nation."

The area's first drive-in theaters opened in the 1930s, and by 1966 more than 30 were in operation. Drive-ins like the Jolly Roger, Blue Sky, and Miracle Mile justifiably earned reputations as "passion pits" for teenagers whose antics were clouded by steamy windows. Today, however, cable television, changing sexual mores, and the prohibitive cost of land has left only one local drive-in—the Ford-Wyoming in Dearborn—in business.

Detroit has had several opera houses during its long history, but the best remembered is the one that stood on Campus Martius, just east of Woodward. Erected in 1868, it burned down in a spectacular blaze in 1897, but was quickly rebuilt. The resurrected building reopened a year later and continued to showcase the finer dramas of the day until 1937, when, to the horror of the silk-stocking set, it was made into a department store. In 1963 the building fell to the wrecking ball. In 1996, the Michigan Opera Theatre ended several years of performing at various locales with the opening of a new Detroit Opera House on Broadway, across from the Detroit Athletic Club. The multimillion-dollar makeover of what had been the long-closed Grand Circus Theatre was celebrated with a gala inaugural concert by Luciano Pavarotti.

The Detroit Symphony Orchestra was organized in 1914 by several socially prominent women who were able to convince a brilliant Russian pianist, Ossip Gabrilowitsch, to become conductor in 1919. To entice him, DSO backers hurriedly built Orchestra Hall at a cost of $700,000. On opening night, October 23,

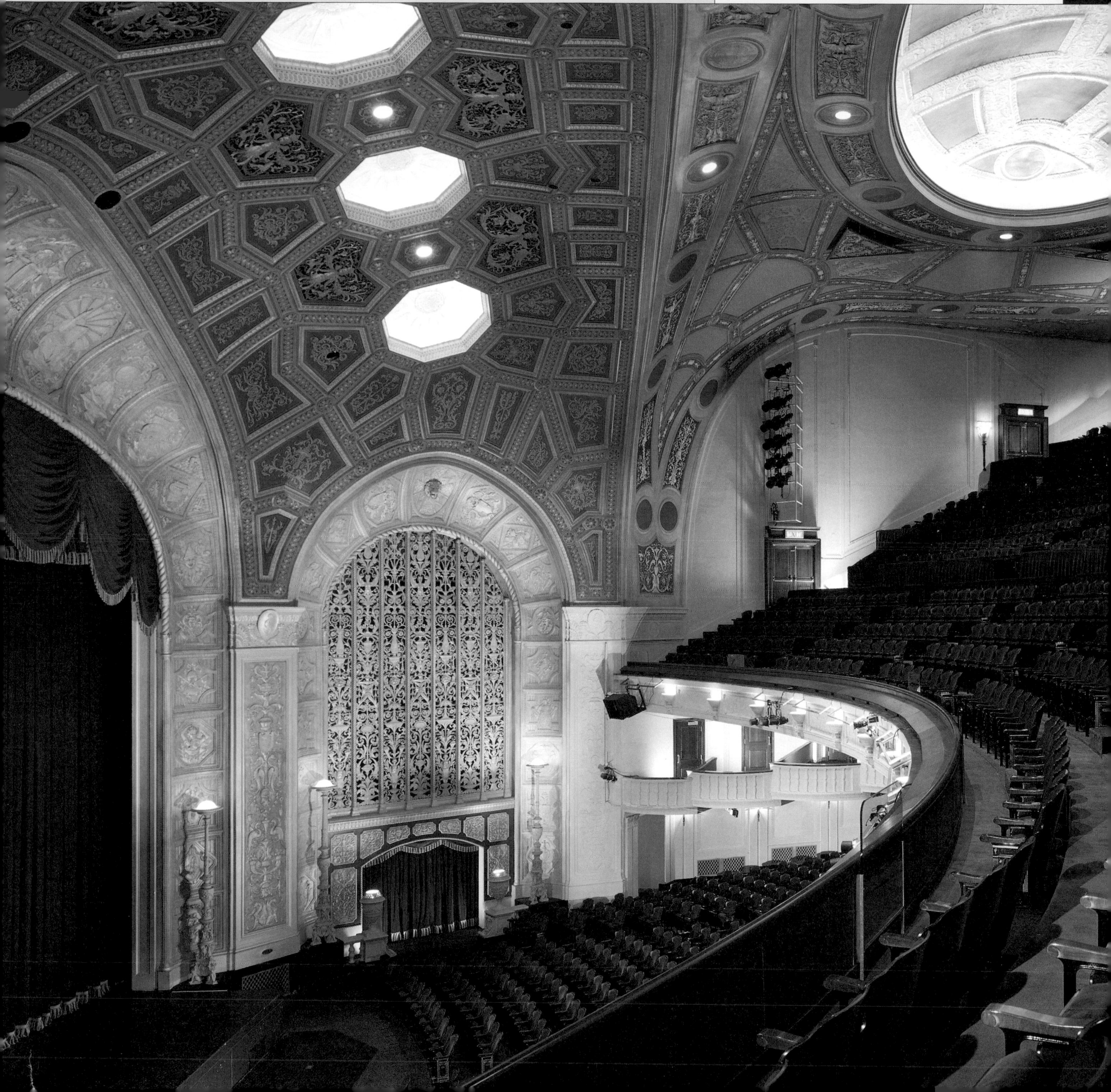

Pewabic Pottery

In the early 1900s, the international Arts and Crafts movement began to flourish as artists reacted to the "aesthetic decay" that resulted from the automated and depersonalized industrial revolution—a decay, some suggested, that was represented best by Detroit's auto industry. Progressive artists were stressing craftsmanship and the beauty of handmade objects in daily life.

Detroit's proudest contribution to the Arts and Crafts movement is Pewabic Pottery, founded in 1903 by potter Mary Chase Perry Stratton and her neighbor, Horace J. Caulkins, a Detroit dental supplier who had invented the Revelation kiln. Nearly a century later, Pewabic Pottery still operates at 10125 East Jefferson Avenue, across from Waterworks Park. The charming English Tudor-style building, with its distinctive 40-foot tiled chimney, was designed by Stratton's architect husband, William Stratton.

Mary Chase Perry Stratton quickly established a reputation for her vases and vessels, but it was her Pewabic tiles that brought her national acclaim. The brilliant and luminous iridescent tiles were used by many famous architects across the country. Her work led to numerous commissions, such as the National Shrine of the Immaculate Conception in Washington D.C. Her tile work is found throughout many famous Detroit homes and buildings, including the Guardian Building, Christ Church Cranbrook, the Detroit Public Library, the Institute of Arts, and Holy Redeemer Church.

Stratton named the pottery "Pewabic" after an Upper Peninsula copper mine located near her Hancock birthplace. In 1937 she told a reporter: "I was trying to decide what I wanted to do, and had gone to spend a week at the lake shore to think the thing over. A piece of paper fluttered along the beach and I picked it up. There was an article printed on it headed 'Develop the Resources of America.' The article outlined the rich possibilities in our own soil for making the clays for pottery. Ever since I have been trying to develop

the resources of America by using the clays found in our soil."

Stratton's most important supporter was Detroiter Charles Lang Freer, a railroad magnate and an avid art collector. Freer exposed her to his vast collection inside his Ferry Street home, which included rare and distinctive Oriental glazes.

In 1906, as Pewabic Pottery was becoming established, Stratton helped form the Detroit Society of Arts and Crafts (now the Center for Creative Studies), in part as a reaction to the Industrial Revolution. "We had been given a flood of the commonplace, the crude, and the unlovely," she explained. "That is why it was important for the individual craftsman to keep working and to keep his place in the community, to train our eyes to recognize the fine things."

When Stratton died in 1961 at the age of 94, local lore has it that she took her famous glaze formulas to the grave, forcing new generations to create their own mark. She almost took Pewabic Pottery with her. The pottery eventually fell into neglect until the Pewabic Society, founded in 1981 by concerned artists and preservationists, saved the national historic site.

Today, Pewabic Pottery carries on its founder's original mission, producing not only commissioned work, but also a store full of pottery and tiles for an appreciative public. Through experimentation, artists have been able to recreate some of Stratton's most distinctive glazes and designs. In addition to providing classes for adults, children, and emerging artists, the pottery's museum and archives are used by researchers to study Stratton's work and those of her peers from the Arts and Crafts movement.

Λ *Mary Chase Perry Stratton started Pewabic Pottery in 1903. A century later, the company continues making tiles for commercial purposes, including Comerica Park.*

1919, a full house of 2,018 greeted Gabrilowitsch with a five-minute standing ovation. With his high, pointed collar and shock of hair, the maestro cut an imposing, romantic figure with the baton. He delighted in what he called "two-collar nights," when his passion required a change of neckwear during intermission. By the time of his death in 1936, musical geniuses like Igor Stravinsky, Isadora Duncan, and Pablo Casals had accepted invitations to perform inside Orchestra Hall, establishing Detroit as an important symphonic venue.

Detroit has a tradition of popular songwriting, beginning with the unlikely Jerome Remick. The owner of the Detroit Creamery Company couldn't write or play a note, but he had an intuitive sense of what the public would buy. Between 1905 and 1928, his publishing company put out 60,000 tunes. Among them were such standards as Neil Moret's "Hiawatha" and Percy Wenrich's "Moonlight Bay."

⌄ *"Dixie Doodle Girl" and "Oceana Roll" were just two of some 60,000 songs put out by Jerome H. Remick & Co.*

Other locally written favorites include Henry Von Tilzer's "I Want a Girl Just Like the Girl (That Married Dear Old Dad)," Sam Lerner's "Popcyc the Sailor Man," and the gridiron standard, "You Gotta Be a Football Hero," composed by Buddy Fields and Al Lewis. In addition, Highland Park's Bill Haley wrote and performed "Rock Around the Clock" in the film *Blackboard Jungle*, a landmark moment that introduced rebellion—with a beat—to a sizable chunk of Eisenhower era teenagers.

Finally, it wouldn't be fair to overlook Larry LaPrise, who in the late 1940s wrote that staple of weddings and bar mitzvahs everywhere, "The Hokey-Pokey." The Detroit native found neither fame nor fortune with his group, the Ram Trio, ultimately retiring as a postal worker in Boise, Idaho. "He wrote several other songs, probably none of which you've ever heard," his daughter said after his death in 1996. "Sitz Mark Samba" was one of them. "You know," she said, "the sitzmark is the hole left in the snow after you've gotten up from falling down skiing."

As the Motor City's alternative nickname, Motown, suggests, popular music is the city's major export after cars. In fact, insisted Motown songwriter Sylvia Moy, one "can hear the cars and factories in our music."

The 20th century saw an influx of southern job-seekers to Detroit, giving musicians a range of folk, blues, gospel, country, and jazz influences to pick and choose from. "Blacks began to migrate here and formed, at the bottom of the city, Black Bottom," said Moy. "They brought with them their music, which was gospel,

⋏ Top: *The world knows him as Kid Rock, but friends growing up with the raunchy rap-rock artist called him Robert Ritchie. Either way, in the late 1990s the Macomb County native made one of the biggest splashes in pop music with his breakthrough* Pimp of the Nation.

⋏ Above: *Madonna Louise Ciccone grew up in Rochester Hills and compensated for a thin voice with loads of ambition and a genius for marketing and self-invention that has made "The Material Girl" one of the most enduring acts in pop culture.*

jazz—our music. Because of the factories, our music got a little louder."

That heritage has spanned the generations, from McKinney's Cottonpickers in the 1920s to blues legend John Lee Hooker, who was working as a janitor at Dodge Main when he recorded "Boogie Chillen" in 1948. The thread runs through such 1960s rockers as Mitch Ryder and the Detroit Wheels to rhyme-slinging rap-rocker Robert Ritchie of Royal Oak, a.k.a. Kid Rock.

"Detroit has always been a hard-working town," said Wayne Kramer, guitarist for the Motor City Five, whose "Kick Out the Jams" is a rock standard. "The people work hard and they want the music to work hard, too. And the rise of techno makes perfect sense . . . . More than anything else, there's a physicality to our music that makes it from Detroit."

In an area filled with remarkable musical success stories, none is greater than that of Motown Records. "It was a musical phenomenon that brought people together," said Harold Skramstad Jr., who in 1998 organized a 40-year retrospective of Motown memorabilia. "This was feel-good music in the best sense of the word. It had a story, it had emotion, it had all those things that make music memorable, and it was different.

"That's what really hit me: This was a new kind of sound, and it really resonated with a whole lot of people. This issue of white or black was not the issue at all. The issue was that it was very expressive of where we were as a people."

During the 1960s Ike McKinnon served a stint in Vietnam, where homesick soldiers turned to harmonizing as a way of chasing away the blues: "Street-corner symphonies we used to call it," said the retired Detroit police chief. "Even when I was in Vietnam, you'd hear it coming from the tents and the barracks. Everybody, black and white, tried to do the Motown sound. Everybody especially tried to do the Temptations. But there was one thing you'd always hear people say: 'Don't mess with Smokey.' If you can't sing 'Ooo Baby Baby' and hit that note like Smokey, don't even try it."

Motown, dubbed "Hitsville U.S.A." by founder Berry Gordy Jr., lives on in the same two-story dwelling at 2648 West Grand Boulevard where Marvin Gaye, the Supremes, the Contours, the Marvelettes, Smokey Robinson, the Temptations, the Four Tops, and a host of other eager acts from the projects created the Motown sound in the 1960s. Today it's a museum. For visitors, the most fun is squeezing

◄ *Opposite page: Another form of homegrown music is making Detroit famous. Techno is an electronic, futuristic sound created principally by drum machines and synthesizers. Unexpected proof of its popularity came during a three-day event held at Hart Plaza in May 2000, when an estimated one million people attended the inaugural Detroit Electronic Music Festival.*

▼ *Television movie host Bill Kennedy (left) with Liberace in 1965. Kennedy, a former bit actor, was Detroit's Hollywood connection during his three decades on local airwaves.*

Lunch with Soupy

On July 4, 1955, a skinny, rubber-faced comic named Soupy Sales introduced his zaniness to a national audience as a summer replacement for *Kukla, Fran and Ollie. Lunch with Soupy* was the first network show ever to originate from Detroit. While the hyperkinetic host in the stovepipe hat and bowtie stuck around town for a relatively short time, from 1953 to 1960, his loopy antics with Black Tooth, White Fang, and Pookie the Lion remain perhaps the most enduring of all images from the kiddie-show era.

"When Soupy told the kids to eat a peanut butter sandwich and a bowl of tomato soup for lunch, man, kids did it," recalled Bob Beemer, who once managed Soupy's personal appearances. "It was like the voice of God coming down into the living room."

Sales was born Milton Supman in 1926. He grew up in Huntington, West Virginia. "When I was a kid my friends used to call me Soup Man," he recalled. "Then it was Soup, then Soup Bowl, and finally Soupy. When I worked in Cincinnati they changed my last name to Hines, so when I moved to Cleveland to do a radio show there, I was known as Soupy Hines."

John Pival, the general manager of Detroit's WXYZ, changed it again when he hired the 27-year-old disc jockey to host the lunchtime show in 1953. The station was trying to land C.F. Smith, the grocery store chain, as a sponsor for the program. "Smith was a competitor of Heinz foods," said Soupy. "They didn't like the idea of people watching me and thinking of Heinz pickles." Soupy went the first couple of shows without a last name, until Pival ran his finger down a telephone directory and came across the name Sales.

Lunch with Soupy quickly became an institution, racking up the best ratings of any local show in the nation.

"The thing was, all the kids would go home and have lunch with me at noon," said Soupy. "Every day would be a different menu." In between the slapstick, silent movies, and the several pies he took in the face, he would dispense his daily "Words of Wisdom." These included such gems as "Show me a pharaoh who ate crackers in bed and I'll show you a crummy mummy," and "Be good to your gums and your teeth won't be false to you."

"Soupy was a genius in improvising, and he loved slapstick," said Clyde Adler, the show's stage manager and off-camera voice for White Fang, among others. Adler also threw all those cream pies.

"Clyde was good," remembered Soupy. "He could tear your head off from 10 feet away."

According to Adler, White Fang originally was just a voice. "Soupy had that character on tape from his radio show in Cleveland. In the beginning, that's all we used. But one day the engineer couldn't find the tape, so in a pinch I imitated White Fang's voice." That evening, a stagehand's wife made up a white claw using a bath towel, and suddenly Adler had a prop to go with the voice.

Other characters followed, including Black Tooth, "The Kindest Dog in the Whole U.S.A." White Fang and Black Tooth would paw Soupy's face while he translated their "loo oo, loo oo" canine jargon to the audience.

"Actually, the show always had an undercurrent of adult humor in it," laughed Adler. "We knew that as many adults were looking in as kids, so we did a lot of *double entendres* that went over the heads of children but were picked up by parents."

Mason Weaver directed the live show. "Sometimes we put half vodka in Soupy's orange juice," he remembered. "He slugged it down. I used to slip dirty notes into his pancakes. Each time he lifted one to put syrup on, he'd crack up."

Moms and dads could also catch Soupy on his local evening show, *Soupy's On*. The half-hour program was notable for featuring some of the country's finest jazz musicians, including Charlie Parker, Chet Baker, and Lester Young.

Soupy's rise mirrored the phenomenal growth of television, or what was called "video" in its early years. There were 3 million TV sets in use across the country in 1950, a number that exploded to 40 million in 1955. By the end of the decade, nine of every 10 American homes had a set. Soupy saw his salary soar from $11,000 in 1953 to more than $100,000 in 1957, by which time he was also opening the ABC network's national programming on Saturday mornings.

"Soupy made a lot of money for Channel 7," claimed Beemer. "Hell, he built Broadcast House"—the new television facilities in Southfield that WXYZ moved to in 1960. That same year, Soupy decided to go for the big time, taking both of his shows with him to Hollywood.

"Initially, we were pretty popular out there," said Adler, who accompanied Soupy to the West Coast. "But it became clear that the regional kind of humor we had in Detroit didn't always translate that well nationally." Adler came back to Detroit, while Soupy tried his luck in New York, where he has lived since 1964.

Many aging baby boomers insist that Soupy's lunchtime show could be successful today, but Soupy is not sure. "I don't know," he mused. "When you can watch a couple screw on the soaps, who wants to watch me get hit with a pie?"

◄ *Opposite page: Soupy mugs with members of his "Birdbath Club" at a holiday show, circa 1955.*

◄ / ▲ *Detroit's airwaves were filled with locally produced versions of nationally franchised children's shows during the 1950s and '60s. Among the favorites were* Romper Room, *hosted by Ardis Kenealy, and* Bozo the Clown, *starring former circus clown Bob McNea.*

The bus driver took us to these tacky little brownstone buildings with a homemade sign it the window that said "Hitsvile." We couldn't believe it. We said, "We want the main office at Motown," and he said, "This is the only Motown I know." But once you got inside that little house, you knew they were the hottest thing going. — *Songwriter Valerie Simpson describing her first visit to Motown Records.*

into the impossibly small Studio A, where many of those songs that a generation still sings in the shower were recorded. In fact, a shower stall may be larger.

Gordy was a product of the Great Migration. He was born in 1929, not long after his father had moved the family from Georgia to Detroit and opened a grocery store. Gordy gave boxing and the assembly line each a try, but in 1959 the budding producer borrowed $800 to form Motown Records. He had already cowritten and produced "Got a Job" for Smokey Robinson and the Miracles. Robinson, gifted with a velvet voice and superior songwriting skills, was responsible for much of Motown's early success. In February 1961, a year after Gordy moved the company into the house on West Grand Boulevard, the Miracles' "Shop Around" became Motown's first million seller and number-one rhythm and blues hit. It also reached number two on the pop charts. Later that year, the Marvelettes—a group of teenage girls discovered at an Inkster High School talent show—scored Motown's first number-one pop hit with "Please Mr. Postman."

Motown was off and running. Gordy soon signed up several more acts, including a skinny girl with a thin voice named Diane Ross. Ross was a neighbor of Robinson's and the daughter of the head of United Auto Workers Local 174. She was perky and ambitious and in time became Gordy's lover. Ross, a diva-in-progress, changed her name to Diana and gladly accepted much of the credit for transforming the lukewarm Primettes into the hot-selling Supremes. Others thought the credit was more properly due to the songwriting and producing talents of Lamont Dozier, Brian Holland, and Eddie Holland, the marketing genius of Gordy, or the throbbing grooves of the jazz-steeped studio band, the Funk Brothers. In any event, beginning in the summer of 1964, the Supremes reeled off five consecutive number-one songs: "Where

◄ / ▼ No music has ever defined Detroit better than the Motown sound. The label, started by one-time autoworker Berry Gordy in 1958, had a roster that included such artists as Marvin Gaye, Smokey Robinson and the Miracles, Diana Ross and the Supremes, the Temptations, Stevie Wonder, and the Four Tops.

Come and Get Those Memories

AS THE LEAD SINGER OF MARTHA AND THE VANDELLAS, ONE OF MOTOWN'S MOST SUCCESSFUL GROUPS, DETROITER MARTHA REEVES DELIVERED MILLION-SELLING HIT RECORDS LIKE "NOWHERE TO RUN," "JIMMY MACK," "COME AND GET THOSE MEMORIES," AND WHAT HAS BEEN CALLED THE NATIONAL ANTHEM FOR URBAN AMERICA IN THE 1960S, "DANCING IN THE STREET."

Our "Dancing In the Street" is an anthem of Motown. Detroit knows what dancing in the street means. It quenched our anger. It got us loving again. It didn't matter what you wear, or how you danced, as long as you danced together. It is a unity song. I didn't write it but I was allowed to sing it the way I felt it, from my heart.

I always felt that when we were on the road that we represented Detroit. I still feel that way as I tour 40 weeks a year now. I never knew why you had to defend that you are a Detroiter. We should be proud that we are from here. I have always had a sense of pride about this area.

My family moved to Detroit from Eufaula, Alabama in 1942, when I was 11 months old. I grew up on the east side where the Pepsi Bottling Distribution plant is located, near Riopelle and Leland. My home, and schools, Russell Elementary and Northeastern High, have all been torn down.

My father worked in the factories trying to support my mother and 12 kids. Growing up in the '50s, I remember there was a strong sense of neighborhood, where everybody knew everybody else and looked out for each other. The school system was also benevolent and considerate. As a child from a large, poor family, I was undernourished, and I recall being placed in a special part of the school.

I was three years old when I first dreamed of being a professional singer. I went to see Lena Horne at the Paradise Theater, or what is now Orchestra Hall. I'll never forget seeing this real pretty lady on stage and the magic she had. I wanted to be where she was and know what that felt like.

I grew up in a very musical house. We didn't have television, so Momma entertained us with her voice and taught us songs. Dad played guitar when he felt like it. It was a magic moment when he'd take his guitar off the wall and play blues and gospel songs he learned as a child. If there was a problem, we sang our way through it and had a big sing. I am an extension of my Momma's dream. She wanted to be like Billie Holiday. I do a tribute to Billie and my Mom when I have a chance to perform.

Mrs. Emily Wagstaff at Russell Elementary realized I could sing, so she taught me all the tunes like "Only A Rose" and "This is My Country." I could retain lyrics and remember melodies. After teaching me a song, she would have me perform it in front of my classmates even when the bell was ringing. I also sang gospel music in church.

One of my favorite things to do at Northeastern High was to go to the park across from the school and doo-wop under the trees. After school, kids would meet at the park with the friends they sang with in choir or glee club and blend voices. I remember doing Ray Charles's numbers because he had such good harmonies with the Raylettes. Another favorite was "Since I Don't Have You" by the Skyliners. There was a lot of talent at Northeastern and several future stars practiced at that park. People like Mary Wilson of the Supremes and Bobby Rodgers of the Miracles sang there.

Abraham Silver at Northeastern, who later taught music at Wayne State, was the one who encouraged me to go further. He was such a great mentor, and he taught me so much. A real highlight for me occurred in 1959 as a senior when our choir at Northeastern got to sing a couple of times at Ford Auditorium in front of 4,000 people. At my graduation ceremony there, I was the featured soloist to sing "Alleluia." The acoustics there were the best I can ever remember. I would love to sing there again someday.

In 1960, my professional career began with a false start—briefly in Boston as a solo singer and later when I joined a girl group called the Del-Phis. Rosalind Ashford and Annette Beard of that group later became the original Vandellas. My big break came in October 1961, when I won a contest to sing at the fabulous Twenty Grand at 14th and Warren. At the time I was working for City-Wide Cleaners. The

➤ *Motown gold: Martha and the Vandellas with Marvin Gaye.*

"I WOULD LIKE TO SEE MORE MONUMENTAL THINGS HERE, LIKE A STATUE OF BERRY GORDY, SMOKEY ROBINSON, AND STEVIE WONDER. WHEN YOU THINK OF DETROIT YOU THINK OF THE AUTO INDUSTRY AND MOTOWN. SO GET A CADILLAC OR FORD AND PUT A MONUMENT OF THE FOUR TOPS RIDING IN ONE NEAR THAT BIG TIRE ON I-94..." — *Martha Reeves*

Twenty Grand was a real stomping ground. Many of the '60s stars were shaped or discovered there. It had a bowling alley, a fireside lounge, a pool room for youngsters, and a big room for performing. Everyone wanted to play there. I sang "Gin House Blues" and "Fly Me to the Moon" in a calypso beat. After the show, William "Mickey" Stevenson, the A&R Director for Motown Records, gave me his card and said come to Hitsville USA for an audition.

The very next day I was supposed to go to my job at the cleaners, but instead I took the bus to 2648 West Grand Boulevard. I was a little disappointed to see it was just a house with a Hitsville USA sign on the top of it. When the secretary got Mickey Stevenson, he looked at me and said, "What are you doing here?"

I didn't know procedure or how to audition. I wanted to cry. The phone rang in his office and he said, "Answer that phone, I'll be right back." In the three hours he was gone I had a stack of messages. I met all the A&R people and observed a beehive of activity with people humming and singing, like Smokey Robinson. He really needed a secretary. After working there for three weeks without pay, my Dad said, "You gotta get paid or find another job." They gave me a $35 a week salary.

One day while working as a secretary, I needed to contact the Andantes, Motown's house background singers, for a session with Marvin Gaye. I discovered they were in Chicago and thought I better get somebody as good as or better than them. I knew I could blend my voice with the Del-Phis, so I called Annette, Gloria, and Rosalind.

I knew Marvin Gaye as one of the session drummers. Now he's going to sing? I thought, *I gotta see this.* When he came to a session he would wear his hat over his eyes, a pipe in his mouth, always looking down and calling everybody "baby." You knew he was hip and talented because he played good drums and piano.

We were real nervous and anxious to sing behind him. When he took off his hat and glasses, I thought, *Oh my God, he looks like Sam Cooke.* He was fine.

The first song we did was "Stubborn Kind of Fellow." We nailed it in two takes. After we did such a good job on backup, a couple of days later they had us record "Hitchhike" and "Pride and Joy" with him. It was one track for singer and background singers. There was no overdubbing and we were directly behind him singing. He had one of the prettiest voices. We made him sing to another place, maybe back to his gospel roots. There was a certain magic between us and we fed off of each other.

After those sessions, the girls and I recorded "Let Him Go," which never sold, then "Come and Get Those Memories," which was our first hit.

We couldn't use the name Del-Phis. One day Berry told us we had 15 minutes to come up with another name for the release. As for the "Van," I thought of Van Dyke Street near our east side family home. There was a big thing about the east and west sides. I remember if you went to the west side you could get beat up. It was important that I could now go to the west side and get along and become famous with a lot of west siders. The "Della" in Vandellas honors Della Reese, a Detroiter who influenced me more than any other singer. I'll never forget hearing her sing "Amazing Grace" at New Liberty Baptist Church. The spirit was so full, she touched me.

When I first heard "Come and Get Those Memories," I was sitting in my mother's living room listening to WCHB. It was wonderful. I was screaming, jumping around and having a fit. Momma said, "Sit down and shut up with all that noise."

Nine months after I had started as a secretary at Motown, I was on the Motown Revue bus with the Contours, Supremes, Temptations, Little Stevie Wonder, and I had "Come and Get Those Memories" playing on the radio. On those bus rides down South we were even shot at because I guess they thought we were freedom riders.

We were a team at Motown. There was such a closeness with the Funk Brothers, the house band made up of fabulous musicians like James Jamerson, Benny Benjamin, Maurice King, and Beans Bowles. Those guys had a different sound for each artist. The Motown Sound varied for everyone: the Temptations, the Supremes, the Four Tops, Marvin Gaye, Stevie Wonder, the Miracles. They allowed the artists to be heard, unlike today where musicians don't care if the singer is heard.

We didn't compete against each other. We competed against the Ronettes and the Crystals. We weren't jealous of the Beatles, either. When we went to England they received us the same way they were received here. We were deafened by screams, too. It was a great exchange, and we still have a loving relationship with many of the British artists.

Then there was that July night in 1967. I'll never forget being onstage at the Fox Theatre, getting ready to introduce "Jimmy Mack." We were ready to stomp it off and a man from the side says, "Come here." I thought I had done something wrong, so I went to the edge and said "What is it?" He said, "You gotta go home because there's a riot in the city and a curfew." We stopped the music and told the audience not to panic. I ended up bringing four or five fans home with me because their parents couldn't get there. There were gunshots and sirens going off, panic. It was awful. I didn't feel it coming. We were having so much fun making music.

When Motown left for Los Angeles in 1972, I didn't see that coming, either. I was left here. I thought Motown would be in Detroit forever. Berry wanted to make movies and couldn't house so many artists here. When they left, Motown kind of lost its family unity.

I later lived in New York, San Francisco, and for about 14 years Los Angeles. I realized home was Detroit so I moved back. In Detroit I have family, and people I went to school with. There's much love for me here. I like the different seasons and the cleaner air. I work with different societies and enjoy doing special functions at the Motown Museum. I still visit the Hitsville Building maybe twice a month.

To me, the Motown Sound makes me young and happy when I hear it. It's a tool to soothe the soul. When I hear a Motown song in the car, I turn it up and bop the whole time and try to hit those high notes. Someday I would like to start an academy where we can help aspiring singers and musicians become full rounded entertainers like Motown did for us, from top to bottom, everything from teaching music theory to learning the business side. We learned how to walk on stage and the etiquette of meeting kings and queens. There's a lot of talent in this city, there's just no outlet.

People need to get over Motown leaving the city. I know there is still resentment, but we need to honor our own. The first thing about faith and religion is forgiveness. We should thank Berry Gordy for all the artists he turned into performers. He spent the best years of his young life doing that. The Hitsville Building was open 24 hours a day from 1959 to 1972.

I would like to see more monuments honoring Motown's greats here, like a statue of Berry Gordy, Smokey Robinson, and Stevie Wonder. When you think of Detroit you think of the auto industry and Motown. So get a Cadillac or Ford and put a monument of the Four Tops riding in one near that big tire on I-94. When you land in a plane and get off you should see Motown. You shouldn't have to just go to 2648 West Grand Boulevard to see Motown.

➤ *The original Supremes consisted of Mary Wilson, Diana Ross and Flo Ballard. The trio, known as the Primettes when they signed with Motown in January 1961, became the first American group to record five straight number-one songs, including such classics as "Baby Love" and "Stop! In the Name of Love."*

⌄ *Stevie Wonder wows the crowd, circa 1965. The Saginaw native, blind since birth, was still a skinny teenager billed as "Little Stevie" Wonder. After a series of hit singles, including "Uptight (Everything's Alright)" and "Fingertips (Part 2)," Wonder matured into an accomplished writer, singer and producer of increasingly complex and creative works.*

Did Our Love Go," "Baby Love," "Come See About Me," "Stop! In the Name of Love," and "Back in My Arms Again." No American group—before or since—has done that.

This was a decidedly more innocent time in popular music.

"I'll never forget the day they brought Stevie Wonder to the studio," said Martha Reeves, one of Gordy's early protégés.

"I was still a secretary at that point. Ronnie White of the Miracles told Berry Gordy about Stevie. When this 11-year-old walked in he was very busy. He feels my typewriter without any paper in it and plays a rhythm on it. I said, 'Leave my typewriter alone' as I fixed all my stuck keys. I started following him around to the piano. He puts his hand on my face and says, 'You sound like a nice person, I want to see what you look like. Can you sing?' I said, 'Yeah.' All of a sudden he starts singing the Mighty Mouse theme—you know, 'Here I come to save the day.' We sang it in harmony. The guy was fabulous. He went to every area of the studio and played everything. Stevie is the most talented person I have ever met in my life."

Gordy's sister, Esther Gordy Edwards, recalled Motown in its prime:

"We really were like one big family," she said. "And that included the staff. We'd call everybody in for different things. If we needed hand-clappers, foot-stompers, we'd just go around the house and say, 'Hey, come into the studio, we need some foot-stompers for 'Twenty-five Miles to Go.'

"Sometimes the groups would be out performing until 2 or 3 o'clock in the morning, and instead of going home they'd come by Motown just to sit and talk on the porch about what they were doing next, or to rehearse a song or watch one of the other groups rehearsing or sit in on another group's session. The togetherness, the happiness, the camaraderie, the respect and the honor for one another, and the love was just tremendous."

The Motown story was not without its tragedies. Florence Ballard, one of the original Supremes, was replaced by Cindy Birdsong in 1967 and died on welfare nine years later. Marvin Gaye, the headstrong son of a preacher who arguably was Motown's most versatile and gifted talent, was shot to death by his father in 1984. Mary Wells, Motown's first female star, left in a dispute over money in 1965 and saw her career fizzle, ultimately dying of cancer of the larynx as friends mobilized to pay her medical bills. In addition, many performers and songwriters feel to this day that they were cheated out of millions of dollars in royalties by the company.

This unique era in Detroit and pop music history skidded to a halt in June 1972, when Gordy, anxious to expand into other avenues of entertainment, announced he was moving the country's largest black-owned business to Los Angeles. The *Free Press* joined the community in lamenting the move. "Where did our love go?" the paper asked in an editorial. "To L.A., baby."

Detroit's music scene, rich and varied as it has been in the decades following the label's move, has never found another civic signature to replace the Motown sound. Most folks, even some on the Left Coast, feel that Gordy's restructured Motown Industries was never able to infuse the soulful quintessence of Detroit— "the rhythmic din of the assembly line," according to music critic Susan Whitall— into its many media ventures.

"Since its move to Los Angeles," concluded music writer Nelson George, "Motown has had moments of glory, but the magic of the production line has been lost, discarded, or buried."

⋎ From the time she was a young girl thrilling the congregation at New Bethel Church with her rendition of "Precious Lord," Aretha Franklin has married gospel and soul like no artist before or since. The multiple Grammy Award-winner recorded her signature song, "Respect," in 1967 when she was 25; everything that followed has reinforced her standing as the uncontested Queen of Soul.

Fran Harris and the Early Days of Television

FRAN HARRIS ENJOYED A LONG, DISTINGUISHED CAREER AS A BROADCAST JOURNALIST WITH DETROIT STATION WWJ. IN ADDITION TO HER REGULAR RADIO RESPONSIBILITIES, SHE ALSO WAS INVOLVED IN THE STATION'S VERY FIRST TELECASTS, PRODUCING SEVERAL EARLY TELEVISION PROGRAMS AND HOSTING THE CITY'S FIRST CHILDREN'S SHOW, *JUNIOR JAMBOREE*.

I never gave television that much thought, but the guys around the station were talking about it, saying how exciting it would be. We immediately assumed that this new medium would also operate on telephones so we would be able to see the people we were talking to. That was a common feeling, that if you could have pictures that talked, for heaven's sake, you'd just hook it up to a phone, too.

The Dumont Corporation placed twelve of their sets around town for WWJ's first telecast in October, 1946. This was the first telecast ever in the city, and the station used the WWDT call letters. Dumont had one set at WWJ on Lafayette, another at Convention Hall at Woodward and Garfield avenues for the public to watch, and another at the Booth family home in Bloomfield Hills. The Booths were part owners of the *Detroit News*. Then there were other sets placed inside hotel lobbies and the offices of potential sponsors. Today there's still one set at the Detroit Historical Museum.

When WWJ decided to have television, they simply transferred radio programming and performers to TV. I remember that on that first trial telecast newscaster Ed Hinkle sat in a folding chair and read the news, while *Coffee Club* host Dave Zimmerman tried to do his audience participation show—without an audience, of course. Bela DeTuscan put on a fencing exhibition with his wife, and I conducted an interview with Lillian Ramon, a little French chanteuse who was my boss's friend.

What else do I remember about that day? Well, it was broadcast from the highest spot in town, the 47th floor of the Penobscot Building downtown. It was broadcast over WENA, WWJ's sister station and the first FM station in Michigan. The elevator stopped at the 45th floor, so you had to walk the rest of the way up to the makeshift studio, which was created by hanging what I thought was a giant white bed sheet across a wall. Then we took our turns standing in front of the sheet, facing this giant, unwieldy looking black camera, and delivering what was basically our radio programming.

Do you know we wore blue makeup that day? I had it on my lips, cheeks, and eyebrows. That's because the cameras we had then couldn't project the color red. We all looked pretty ghoulish. It really didn't matter, since the picture was probably more snow than anything.

Between that first telecast in October of 1946 and the following June, the station did a lot of experimenting, but there wasn't any regular programming. During this time adjustments were made, cameramen were created, and even WWJ's largest radio studio was sacrificed to the cause. And, oh, the color of our makeup changed—to brown.

When WWJ-TV finally went commercial in June 1947—the station had changed its call letters from WWDT—it featured a cooking show hosted by Jean McBride, who was a food writer for the *Detroit News*. Jean proved to be a fine performer, and the crew loved her. That's because after each show the director, stagehands, and cameramen would gobble up all the edibles. There'd hardly be a crumb left. The crew's favorite show was on Thanksgiving, as this gave them a chance to demolish a turkey and all of its trimmings. Once, though, Jean concocted spinach ice cream on her show. There were no takers.

Sports helped fill a lot of programming, though in the early years owners just couldn't understand that television would help rather than hurt attendance. They were afraid TV would clear out the bleachers and no one would come to the games. How wrong they were. That's how hockey and wrestling got such a hold. They were just beginning then. They were looking for exposure of any kind. We started airing the Red Wings' hockey games and suddenly Olympia Arena started filling up. Pretty soon the football Lions and baseball Tigers were televised, too. These were primarily home telecasts, since there was still trouble hooking up audio and visual on remotes.

That first summer of television, sets just weren't selling. They were too expensive. People at RCA, Philco, and General Electric were very unhappy because nobody was buying them. I believe it was RCA's idea to have a children's show. I was called up to the boss's office and was told, "Hey, we want to put on a show as good as *Kukla, Fran, & Ollie*."

"What kind of show is that?" I asked.

"You know, puppets," he said. "A little man and a puppet talk to a woman named Fran Allison."

"So you want puppets?" I asked.

"That's right. And anything else you can think of to make kids watch TV."

➤ *Opposite page: Curious Detroiters pack Convention Hall in 1946 to watch an experimental television broadcast.*

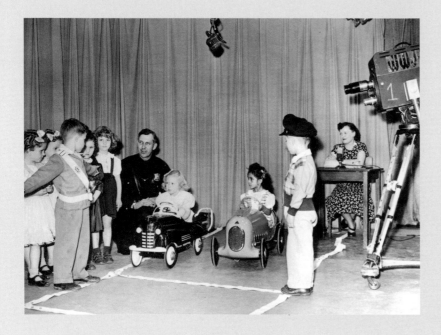

Thank goodness I had three children at home. My daughter was 11 years old. My youngest son was a year old; my other son was five or six. So I'd check with the two oldest to see what interested them in *Highlights for Children*, a magazine which at that time was called *Children's Activity Book*. They'd tell me what they liked and I just translated that to the children's show, which was called *Junior Jamboree.*

I don't really remember very much about the very first show of *Junior Jamboree* except that the studio was in the Detroit News Building on Lafayette, in the printing area. The studio was twice the size of my living room and the lights were so hot. It was about 120, 130 degrees under those lights. I had a zero budget. I did get an extra $15 a show. This was on top of my regular salary of $150 a week.

We didn't actually have a puppet, but a marionette named What Now. Jo Alexander, who worked at the Detroit Public Library, would stand out of sight on a chair and pull the strings. Jo had learned how to make it by reading some books at the library. What Now and I had some wonderful conversations on the show, and he'd put on some virtuoso performances at his toy piano.

Jerry Peacock was our artist. Because cameras still couldn't pick up the color red, Jerry would sketch his drawings beforehand in red on a large sheet of white paper. Then, when we were on the air, he'd simply trace over them with a black crayon. Perfect drawings every time.

Each show typically would include an artist, sports celebrities like Ted Lindsay of the Red Wings and Dizzy Trout of the Tigers, and animals. On Fridays the Humane Society brought in a kitten or puppy. Children would write in, asking for a pet, and each week we'd give it away to whoever wrote the best letter. Karroll Fox, who years later replaced Clare Cummings as Milky the Clown, performed magic tricks, and we'd have policemen and firemen on the show, too, teaching safety tips.

All of this was live. Was I worried? Of course. But if anything went wrong, we told the audience right away and brought them into the act. If Jo didn't show up, we'd tell the audience, "Well, Jo isn't here yet, so we're going to do it this way." It was fun. I often used to think, *Isn't it great to get paid for having such a good time?*

At the time cartoons hadn't yet invaded the airwaves. Instead, each day after school WWJ-TV presented three live programs, all geared to children, and all sponsored by television manufacturers. At 4:30 there was *The Story Lady*, who read stories to the kids. That program was sponsored by Philco. At five was *Junior Jamboree*, which was sponsored by RCA. They typically ran two commercials during our show. Then at 5:30 General Electric ran nature films.

Sales of television sets picked up soon afterwards. The increased sales were attributable in large part to children's shows. That's because children would demand that their parents buy a set. The first few months of *Junior Jamboree*, into early 1948, someone figured that an average of eight people watched each set. Someone on the block would have a TV and everyone would assemble in that living room to watch.

Junior Jamboree was cancelled after about 18 months. Sales were under way so there wasn't really a need for it anymore. I was disappointed, that's all. But heavens to earth, I was still doing my news and interviews every day on radio. I also figured that I would just do something different on TV, which I did.

In 1948-49 I put on an accident show called *Wagon on the Way*. We called it that because that's what the police would shout when they were ready to go on a call. At the time, the Red Cross was trying to find missing veterans. The Detroit Police Department was always trying to find missing persons. So I combined the two and each week showed four or five pictures of missing persons on the show, asking the public for help in finding them.

One week I showed a picture of this man in his thirties, wearing a hat at a sort of a rakish angle. After the show I got a phone call.

"Whaddya mean I'm missing?" this bleary sounding voice said. "I know where I am."

"Where are you?" I asked.

"I ain't talking," he said. "You'd tell my wife."

I'd always been interested in city operations, and that was reflected in the interviews I did on my radio show. It occurred to me that it might be fun to have a court show. So in 1950 I dreamed up a live program called *Traffic Court*. We used actual cases that had been closed and were a matter of public record. We used all the actual people involved in the case, including the witnesses and policemen. But someone else—a police officer—always played the defendant. The show ran once a week in the evening. It was the first court show in the country. The inspiration for Judge Wapner? Little did we know.

The Detroit Bar Association was up in arms over the show, saying it reflected poorly on the dignity of the court. But we didn't broadcast from the courtroom, and the number of traffic offenses did go down in the city, so the show continued. We alternated Judges Watts and George Murphy, both of whom were great hams. I know the bar association was very unhappy because by having Judge Watts on every week, we assured him of reelection. By the way, Judge Watts is a footnote in TV history. He was bald, and the overhead studio lights reflected off his head, so we had to powder his head before air time. He was a good sport about it, though.

By the early '50s, television had really taken off. Those first few years you could buy a set at department stores like Grinnell's, Hudson's, or Kern's. The specialty shops came later. Of course, my own husband wouldn't let me buy a TV set until after I'd been on the air for about three years. My own kids couldn't watch *Junior Jamboree*, which perhaps was just as well.

◄ *Opposite page, far left: From behind a desk, Fran Harris oversees a traffic lesson during an early episode of* Junior Jamboree.

⋎ *Detroit's WXYZ-Channel 7 produced more local kids programming than any station in the country during the '50s and '60s. Johnny Ginger (born Galen Grindle) portrayed a bumbling stagehand while Irv Romig (a descendent of the family that, in Detroit in 1906, created the country's first Shrine Circus) kept kids laughing with his antics as Ricky the Clown.*

CITY OF CHAMPIONS

In Detroit, sports are literally larger than life. All one has to do is take a look around downtown, where side-by-side stadiums, heavily funded with tax dollars, are being viewed as the cornerstone of the city's rebirth. Where a two-ton fist dangles menacingly at the foot of Woodward. And where, for years, eight-story paintings of Lions running back Barry Sanders and Michigan hoops star Chris Webber—part of Nike's "Hero Wall" series—filled the sides of office buildings overlooking Cadillac Square.

It goes without saying that early Detroiters would have been staggered. Recreation in Cadillac's Detroit centered around activities of skill that had practical applications in everyday life: rowing, shooting (bow and arrow and firearms), wrestling, swimming, and foot racing. A heavily padded man running around with a pig bladder tucked under his arm and some kind of birdcage jammed on his head would have left the habitants staring in bewilderment or reaching for their muskets.

Still, historian Clarence Monroe Burton reminds us, French frivolity was a big part of everyday life three centuries ago. One feels the habitants would have adjusted just fine to the notion of jamming a large rubber ball through a peach basket, or slapping a frozen disc into a net, or standing on the sidelines and cheering those who did.

◄ *The "Monument to Joe Louis" on Woodward.*

➤ *A trio of Tigers from 1940. From left: Barney McCosky, Rudy York, Charlie Gehringer.*

The Sports Scene in 1859

Although such popular modern pastimes as football and basketball had yet to be invented, Detroit's sports scene nonetheless was an active one on the eve of the Civil War.

On April 12, 1859, the city hosted the first national championship billiard match, with Michael Phelan of New York defeating local favorite John Seereiter for the $15,000 top prize. Amidst all the excitement, the *Detroit Free Press* enthusiastically reported that "Detroit is really getting to be a sporting city." As proof, it cited the existence of two cricket teams, the Peninsulars and the Detroits; a yacht club; "first-class" billiard players like Seereiter; and a boat club (the Detroit Boat Club, formed in 1839 and today the nation's oldest). Also mentioned was a local chess club "that has just come off victorious in a match with the Cleveland chess club." Then there were the three race courses operating in or near the city. "Our citizens really seem to take great pride in fast horses," the paper observed, "for the display of which our broad avenues are finely adapted."

There was one glaring omission in the newspaper's rundown of the city's sporting activities. Significantly, at that time of the year when future generations of Detroiters would eagerly anticipate the first cry of "Play ball!", there was not a single mention of a baseball team in the city.

The oversight was understandable. Although baseball would within a few years become wildly popular in Detroit, in the spring of 1859 it still was running second to its British cousin, cricket, in popularity among the city's sporting types.

This began to change one afternoon that summer. On August 8, 1859, a large crowd of curious citizens attended the first game ever played between competing nines in the city. Meeting on the grounds of the Cass farm, the Detroits—a team comprised of some of Detroit's leading citizens—routed the Early Risers, a recently organized squad of clerks who practiced mornings before reporting to work, by a 59-21 score.

This historic match demonstrated the qualities of the emerging national pastime. Whereas a cricket match was interminably slow, often taking two or three days to complete, a baseball game was usually over in less than 90 minutes. Soon several more ball clubs were organized locally, the *Free Press* joining other editorial voices in proclaiming baseball as the perfect game for a young, virile America.

➤ *The Detroit Athletic Club's cricket team in 1890.*

"The soldiers who came with Cadillac were Frenchmen who had entered the army in France and were therefore familiar with the soldiers' life in the old country," observed Burton. "This life was not one of seclusion, or of toil only, but was interspersed with all the hilarity and joy-making that could be obtained in such a situation and such a life. They undoubtedly played all the games that were common in their day, such as quoits, bowling in the narrow streets of the village, card playing, and other similar indoor amusements in inclement weather."

Native Americans introduced white settlers to a favorite pastime, lacrosse, as well as to an early ball-and-stick game called "Baw-qua-quat" that was a primitive predecessor to that great American pastime, baseball. Although there were nearly no horses to be found in Cadillac's Detroit,

within a century of his arrival the equine population had grown to the point that horse racing was a favorite sport, especially on ice during the long months of winter.

The rise of spectator sports in Detroit and elsewhere was a direct result of the industrial revolution and America's growing urbanization. Young men who left their farms for the city found themselves with time on their hands and a few coins in their pocket. Although many amateur clubs were formed during the 19th century—most notably the Cass Club, the Aetnas, and the Detroit Athletic Club—by the time of the Civil War far more clerks and factory workers were watching than participating in organized pastimes. This development led many social critics to decry America's growing flabbiness while causing a new breed of opportunists—professional sports promoters and athletes—to rub their hands in anticipatory glee.

Detroit's first major spectator sport, baseball, was played with enthusiasm by amateur clubs beginning in the 1850s. By the summer of 1867, the game's popularity had grown to the point that thousands of citizens were willing to pay up to 50 cents to watch a three-day tournament featuring teams from as far away as Pennsylvania. The "Great Base Ball Tournament," held at the cricket grounds on Woodward Avenue north of Grand Circus Park (where the Vernor's bottling plant later stood), helped demonstrate the great commercial appeal of sports in the growing city.

In 1879 local promoters built Detroit's first enclosed ballpark, Recreation Park, and stocked it with the first professional team to represent the community, Hollinger's Nine. Unlike the rosters of local amateur teams, all members of this pay-for-play squad hailed from out of state. Local fans saw nothing strange in having the "home team" comprised of imported professionals who, if the money was right, would be just as happy playing ball in Toledo or Grand Rapids. All the "bugs" and "cranks" (as fans came to be called) cared about was the vicarious thrill of cheering for a champion.

In 1881, Mayor William B. Thompson helped secure a National League franchise

⋏ *Recreation Park opened in 1879 and was Detroit's first enclosed ballpark. The city's first major league team, the National League's Wolverines, played there from 1881 to 1888. The park was torn down in 1894.*

⋎ *Hall-of-Fame first baseman Dan Brouthers was one of the stars of the 1887 Wolverines, who won the National League pennant and that fall's "world series" against the St. Louis Browns of the American Association.*

for Detroit, giving the city a presence in organized base-ball's most respected circuit. Detroit may have been gar-nering some national attention for its growing indus-trial might, but with the coming of the Wolverines its citizens could really feel good about themselves. In their eyes, and in the eyes of the rest of the country, Detroit was now officially a major league city.

Interest was ratcheted up several notches when, after several so-so seasons, Frederick Stearnes, whose family had made its fortune in pharmaceuticals, bought the team and promised the city a winner. In 1886 the young owner rocked the sports world by purchasing Buffalo's "Big Four" infield for the princely sum of $8,000. The following summer the Wolverines won the pennant and the ensuing "world series" against the St. Louis Browns of the American Association. The Wolverines' success foreshadowed some of the more unseemly aspects of 20th century sports, where impatient and deep-pocketed owners like Walter Briggs and Mike Ilitch tried to buy their way to a championship.

The Detroit Tigers debuted in 1894 as a member of the minor Western League; six years later it was a charter member of the American League. Original owner George Vanderbeck sold the franchise to local millionaire Bill Yawkey, a playboy with little interest in the team beyond what social cachet its ownership might convey on him. Over time, he allowed his stone-faced bookkeeper, Frank Navin, to buy up stock in the team until he owned it. Under Navin's penurious but capable management, the Tigers wound up win-ning three straight pennants from 1907 to 1909, losing the World Series each time. The catalyst was a thin-skinned, rolling ball of hell named Tyrus Raymond Cobb.

Perhaps no athlete has personified Detroit better than the red-haired outfielder from small-town Georgia, who broke into the lineup one August afternoon in 1905 and spent a contentiously brilliant 22 seasons in a Tigers uniform.

▼ *Ty Cobb won a dozen batting titles and stole 894 bases during his 24 big-league seasons, all but the last two spent in Detroit.*

According to biographer Charles C. Alexander, "Cobb's future, as both baseball player and businessman, was intimately tied to the rise of Detroit as the hub of world automobile production in the century's early decades. In his hustle and drive, his ingenuity, his willingness to take chances, in his competitive ruthlessness as well, he often appeared to personify that city in its heroic age, a time when the automobile became central to American life and Cobb became central to American baseball."

The "Georgia Peach" brought a blowtorch intensity to the diamond. Future Tigers like Kirk Gibson and Bobby Higginson, whose hustle reminded some modern commentators of the old master, paled by comparison.

"His determination was fantastic," one awed opponent said of Cobb. "I never saw anybody like him. It was *his* base. It was his game. Everything was his. The most feared man in the history of baseball."

"My idea was to go on the attack and never relax it," was Cobb's explanation. "An offensive attitude is the key to making any play, and if it meant gambling and getting tough, I was willing. If they roughed me up, I knocked them kicking with my spikes. I used my legs like an octopus when I was thrown out."

Cobb found it impossible to dial down his "vying nature," which was leavened with a streak of cruelty. He had a reputation for deliberately trying to spike infielders and catchers, and his off-the-field run-ins are simply too numerous to list. A tiny sampling of his many skirmishes include a bloody fistfight with umpire Billy Evans under the stands in Washington; climbing into the stands in New York to beat up a crippled heckler; knifing a watchman inside a Cleveland hotel; and punching a black laborer outside the Pontchartrain Hotel in Detroit. On one infamous occasion he was tossed into jail after coming to blows with a butcher boy who had sold his wife five cents worth of bad fish.

After leaving Detroit as player-manager in 1926, Cobb spent two more seasons in Philadelphia before he retired, holding more than 90 records. In 1936 he was the

⋀ *Cobb and his counterpart on the Boston Red Sox, center fielder Tris Speaker. "Good as I was," Speaker once admitted, "I was never close to Cobb, and neither was Babe Ruth or anybody else." In 1936, the Georgia Peach was the first player voted into the Baseball Hall of Fame.*

WITH YOUNG COBB IN THE GAME, THERE'S NEVER ANY TELLING WHAT MIGHT HAPPEN: WHETHER HE'S AT BAT, ON BASE, OR IN THE FIELD, THE FANTASTIC, IMPOSSIBLE TWIST IS AN EASY POSSIBILITY AND WE SIT THERE LIKE CHILDREN WONDERING WHAT MIRACLE HE WILL PERFORM NEXT. — New York World, 1907

⋏ *Cobb, a "genius in spikes," evades the tag, circa 1910. "The whole secret of sliding," he once explained, "is to make your move at the last possible second. When I went in there I wanted to see the whites of the fielder's eyes."*

➤ *Opposite page: Clockwise from top left: The Tigers' potent outfield of Bobby Veach, Cobb and Sam Crawford in 1915; Davy Jones battles snow flurries in an April game at Bennett Park in 1911; opening-day ceremonies at Navin Field in 1925.*

⋎ *Pages 232-233: Bennett Park was the home of the Tigers from 1896 to 1911.*

first man elected to the Baseball Hall of Fame. Some of his most notable records have since been eclipsed, though his .367 career batting average and dozen batting titles are untouchable.

Cobb's agile mind served him well off the field. He invested his salary in real estate and in Coca-Cola and General Motors stock, ultimately becoming the first athlete to be worth a million dollars. He indulged his passion for fast cars, big game hunting, and golf, while regularly embroiling himself in embarrassing situations. He generally made life uncomfortable for everyone around him—family members and teammates included—until he died in his native Georgia in 1961.

Unfortunately for Cobb, his deeply flawed character will always be the cornerstone of his legend. Several years ago, Pete Rose was in the process of overtaking Cobb as baseball's all-time base-hit champion when a reporter asked him if he thought the Georgia Peach was watching the proceedings from heaven.

"From what I've heard," said Rose, "that's not where he's at."

The decade that defined Detroit as the "City of Champions" was the 1930s, when newly-minted heroes uplifted the spirits of Detroiters mired in the Great Depression. While Joe Louis captured the hearts of black and white Detroiters with his climb through the heavyweight ranks, the Tigers, the newly formed Lions, and the Red Wings all won their first championships during a six-month period in 1935–36.

Baseball was still king. Prior to the 1934 season, Frank Navin purchased the Philadelphia Athletics' star catcher, Mickey Cochrane, for $100,000 to call signals and to manage a young, talented team that needed direction. Years later, pitcher Eldon Auker said, "Cochrane formed a relationship between himself and us. We were like a family. We followed him around like kids and would do anything Mike wanted us to do."

Cracker Jack
BALL PLAYERS

COBB, DETROIT - AMERICANS

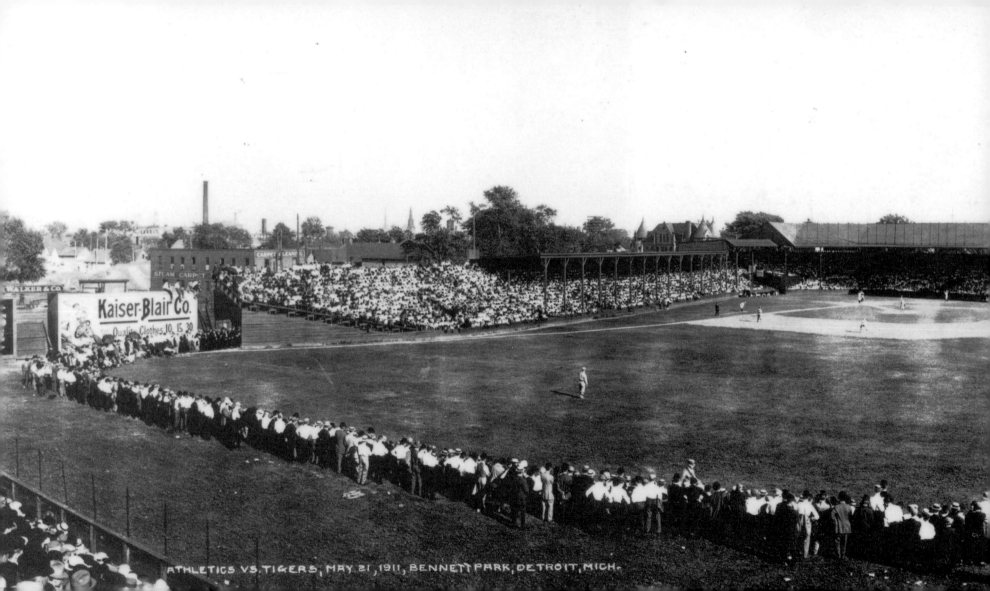

ATHLETICS VS. TIGERS, MAY 21, 1911, BENNETT PARK, DETROIT, MICH.

COPR. TRIPP AND McCURDY.

A League of Their Own

During the apartheid era of professional baseball, a period that ran from the late 19th century through the end of World War II, Negro ballplayers were forced to organize and compete in leagues of their own. None was as successful as the Negro National League, a circuit that between 1919 and 1931 included the Detroit Stars.

The Stars were owned by the league's founder and driving force, Chicago-based Rube Foster, and managed for their first several seasons by local numbers operator Tenny Blount. League games were played at Mack Park at Mack and Fairview. The wooden park was owned and operated by John Roesink, a downtown clothier who was well known for his support of amateur and professional athletics. Roesink (who brought the first National Football League franchise to the city in 1920) bought the Stars after Foster's untimely death in 1925. He operated them until selling the club to Everitt Watson, a Black Bottom numbers racketeer, in 1931.

"We used to fill that Mack Park on Sundays," recalled Ted "Double Duty" Radcliffe, who played three seasons with the Stars. "They'd be lined up on the streets when we opened the gates. We could only get seven or eight thousand in the place, but there were some days that we'd outdraw the Tigers."

Due to Mack Park's cozy dimensions, the Stars generally were a competitive and lively hitting team during their existence, though the closest they ever came to a pennant was a 1930 playoff loss to the St. Louis Stars. The lineup boasted sluggers like Edgar Wesley, a hulking first baseman who during the 1920s won or shared three home run crowns and captured a batting championship, and Norman "Turkey" Stearnes. The quiet, bladelike center fielder from Nashville joined the team in 1923 and immediately made his presence felt, winning his first of several home run titles. "The reason they called him Turkey," recalled longtime fan Gussie Weaver, "was because of the way he'd flap his arms as he trotted around the bases. Everybody got a kick out of the way he ran."

Other standouts on the Stars included catcher-manager Bruce Petway, shortstop Orville "Mule" Riggins, and pitchers Bill Holland, William Force, and Andy "Lefty" Cooper. Although the roster was leaner and the substitutes generally were of lesser talent than their white major league counterparts, in the many head-to-head exhibition meetings between black and white teams the Negro leaguers came out on top more often than not. In a three-game series at the end of the 1923 American League season, for example, the Stars twice beat the St. Louis Browns by staging improbable ninth-inning rallies before a packed house at Mack Park.

A disastrous fire at Mack Park prior to a game with the Kansas City Monarchs forced the stars to relocate to Hamtramck Stadium halfway through the 1929 season. The Depression caused the Stars and the rest of the Negro National League to fold after the 1931 season. The Stars were rein-

Y *Detroit Stars catcher Leon "Pepper" Daniels was a Mack Park favorite from 1921 to 1930. "The Mack Park crowd is intensely partisan but at the same time good-humored," one observer wrote in 1922. "There is more 'kidding' than 'panning.' Only the star who is having a bad day is made the target for the sort of abuse that Babe Ruth and Ty Cobb receive on foreign grounds."*

carnated as a short-lived member of a revamped Negro National League in 1933, and then later as a charter member of the Negro American League in 1937, but in each case hard economic times caused the local nine to disband after one season. Yet another version of the Stars appeared in the 1950s, but by that time the Negro leagues were just a shadow of their former greatness, the result of the majors' desegregation after Jackie Robinson's historic 1947 breakthrough with the Brooklyn Dodgers.

Belated recognition of the Stars has come in the recent elections of Stearnes and third baseman Ray Dandridge (who began his long career with the 1933 Stars) to the National Baseball Hall of Fame. And once each summer, the Tigers and their opponents for the day play an official league game in reproduction Negro League uniforms.

But even in their own time the Stars were afforded grudging respect by white sportswriters. "You can usually see a game at Mack Park that will produce about as many sparkling plays as one at Navin Field," Eddie Batchelor observed in 1922, "and invariably you will hear rooting that even the bleacherites at Trumbull and Michigan would find it impossible to equal."

∨ *The Stars line up inside Mack Park in 1923. Standing sixth from the left is Norman "Turkey" Stearnes, a rookie center fielder who went on to win several home run titles with Detroit. After leaving the game nearly a quarter-century later, Stearnes worked at the Ford Rouge plant. He died in 1979 and was elected to the Baseball Hall of Fame in 2000— a belated honor for one of the Negro Leagues' true superstars.*

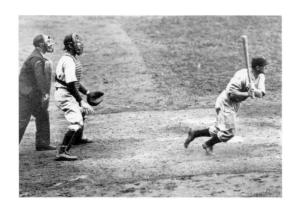

⋀ Mickey Cochrane bangs out a hit against the Yankees.

⋁ The Tigers' regular lineup and batting order in 1934-35 included (from left): Pete Fox, Mickey Cochrane, Charlie Gehringer, Hank Greenberg, Goose Goslin, Billy Rogell, Gee Walker, Marv Owen and Schoolboy Rowe.

In 1934, Cochrane's Tigers, featuring future Hall of Famers Charlie Gehringer, Hank Greenberg, and Goose Goslin—the "G-Men"—won the club's first pennant since 1909. They extended St. Louis's Gas House Gang of Dizzy and Daffy Dean to the seventh game of the World Series before falling, 11-0, at Navin Field. The drubbing was highlighted by a near-riot by Detroit fans, who showered Cardinals left fielder Ducky Medwick with fruit following a spiking incident with Tigers third baseman Marv Owen. One year later, following another pennant win, the Tigers beat the Cubs, 3-2, in the sixth game of the World Series. Cochrane streaked across the plate on Goslin's ninth-inning bloop single, giving Detroit its first world championship since the 1887 Wolverines and touching off a wild celebration that lasted until the following day.

"I believe we helped bring Detroit out of the Depression," Auker said of those years. "We helped change the attitude of the state. We gave people hope, and they became proud of Detroit and their Tigers. They were crazy for us."

While the Tigers owned Detroit, pro football finally became established after several previous attempts to launch an NFL franchise failed in the 1920s. In 1934, the Detroit Lions, owned by WJR radio magnate Dick Richards, opened their inaugural season at the University of Detroit's Dinan Field. Featuring the playmaking of Earl "Dutch" Clark, the Lions won their first 10 games, including shutouts of their first seven opponents.

"Dutch was the finest athlete I ever had the pleasure to know," said sportswriter Eddie Hayes. "First of all, he was a super, gifted athlete. Beyond

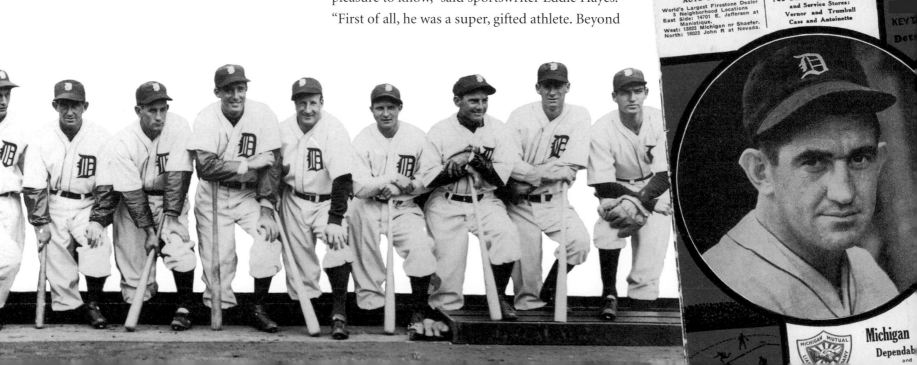

that, he was a fine gentleman. He had class. I remember once when a bunch of Lions were up in one of the players' rooms at Webster Hall, where the Lions stayed during the season.

"They were watching dirty movies, when someone came in and said, 'The Dutchman's just come into the lobby.' They wouldn't have gotten into any trouble, but they put the movies away all the same. They thought so highly of Dutch they wouldn't run them in his presence."

A longstanding Detroit tradition began that Thanksgiving when the Lions hosted Bronco Nagurski and the Chicago Bears before a packed house. Listeners from coast to coast tuned into the radio broadcast of the game. The Lions lost, but fans were already looking forward to next season.

⋏ Top: Excitement over the Tigers was so great during the 1934 World Series that temporary bleachers were built around the houses on Trumbull Avenue.

⋏ Above: Navin Field in 1912.

Spartan Seasons

BORN IN 1905, GLENN PRESNELL IS THE LAST SURVIVING MEMBER OF THE ORIGINAL DETROIT LIONS TEAM OF 1934. ALONG WITH FELLOW BACKFIELD STARS EARL "DUTCH" CLARK, LEROY "ACE" GUTOWSKY, AND ERNIE CADDELL, PRESNELL LED THE LIONS TO THEIR FIRST CHAMPIONSHIP AND HELPED ESTABLISH THE NATIONAL FOOTBALL LEAGUE DURING THE UNCERTAIN DAYS OF THE DEPRESSION.

I started my NFL career with the Portsmouth Spartans in 1931 after having played at the University of Nebraska, where I made the All-American team. Portsmouth was a small mining town in southern Ohio, right on the Ohio River. There were some tremendous fans in Portsmouth, but most people had very little money because of the Depression. I stayed with the Spartans until the team was sold and moved to Detroit, where we became the Lions.

In '31 and '32 Portsmouth just missed winning the championship. I played in that famous 1932 playoff game—the first NFL postseason playoff ever—against the Chicago Bears inside Chicago Stadium. It had been moved from Wrigley Field because of bad weather. Because it was being played indoors and the building was so small, the field was only 80 yards long. The field consisted of dirt from a recent circus, so all afternoon we had to play with the foul smell of animal droppings in our noses. I remember we were handicapped by the small field. There were no long runs and it was difficult to pass because it was so confining. It was hot and close, and in the second half, the dust clouds got kind of thick. We lost 9-0 on a disputed call at the end of the game. Can you imagine playing what was then the equivalent of the Super Bowl in that kind of environment today? But that was professional football in those days. The league was nothing like what it is now.

In 1933 I led the league in scoring and was second in passing, but I never got paid for the last four games with Portsmouth. They gave me $360 in stock instead. The small towns just couldn't make it during the Depression and the crowds really dwindled. After the season I left for the University of West Virginia to coach.

In 1934, G.A. Richards, the owner of radio station WJR, bought the Portsmouth team. He wanted me to play for the Lions, but I held out. Finally, he brought my wife and me into Detroit on an all-expense-paid trip and talked me into playing. I set my salary as high as I thought I could get in those days. I got $4,000, but other stars around the league, like Bronco Nagurski and Red Grange, probably were paid more.

By the way, my wife and I were the ones who selected the Lions' colors. At our meeting with Richards he asked us to look at the different colored jerseys in the next room. Everything from orange and black to red and white were there. We saw the Honolulu blue and silver and we told him that's what we liked.

The difference between Portsmouth and Detroit was like night and day.

Besides the pay, the University of Detroit stadium was much nicer than what we were used to playing in. It held about 25,000 people. It was quite an experience for an old country boy like me from Nebraska to live in a big city like Detroit.

I played safety on defense and quarterback on offense. I also did the placekicking. Remember, in those days before free substitution, if you were replaced you couldn't play the rest of the quarter.

That first Lions team in '34 was probably the greatest defensive team ever. We had George Christiansen at tackle, Ox Emerson at guard, and Ed Klewicki at end. Tremendous players. We were not scored upon in our first seven games of the season. It's a record that will never be broken. I remember in the third game against the Packers, I kicked a 54-yard field goal to win the game, 3-0. It stood as the league record for the longest field goal for about 20 years. In the eighth game, the Pittsburgh Steelers finally scored on kind of a fluke play, but we still beat them, 40-7. That year we gave up only 59 points in 13 games. That's less than five points a game.

The biggest game of the '34 season was the very first Thanksgiving Day game, which pitted us against the Bears for the Western Conference title. It was a beautiful day with a sellout crowd at U of D. We played in the morning so that people could go home and eat their turkey dinner. Prior to the game, Mr. Richards got a bear from northern Michigan, and we were told that we were going to have a bear dinner after the game.

The Bears beat us late in the fourth quarter when Bronco Nagurski, who you didn't normally think of as a passing back, jumped in the air and lobbed the ball with both hands to a teammate in the end zone. He was the best player by far. He could run inside for power or take a pitchout and run wide. Nagurski would run his own interference. He would come up with his forearm under you and try to knock you off. He was a very powerful man.

During the football season the entire team lived at Webster Hall, which was on Cass Avenue near Wayne State University. Even the married players like myself had to stay there. We had a big room in the basement called the Lions' Den. That's where we loafed and played cards when we weren't practicing. It was really nice, with a swimming pool and handball courts. Anyway, the hotel staff had prepared the bear, and sure enough we ate it. But after losing that first Thanksgiving Day game to Chicago, it didn't taste very good.

In 1935 we beat the New York Giants for the World Championship at

U of D stadium, 26-7. I remember that it was a snowy day, very cold, and there were far less fans there than on Thanksgiving. In those days, people didn't go very often when it wasn't nice weather.

I was the starting quarterback that game and for most of the season. Potsy Clark, our coach, liked to start me and see what was going on before sending in Dutch Clark. The one thing that stands out in my memory is that we scored in the first two minutes. I had thrown a flat pass to our blocking back on a fake for a 60-yard play to about their four-yard line. Ace Gutowsky punched it over for the score and I kicked the extra point. If we celebrated when we made a touchdown like the way they do today we would have been hooted off the field.

For winning the championship, we each received $300. We never got a championship ring like they do now, but it was certainly one of my proudest moments. Remember, professional football was not nearly as popular as college football and major league baseball. It was much more exciting to play college football at Nebraska in front of 40,000 people. The NFL simply was a way to make a living during the Depression.

I quit playing after the '36 season because I wanted to get into college coaching, which offered more security. For a little less money I became the backfield coach at the University of Kansas for one year. I then coached at Nebraska and later became the head coach at Eastern Kentucky. I retired as their athletic director in 1974.

Those first two winning seasons in Detroit, 1934–35, really brought out the fans. If we hadn't won, I doubt the franchise would have stayed there. There were other teams that had tried Detroit but couldn't make it. The Lions were a well-run organization and everyone liked each other. There were no petty jealousies. We didn't make the money they do now, but I still had a lot of fun and met a lot of people.

▼ *The Detroit Lions of 1935, champions of the National Football League.*

➤ *Green Bay's muddied halfback, Paul Hornung, runs to daylight in the 1961 Thanksgiving Day game against the Lions at Tiger Stadium. The Lions' Turkey Day tradition began in 1934 and continues today.*

Y *Hall-of-Fame back Earl "Dutch" Clark helped establish professional football in Detroit.*

➤ *Opposite page: Action from the final game of the 1937 Stanley Cup finals between the Red Wings and New York Rangers. Detroit won the game to clinch its second straight Stanley Cup.*

As with the Tigers, 1935 would prove to be the magic year for the Lions. On a muddy field flecked with snowflakes, the second-year franchise defeated the New York Giants, 26-7, at U of D stadium for its first National Football League title.

Detroit's sports trifecta was completed the following April, when the Detroit Red Wings captured their first Stanley Cup championship. Stars Ebbie Goodfellow, Herbie Lewis, and Larry Aurie led the way in defeating Toronto in the finals. The following year, the club repeated as Stanley Cup champions, this time shutting out the New York Rangers in the last two games of the finals at a jam-packed Olympia Arena.

For general manager and coach Jack Adams, his 10-year effort to establish hockey in Detroit had finally paid off. Adams came to Detroit in 1927, the year Olympia was built and one year after the Detroit Cougars entered the National Hockey League. In 1932, Chicago millionaire James Norris bought the franchise, renamed the team the Red Wings, and let his temperamental but brilliant hockey man put the pieces together. Adams, a penny-pincher, was known to award his players with varsity jackets instead of bonuses. But his record speaks for itself. Before retiring as the Wings' general manager in 1963 after 36 years, including 20 as a coach, his teams won 12 regular season titles and seven Stanley Cups.

By the end of the 1930s, Detroit's three major sports franchises had developed a loyal fan base. In 1938, new Tigers' owner Walter Briggs finished expanding Navin Field to 52,000 seats, renamed it after himself, and then welcomed the Lions—whose growing popularity demanded a more suitable venue—as tenants. The town was rewarded with a World Series championship in 1945, as Hank Greenberg returned to the lineup after four years in uniform and hit a grand-slam home run on the final day of the season to clinch the pennant. In the Series, former Detroit sandlotter Hal Newhouser whipped the Cubs in the decisive seventh game at Wrigley Field. Greenberg and Newhouser would both wind up in the Hall of Fame.

The "fabulous '50s" belonged to Jack Adams's Red Wings and coach Buddy Parker's Lions, as both teams established dynasties in their greatest decade ever.

When Adams signed 18-year-old right winger Gordie Howe from Saskatoon in 1946, he knew he had something special. The slope-shouldered youngster was sneaky fast, tough as nails, and had an uncanny ability to find the net. Adams placed him with left winger Ted Lindsay and center Sid Abel, forming the most famous line in hockey, the "Production Line."

"Gordie Howe is the greatest young player I've seen," Adams said at the end of 1949, a season that marked the start of a record seven-year run at the top of the regular-season standings. The 21-year-old Howe was selected to the All-Star game, the beginning of a remarkable 21 consecutive All-Star berths. The following year, the famous trio finished 1-2-3 in scoring, leading the franchise to its fourth Stanley Cup championship. During the semifinals against defending champion Toronto, Howe nearly died from a fractured skull when he fell headfirst into the boards after a run-in with the Leafs' Ted Kennedy. Playing without Howe, the Wings took the Rangers into a seventh game at Olympia. Little known Pete Babando, acquired in the off-season by the crafty Adams, scored in overtime to end several years of post-season frustration. Afterward, Ted Lindsay launched a Stanley Cup tradition by

⋏ *Detroit's boys of winter scrimmage outdoors in 1927. Prior to being named the Red Wings, the club was known as the Cougars and the Falcons.*

◄ *Opposite page: Olympia Arena lit up at night in 1938. In addition to hosting rodeos, wrestling and boxing matches, concerts and political rallies, the "old red barn" served as home ice for the Red Wings from 1927 until the team moved to Joe Louis Arena 52 years later.*

LIKE ALL GREAT TEAMS, THE WINGS THAT YEAR HAD A DISTINCTIVE PERSONALITY...A SPIRIT OF BLITHE OPTIMISM AND YOUTHFUL INSOUCIANCE AND JOIE DE VIVRE. THEY COMBINED MATURE PROFESSIONALISM AND RECKLESS ABANDON, DISCIPLINED SELF-CONTROL AND EXPLOSIVE INTENSITY, UNSELFISH TEAMWORK AND INSPIRED, INDIVIDUAL SPONTANEITY. WITH THEIR FEARLESS DASH AND MADCAP HUSTLE AND SHEER WILL TO WIN, THEY WERE A JOY TO WATCH IN ACTION. —*author Roy MacSkimming describing the 1951-52 Red Wings*

➤ Leonard "Red" Kelly was a key member of the Red Wings' four Stanley Cup winners in the 1950s, winning the inaugural Norris Trophy in 1954 as the league's best defenseman and being named to the All-Star team eight straight seasons during the decade.

➤ Opposite page: Hall-of-Fame right winger Gordie Howe was the most dominant player in the National Hockey League for most of his 25 seasons in Detroit. During that time "Mr. Hockey" was the league's MVP six times and leading scorer six times. He retired as the NHL's all-time leading scorer, popping in 786 goals as a Wing.

hoisting the Cup over his head and skating around the rink.

The Wings would raise the Cup three more times before the decade was over, as Adams, known as "Trader Jack," constantly reinvented his lineup through trades and a strong farm system. The "old red barn" at Grand River and McGraw shook as fans cheered not only Howe and Lindsay, but a tight-knit group that included goaltender Terry Sawchuck, defensemen Red Kelly and Bob Goldham, and forwards Alex Delvecchio, Johnny Wilson, Metro Prystai, Marty Pavelich, and Glen Skov. Although their 1955 Cup would be the team's last until 1997, Howe developed into the finest all-around player in NHL history. Rival Montreal superstar Rocket Richard admitted, "Sincerely, I have never seen a greater hockey player." On November 10, 1963, Howe scored goal number 545, breaking Richard's record in front of a delirious Olympia Stadium crowd that gave Number 9 an ear-splitting, 20-minute standing ovation.

The other dominant Detroit team of the Eisenhower decade, the Lions, copped four divisional titles and three championships within a six-year span. In 1952, they beat Los Angeles in a special playoff at fog-wrapped Briggs Stadium in Detroit, then captured the championship with a 17-7 victory over the Cleveland Browns. In 1953, the Lions claimed their second straight championship with a rousing 17-16 win in a rematch with the Browns. Rookie linebacker Joe Schmidt, one of several future Hall of Famers on the squad, was ecstatic. "I had just purchased a new car and I thought, if we win it, I could get out of the hole. Our payout was $2,400, so I was tickled I could pay off that two-door Chevy."

The architect of the comeback victory was the legendary Bobby Layne. With under two minutes to play, the paunchy Texas quarterback tossed one of his trademark

"THERE WAS WATERFIELD. AND GRAHAM. AND UNITAS. NOW, SOME SAY STARR. OTHERS SAY TITTLE, BUT HE NEVER WON THE BIG ONE. BUT FOR THOSE OF US WHO KNOW THE GAME, THERE WAS ONLY ONE QUARTERBACK — BOBBY LAYNE." — *Howard Cosell*

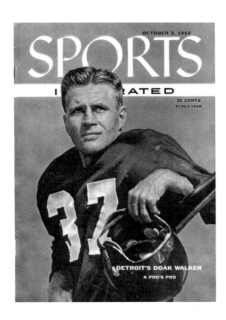

▲ *Doak Walker set an NFL scoring record with 128 points in his rookie season with the Lions, 1950. Although he played just five more seasons, the Texas halfback with the cover-boy looks made it into the Football Hall of Fame.*

➤ *Opposite page: Barry Sanders was poised to overtake Walter Payton as the top rusher in pro football history when he unexpectedly retired after the 1998 season. Here the Lions' running back is being carried off the field at the end of the final game of the 1997 season after becoming only the third back to gain 2,000 yards in a season.*

wobbly passes to Jim Doran for the winning score.

"Bobby was a great competitor," recalled center Vince Banonis. "He was the best two-minute quarterback ever. He knew how to control the clock. Everybody looked up to him."

As for Layne's storied off-field escapades, Banonis insisted that Bobby's passes may have wobbled during the game, but not Bobby himself. "They're great stories. But being the center, I would've been the first to notice if he'd been out all night."

With their annual Thanksgiving Day telecasts and Layne's last minute heroics, by 1954 the Lions had become America's team. Layne graced the cover of *Time* magazine and his old high school buddy, All-Pro halfback Doak Walker, appeared on the front of Wheaties boxes.

The team would win still another title in 1957. The grizzled and capable Tobin Rote replaced the injured Layne late in the campaign and led the team to an improbable comeback over San Francisco in a Western Division playoff. Trailing 27-7 in the third quarter, the Lions carved out a 31-27 victory behind two touchdown runs by stumpy fullback Tom "The Bomb" Tracy. The following week Rote threw for four touchdowns and rushed for a fifth in a 59-14 thrashing of the Browns.

That was the zenith of Lions football. In the 43 years since that cold Sunday afternoon at Briggs Stadium, the Lions have gone through eleven head coaches, a change of ownership, two stadiums (with a third on the way), and scores of stars like Lem Barney, Billy Sims, and Barry Sanders—and they have exactly one postseason win to show for it all. Still, despite the lack of championships, the fans have remained loyal, their grandfathers soothing them with tales of Layne's Lions.

The same year the Lions won their last championship, a new professional team arrived in town. Automobile-piston magnate Fred Zollner brought the Fort Wayne Pistons of the National Basketball Association to the Motor City. The NBA had a

➤ *Opposite page: Gates Brown is mobbed by teammates after his pinch-hit delivered another Tigers victory during the glorious season of 1968.*

⩗ *Al Kaline in the 1950s, a decade that saw the Tigers' right fielder win a batting title and the first of several Gold Glove awards.*

tough go of it at first in Detroit. Somebody asked acidic *Detroit News* sports columnist Doc Greene what he thought of the pro game. "If they held the NBA championship in my backyard," he replied, "I wouldn't lift the window shade." Actually, until moving to Cobo Arena in 1961, the team played games at Olympia Stadium and the University of Detroit. Reflecting the league's low-rent status, in 1960 the Pistons even suited up for a playoff game at the Grosse Pointe High School gym.

While in Fort Wayne, Zollner's Pistons had often been a contending team. However, the move to a larger media market did not ensure success. For years they were the joke of the league. From the late 1950s through the 1960s, the team posted losing records with eight different coaches. Despite their futility, the early Pistons did have some solid performers, like George Yardley, Gene Shue, Bailey Howell, Walter Dukes, and Dick McGuire. Coming along later were the University of Detroit's Dave DeBusschere, who at age 24 was named player-coach, Dave Bing, the 1966 Rookie of the Year, and big Bob Lanier, whose size 22 sneakers had fans shaking their heads in disbelief.

About this time, Al Kaline was also shaking his head. Entering his 16th season as a Tiger in 1968, the 33-year-old right fielder wondered if he would ever play in a World Series. The 1950s and 1960s had been frustrating years for Tiger followers. The previous year, the Tigers had lost the four-way chase for a pennant on the last day of the season, prompting fans to practically dismantle Tiger Stadium in their frustration.

But 1968 would be the Year of the Tiger, a healing force for a city still reeling from the previous summer's riot. For the first time, a Detroit pennant winner fielded an integrated lineup, as black stars Willie Horton, Gates Brown, and Earl Wilson all made huge contributions. "I knew that what we were doing was special," said Brown, the game's most devastating pinch-hitter. "But I never realized how special it was until I went into the neighborhoods and heard people talking Tigers nonstop. None of that other stuff mattered, at least for the time being."

Denny McLain, a flaky fastballer, became baseball's first 30-game winner since Dizzy Dean. The supporting cast of Norm Cash, Mickey Lolich, Jim Northrup, et al. helped grab the team's first pennant in 23 years. Forty times that summer the Tigers came back to win a game when trailing or tied in the seventh inning or later. Their uncanny ability to come from behind continued into the World Series against St. Louis.

With the Tigers down three games to one, and losing 3-2 in the seventh inning of the fifth game at Tiger Stadium, the powerful Cardinals were close to capturing their third championship in five years. In storybook fashion, Kaline came to the plate with the bases loaded for the most important at-bat of his storied career. Injured during the season, the man who had in 1955 become the youngest player ever to win the batting title returned to find the Tigers' outfield in capable hands. Manager Mayo Smith solved the dilemma by shifting center fielder Mickey Stanley to shortstop, a position he had never played.

The gamble paid off. Kaline lined a clutch single over second base, scoring the tying and go-ahead runs. The Series returned to St. Louis, where the back-from-the-dead Tigers took games six and seven. When the pot-bellied Lolich, who won all three of his starts, was lifted off the ground by Bill Freehan after the final out, a spontaneous celebration exploded in downtown Detroit.

The 1970s were an absolutely dismal decade for Detroit sports, as all four major franchises were perennial bottom feeders. However, the Tigers did hire former Cincinnati manager Sparky Anderson in 1979. The white-haired, craggy-faced skipper brashly predicted a championship in five years. His trademark optimism was based on a clubhouse of homegrown talent. Although never a terribly accurate prognosticator, this time the former used-car salesman was right on the money.

The '84 Tigers were not anything like the '68 edition, which had a penchant for winning in the late innings. Sparky's boys blew the opposition out in the first inning. Their strength was up the middle: Lance Parrish behind the plate, Jack Morris on the mound, Cy Young and MVP Winner Willie Hernandez in relief, and what became the longest-running double-play combination in the game's history, shortstop Alan Trammell and second-sacker Lou Whitaker, joined at the hip from 1977 to 1995. The team posted

⋎ *Detroiters take to the downtown streets to celebrate the Tigers' seventh-game victory over the Cardinals in the 1968 World Series. The jubilation helped erase, at least temporarily, the pain from the previous summer's riot.*

an unprecedented 35-5 start, then swept Kansas City in the playoffs. Attendance soared at Tiger Stadium to an all-time high of 2.7 million, with fans doing "the wave" all season.

The streaking Tigers took the World Series against San Diego in five games— their first championship won on home turf since Cochrane crossed the plate half a century earlier. Although Trammell was the Series MVP, the image of a wild Kirk Gibson leaping into the air after his home run sealed the Series remains encased in many a fan's mind.

The Pistons were next to deliver a championship. Like the Red Wings, the drafting of a superstar signaled better things ahead. The Pistons hit the jackpot in the 1981 draft when they selected Isiah Thomas, the multi-talented guard from Indiana University. Within two years Coach Chuck Daly and center Bill Laimbeer arrived on the scene, and with the acquisition of guard Joe Dumars in the 1985 draft, new owner Bill Davidson had secured the triumvirate that anchored two championship teams.

▲ Tigers pitcher Mark "The Bird" Fidrych won over fans in Detroit and the rest of the country with his boyish enthusiasm and peerless pitching during the summer of 1976.

▼ Shortstop Alan Trammell (doffing his batting helmet) and second baseman Lou Whitaker were the cornerstone of the Tigers' 1984 world champions and the longest-running double-play partners in baseball history.

◄ Mike and Marian Ilitch were heralded as civic saviors when they bought the Tigers in 1992. Among the Ilitch family's other sports and entertainment properties are the Fox Theatre, the Detroit Red Wings and Second City.

∧ *Isiah Thomas averaged 19 points a game during his 13 seasons in Detroit, many of them of the clutch variety. The Pistons' guard—one of the most tenacious athletes ever to grace the hardwood—escaped the Chicago ghetto to lead the Pistons to their only two NBA titles in 1989 and '90. He later was named a member of the league's 50th anniversary team.*

With the additions of rebounder extraordinaire Dennis Rodman, hot-shooting guard Vinnie "Microwave" Johnson, and forwards Rick Mahorn and John Salley, the Pistons became one of the dominant teams in the late '80s. The "Bad Boys," a moniker inspired by their rough-and-tumble play, made five straight trips to the Eastern Conference Finals, engaging in some memorable postseason duels with Larry Bird's Boston Celtics. After losing in the seventh game of the 1987–88 finals to Los Angeles, as Thomas played on a badly sprained ankle, the Pistons exacted revenge the following year in their new home, the Palace of Auburn Hills.

Thomas and former Michigan State star Magic Johnson continued their rather odd custom of pecking each other on the cheek before each game, but in the '88–'89 finals, the Pistons swept the injury-plagued Lakers for their first world championship. The following season the Bad Boys beat the Portland Trailblazers in five games for the championship when Vinnie "Microwave" Johnson hit the winning jumper with :007 left on the clock.

Since that game, it has been downhill for the Pistons. Chuck Daly left in 1992, his team no longer focused, as Michael Jordan and the Chicago Bulls began their domination of basketball in the '90s.

The Red Wings own the city's last two championships. In 1982, owner Bruce Norris ended his family's 50-year association with the club by selling it to pizza magnate Mike Ilitch. In his first season as owner, the hapless Wings finished last for the fifth straight year. But the following

⋏ *The Detroit Grand Prix first roared into town in 1982, the Formula One drivers tearing up downtown streets every July until 1989, when the race switched over to CART's Indy-style cars. Three years later the Grand Prix was moved to a temporary course on Belle Isle, though complaints over the track, parking and access to the island left the event's future in doubt after the 2001 race.*

◄ *Brendan Shanahan is mobbed by teammates after his overtime goal completed the Red Wings' sweep of the Anaheim Mighty Ducks in the 1997 playoffs. Detroit has been hockey's winningest team since Scotty Bowman became head coach in 1993.*

◄ *Opposite page: The expansion of professional sports since the 1960s has included a variety of "boutique" leagues, such as indoor soccer, professional softball, women's basketball, and arena football. All have fielded teams in Detroit, universally recognized by promoters, players, reporters, and fans as one of the country's truly great sports markets.*

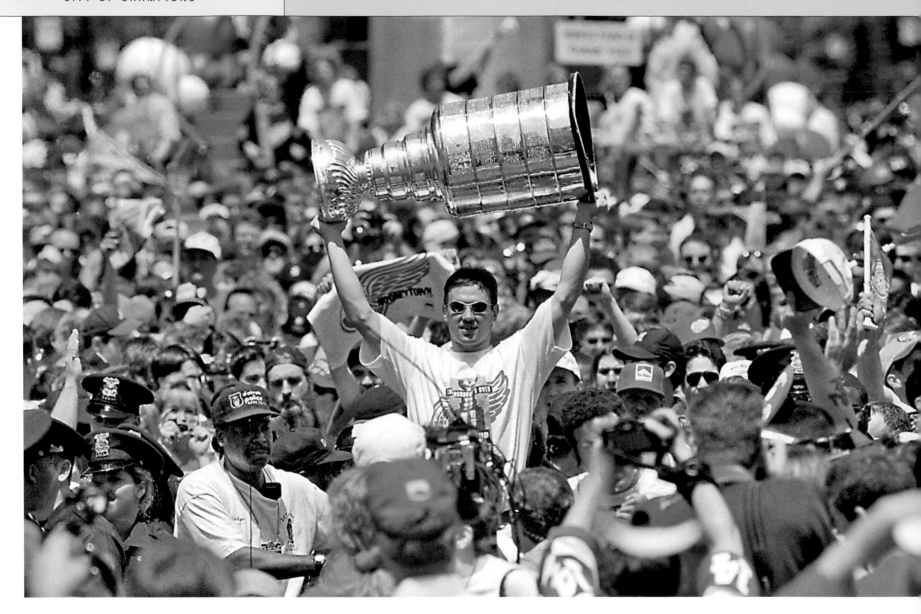

▲ *Afloat in a sea of worshippers, Red Wings captain Steve Yzerman hoists the Stanley Cup in a massive downtown parade celebrating the Wings' 1997 Cup victory.*

➤ *Opposite page: Darren McCarty, who minutes earlier had scored the deciding goal in the Red Wings' 2-1 victory to complete a four-game sweep of Philadelphia in the 1997 Stanley Cup finals, dances around the Joe Louis Arena ice with the spoils of victory. It ended a 42-year championship drought for Wings' fans.*

season hope arrived in the form of 18-year-old center Steve Yzerman. The quiet rookie's 87 points heralded a renaissance in Detroit hockey. The city would become known as "Hockeytown," but it wasn't until legendary coach Scotty Bowman arrived on the scene in 1993 that the Wings were legitimate contenders.

After the Wings were swept in the 1995 Cup finals by New Jersey, the players finally bought into the Bowman system. As a result, players like the high-scoring Yzerman adjusted their game to become more defensive-minded. During the '95–'96 campaign, the Wings set an NHL record for the most wins during the regular season with 62. However, the tough-minded Colorado Avalanche, led by Claude Lemieux, who put Kris Draper in the hospital with a vicious and controversial board check, prevailed in the Western Conference finals.

The following season the Wings beefed up their game by acquiring power forward Brendan Shanahan. An all-out brawl with the Avs during the regular season avenged the playoff hit on Draper and provided the spark plug that rallied the team toward their ultimate goal. With veteran Mike Vernon in net and the "Russian Five" of forwards Igor Larionov, Sergei Federov, Slava Koslov, and blueliners Vladimir Konstantinov and Slava Fetisov skating circles around opponents, the Wings were running on all cylinders. They easily swept the Philadelphia Flyers for their first Cup since 1955. The victory parade that followed had hundreds of thousands of long-suffering Wings fans lining Woodward Avenue. Many had skipped work to be in on the love-fest. "Sorry, boss," read one truant's sign. "I've got Stanley Cup fever."

Tragedy followed triumph. Three days later, the popular Konstantinov and trainer Sergei Mnatskanov were left permanently disabled when the limousine they were riding in slammed into a tree in Birmingham. A pall fell over what just a few days earlier had been an exuberant community. Grim but inspired, the Wings swept through the season, blowing out Washington in the finals. Afterward, Konstantinov was wheeled to center ice, where Yzerman presented him with the Stanley Cup.

In the tumult that followed, assistant coach Dave Lewis took time to suggest that this band of brothers had more than persevered, it had gained perspective. "Everybody on this team looks at things totally different now. That late goal against St. Louis? That's not devastating. A tough loss to Dallas? That's not devastating. We know what devastating is."

⅄ / ➤ *From Tommy Burns to Thomas Hearns, Detroit has produced its share of notable prizefighters. Burns held the heavyweight belt for two years until losing a title fight to the controversial black fighter, Jack Johnson, in 1908. Hearns, under the tutelage of legendary Kronk gym trainer and manager Emanuel Steward, won seven titles in six different weight divisions ranging from 145 to 190 pounds. His bouts with Sugar Ray Leonard and Marvin Hagler during the 1980s are considered ring classics.*

From Tommy Burns to Thomas Hearns, ring champions separated by nearly a century, Detroit has always enjoyed a reputation as a great fight town. Burns, a Canadian who changed his name from Noah Brusso in tribute to his manager, downtown saloonkeeper Jim Burns, was the heavyweight champion before Jack Johnson took the title from him in their controversial 1908 fight in Australia. The tall and gangly Hearns, who hated the "Hit Man" nickname given him during Detroit's "Murder City" era, began his 23-year career at the west side Kronk Gym. He is the only man ever to win seven titles in six different divisions, and his battles in the 1980s with Marvin Hagler and Sugar Ray Leonard are ring classics. In the fall of 2000, he turned promoter, bringing the mercurial heavyweight Mike Tyson to town. Tyson treated his first fight in Detroit almost as a pilgrimage, paying a wide-eyed visit to the former Brewster gym, where Joe Louis had gotten his start nearly 70 years earlier.

Tyson's respect was genuine. No fighter has ever packed more of a cultural wallop than Louis, one of the finest ring craftsmen ever and the greatest athlete ever to represent Detroit. He reigned as heavyweight champ from 1937 to 1949, and ultimately retired in 1951 with a record of 68 wins in 71 fights, including 54 knockouts. But it was the nature of Louis' fights that made him an icon. When he fought the Italian giant, Primo Carnera, Mussolini's fascists had invaded tiny Ethiopia. When he fought German nemesis Max Schmeling, Americans were already mentally preparing themselves for a showdown with Hitler's Nazis. During World War II, he fought numerous exhibitions and donated his entire purses from two title fights to servicemen's relief funds. All Americans, but especially blacks, lived vicariously through his ring battles.

The poet Maya Angelou described a scene from the '30s, when a group of blacks gathered around a radio in her uncle's store to listen to Louis defend his title against one of his white opponents:

"He's got Louis against the ropes and now it's a left to the body and a right to the ribs. . . . It's another left to the body and it looks like Louis is going down."

My race groaned. It was our people falling. It was another lynching, yet another Black man hanging on a tree. . . .

This might be the end of the world. If Joe lost we were back in slavery and beyond help. It would all be true, the accusations that we were lower types of human beings. . . .

"And now it looks like Joe is mad. . . . Louis is penetrating every block. The referee is moving in. . . ."

Champion of the world. A Black boy. Some Black mother's son. He was the strongest man in the world. . . .

It would take an hour or more before the people would leave the Store and head for home. Those who lived too far had made arrangements to stay in town. It wouldn't do for a Black man to be caught on a lonely country road when Joe Louis had proved that we were the strongest people in the world.

▼ *Powerboat racing has been a staple on the Detroit River since 1916, when a boat named Miss Minneapolis beat Miss Detroit—driven by pioneer racer Gar Wood — to capture the Gold Cup. Today's hydroplanes routinely record winning speeds in the 140-to-150-mph range, making heroes out of such racers as Bill Muncey and Chip Hanauer. Death is never far away; since 1962, three drivers have died challenging the three-mile oval course west of the Belle Isle bridge.*

Detroit sportswriter Harry Salsinger once assessed Louis's impact. "Louis did for boxing what Babe Ruth did for baseball, only more so. Joe came into the fight game when it was controlled by the survivors of the bootleg wars. Fixed bouts were the order of the day. Boxing had reached its lowest level, and Louis pulled the game out of the gutter. Louis set a standard for ring conduct and boxing decency. He came closer to being the perfect champion than any man before him. He always did the right thing, instinctively and not by design."

Throughout his career, the man who columnist Jimmy Cannon immortalized as "a credit to his race—the human race," inspired songs, books, movies, paintings, and sculptures. In Detroit, an arena was named after him, and a giant replica of his fist was installed at the corner of Woodward and Jefferson avenues. *Sports Illustrated*, in conjunction with the Detroit Institute of Arts, annually presents the Joe Louis Award to a member of the local sports community.

Since Louis died, the honors have slowed but never really stopped coming. A few years ago, the U.S. Postal Service released a first-class stamp recognizing the fabled Brown Bomber. It was issued before self-adhesive stamps became the norm, giving millions of ordinary Americans the opportunity to do what so many fighters couldn't—lick Joe Louis.

➤ *The heavyweight champion of the world is surrounded by young admirers in Chicago in the early 1940s. "Louis set a standard for ring conduct and boxing decency," declared Detroit sportswriter Harry Salsinger. "He came closer to being the perfect champion than any man before him."*

HEAVYWEIGHT
1937 · 1949
CHAMPION

JOE LOUIS

The Brown Bomber: No Ordinary Joe

Shortly after 10 p.m. on June 22, 1938, heavyweight champion Joe Louis shot from his corner inside muggy Yankee Stadium and, with a pistonlike flurry of punches, knocked German challenger Max Schmeling halfway into 1939.

The first-round knockout not only avenged Louis's sole professional defeat, it literally silenced claims of Aryan supremacy. For citizens of Nazi Germany, who had stayed up until 3 a.m. to listen to the shortwave radio broadcast of the fight, the transmission was abruptly cut short by a mysterious power outage after Louis landed his first punches.

Electricity crackled throughout America that night, however. Blacks and whites alike poured out onto streets and sidewalks to celebrate America's triumph in what had been promoted as a showdown between democracy and fascism.

In Detroit, thousands flooded the black entertainment district of Paradise Valley—hollering, passing drinks, and listening to a local band play a single tune, "Flat Foot Floogie." Above the tumult waved a banner: "Joe Louis Knocked Out Hitler."

"The reaction was just like winning a World Series," recalled Freddie Guinyard. "It was something for people to be proud of. And not only blacks. It was like when Jackie Robinson was with the Dodgers. A lot of whites didn't want Robinson in baseball, but he was so wonderful everyone cheered for him."

Guinyard knew Detroit's fabled "Brown Bomber" from schoolyard to ringside. While his duties officially were those of traveling secretary to the champ, Louis liked to claim that he learned the meaning of the word "manager" from Guinyard when they worked as youngsters on an ice truck in the 1920s.

"Freddie would holler 'ice,'" Louis recalled, "and I'd deliver it."

If the two could have looked through those 50-pound blocks of ice into the future, they would have been amazed by the view. The shy, oversized kid in short pants and skullcap named Joe Louis Barrow would emerge as one of the greatest heavyweight boxers in history. His first-round knockdown of Max Schmeling—arguably the greatest single moment in ring history—would transform him into an American icon.

Through it all, his best friend would remain short, willowy Freddie Guinyard. "For all his skinny self, he was tough and slick," Louis reflected once. "We made a good team."

"We'd meet and play every evening on the playground at the Duffield Elementary School," Guinyard recalled one morning inside his modest Detroit home, not far from the eastside neighborhood where he and Louis grew up.

The two youths, born three months apart in 1914, shared similar backgrounds. Both came up from the south—Louis as a 13-year-old from Alabama, Guinyard as a 9-year-old from South Carolina. Both had parents who, despite poverty, demanded a certain code of behavior from their children, including music lessons and regular churchgoing.

"Occasionally, Joe and I would help ourselves to some fruit at Eastern Market," said Guinyard, recalling some ancient mischief. "Our parents didn't approve of that. We'd have to eat all that fruit before we came home. If they caught us with a banana, they'd ask, 'Did you work for that?'

"I'd think, *Yeah, we worked for it. We had to run like hell.*"

Λ *In 1988, Freddie Guinyard held the bronzed right-handed glove his childhood buddy used to knock out Max Schmeling 50 years earlier.*

➤ *Opposite page: The Brown Bomber impassively watches another opponent hit the canvas. Louis was the heavyweight champion longer than anyone else —12 years, from 1937 to 1949. His 68-3 record included 54 knockouts.*

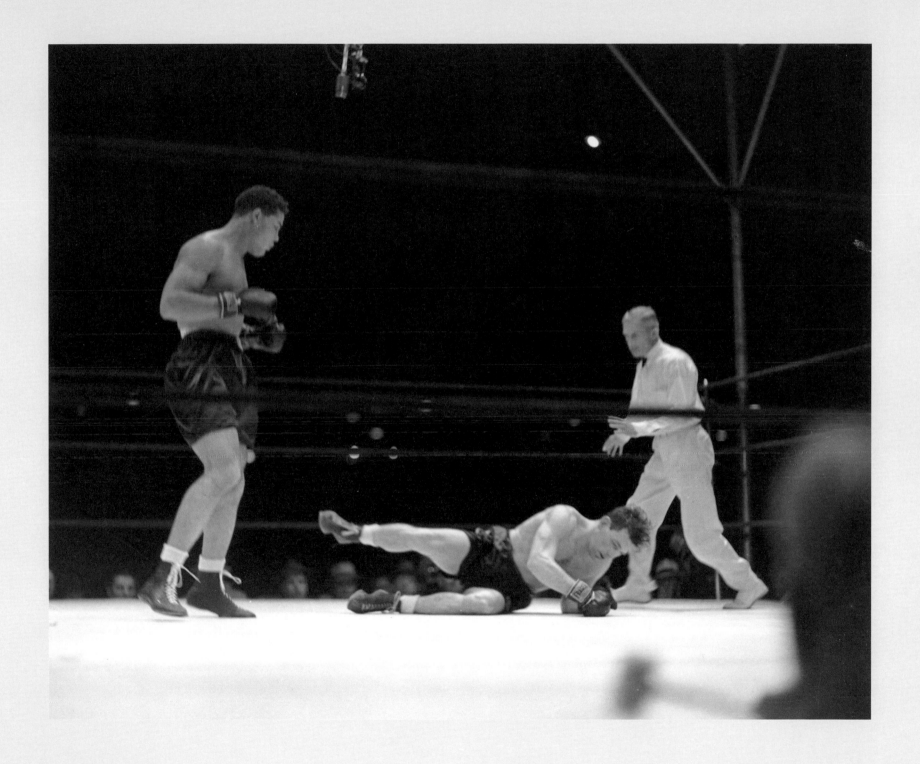

Guinyard remembers Louis as an even-tempered sort who was content to follow, rather than lead, others into minor trouble. It was while he was on his way to his weekly violin lesson that the fate of the young Louis was waylaid by a neighborhood acquaintance.

"Joe's mother used to give him 50 cents for the lesson at a music school," Guinyard recalled. "Thurston McKinney, a friend of ours, used to say, 'Give me the 50 cents and we'll go over to Brewster Center and get some boxing lessons. Forget that music.'"

According to Guinyard, Louis's mother didn't discover that her son was a fighter until his picture was in the paper after he won the amateur Golden Gloves championship in 1933. "His sisters knew it, though. One sister didn't have enough room to sew his entire name on the back of his warm-up sweater, 'Joseph L. Barrow.' So she used an old family name, 'Joe Louis,' and it stuck."

After turning pro in 1934, Louis won his first 27 money fights until Schmeling, a 10-to-1 underdog, administered a fearful beating on June 19, 1936, in a nontitle bout. After Louis was knocked out in the 12th round, Guinyard had to drag Louis's mother, crying and hysterical, from the stadium.

"She never went to another fight," he said. "She never wanted him to be a boxer. After Joe would win a fight, ring announcer Harry Balough would bring a microphone over to him and say, 'What have you got to say, Joe?' He'd say, 'Hello, mom. I had another lucky night.'"

Guinyard shook his head wryly.

"Joe called it luck, but you couldn't tell it by the guy laying on the floor."

Adolf Hitler stamped a swastika on Schmeling's unexpected victory, using it as "proof" of the Nazi party's "master race" theory. President Franklin D. Roosevelt responded by feeling Louis's biceps one day in the White House and declaring them "the kind of muscles we need to defeat Germany."

If the irony of being a symbol of freedom in a segregated America ever bothered Louis, he never let on. He was more concerned with becoming heavyweight champion and then facing Schmeling again. Louis defeated James Braddock on June 22, 1937 to win the heavyweight crown, then stepped into the ring exactly one year later for his rematch with Schmeling. By then, world events had elevated the fight into a symbolic prelude to World War II.

"People with smart remarks is what really got Schmeling whipped," said Guinyard, who was in his usual spot—ringside, kneeling next to a water bucket—for Louis-Schmeling II. "For two years, Joe'd be in a crowd and someone would yell out, 'Look out, Joe, here comes Schmeling!' I'd notice Joe acting kind of sulky afterwards."

With 72,000 people packed into Yankee Stadium and millions more huddled around radios, Louis took only two minutes and four seconds to destroy the 32-year-old German.

"Joe didn't say a word," marveled Guinyard. "He just jumped off the stool. Schmeling got hit in the ribs and hollered like a pig."

The ferocity of the attack shocked observers. The 24-year-old Louis landed an estimated 50 punches and knocked Schmeling down four times before Schmeling's handlers threw a towel into the ring. The battered boxer was taken to New York's Polyclinic Hospital, where he was treated for two broken bones in his back and hemorrhaging of his lumbar muscles.

Years later, Guinyard asked Louis, "Why'd you knock him out so fast for? You should've given the crowd a chance to see the fight."

The typically deadpanned Louis replied: "I wanted to get it over with."

Characteristically, Louis never professed any personal hatred of Schmeling. In fact, his generosity of spirit cost him dearly. When he retired in 1949 after successfully defending his heavyweight crown for an unprecedented 12 years, he had already lost most of his prizefight winnings through bad investments and misplaced faith.

Louis came out of retirement in an attempt to pay back taxes and lost his title to Ezzard Charles. In 1951, Rocky Marciano ended Louis's comeback with a resounding knockout, then cried afterward. Like countless other impoverished youths, Marciano had grown up with the modest Brown Bomber from Detroit as his hero.

"After Marciano retired Joe, he went into wrestling," said Guinyard. "We pleaded, 'Please, Joe, don't.' It was beneath his dignity. Later he went into promotions at Caesar's Palace. He made a nice salary and met a lot of people. I didn't go with him. Maybe I should have."

Guinyard stayed in Detroit, and from then on saw Louis infrequently. He was a pallbearer

◄ *Joe Louis, fresh from a victory over Max baer, returns to Black Bottom in the fall of 1935.*

◄ *Opposite page: Louis was more than Detroit's greatest athlete, a hero to black Americans, and boxing's brightest star. He was a cultural icon, his name and face appearing on everything from tins of hair pomade to bottles of soda pop.*

when his playground buddy, reduced by strokes to a figurehead on the Vegas strip, died in 1981.

"There's more in this little room than there is in most libraries," said Guinyard, leading the conversation into a sunroom wallpapered with boxing memorabilia. One wall has a poster-sized photograph of him and Louis, circa 1938. The men are looking sharp in suits and snap-brim hats. "Twenty-five dollars for that suit," he noted. "And that included two pairs of britches, Jack."

Guinyard proudly produced several relics: the champ's trunks, his shoes, and—the true cross—the six-ounce, right-handed glove used to floor Schmeling.

Given the impact of Joe Louis in and out of the ring, it's entirely appropriate that the glove is bronzed. While Louis never was comfortable being used as a role model for the burgeoning civil rights movement, his boxing success in the 1930s and 1940s made an indelible impression on a society increasingly enamored with sports and its heroes. At a time when southern blacks weren't allowed to vote or attend schools with whites, America could

not ignore the quiet dignity and extraordinary skills of its most famous athlete.

Seated at the dining room table, Guinyard pored over a scrapbook's yellowed pages. "My mother was a domestic," he said softly, flipping through the years. "She was not an educated woman, but she was intelligent. I was young and simple and wanted to know why certain things had to be the way they were. She told me to be patient, that things would change. That's what I preach today to my nieces and nephews.

"Sports did a lot to break the segregation barrier. That's why Joe was so important. Blacks had to be noticed there before we could have a lot of other things."

Like any man, Joe Louis had flaws. Freddie Guinyard understood that better than anyone. But those looking to dig up dirt on the champ soon learned to take their shovels elsewhere.

"No, Joe made it possible for me to make a fairly decent living," he said. "And I appreciate that."

THE GREAT DIVIDE

The Second World War brought a wide range of changes to Detroit, which had fitfully been trying to lift itself out of the Great Depression. On December 7, 1941, Leona Demps Rostkowski was celebrating her seventeenth birthday a day late with friends when word of the Japanese attack on Pearl Harbor came over the radio. "None of us really knew where Pearl Harbor was," the longtime Detroiter reflected. "All it meant to us was one thing—war. Before that day we had never thought of anything like that."

Ben Marsh Jr. was a 25 year old ensign stationed aboard the U.S.S. *Arizona* when Pearl Harbor was attacked. Five days later, his family in Grosse Pointe was informed by telegram that he had died when the battleship exploded and sank. The tragedy made Marsh the first Metro Detroiter to die in a war that would claim the lives of many more area residents before the fighting finally ended four years later.

For those Detroiters fortunate enough to stay out of uniform, the two-front struggle against Japan and Germany proved to be an economic godsend. Auto plants quickly were converted to the production of war goods. By the beginning of 1944, Detroit area industries had been awarded $14 billion in defense contracts—more than anywhere else in the country. The giant Willow Run plant, built about 20 miles west of the city, churned out 8,500 bombers, while the Chrysler Tank Arsenal produced 25,000 tanks. Rostkowski was one of an estimated 610,000 workers employed in area factories.

◄ / ► *Rubble and rifles: the '67 riot.*

➤ *During World War II, Detroit's factories switched from producing cars to manufacturing tanks, airplanes and munitions, gaining the Motor City a new sobriquet: "the arsenal of democracy." Here Ford workers are building Patton tanks.*

∨ *At its peak in 1943, the Willow Run bomber plant employed 44,000 workers, a quarter of whom were women.*

"I got a job working at Lincoln's over on Livernois and Warren," she said. "They switched over from car parts to defense work, so I wound up spot-welding pieces of airplane metal together. There was nothing, really, to my job. Just work this machine with a foot pedal. I wasn't mechanically inclined at all before I got the job. I'd been working in a bakery.

"There were mostly women working in the plants, because most of the men were in the service. The women got paid the same as the men who were working in the plant. I ended up making $1.25 an hour. I was working the afternoon shift, six days a week with Sundays off. They were working 'round the clock, three shifts, seven days a week. So you'd work 48-hour weeks, with one day off a week, but that day varied. I got laid off just prior to the war ending, because they had such a backlog of parts. But the defense work sure helped the economy.

"We had all sorts of things going on back then. People would plant victory gardens, and there were shortages of tires and silk stockings. You had rationing of just about everything—shoes, cheese, butter, meat—but people didn't complain. You got by. A lot of times you forgot there was a war on."

In the first two years of the war, an estimated 350,000 people moved to Detroit to take advantage of the high wages in the defense plants. Fifty thousand of them were black; several times that number were Appalachian whites. The flood of newcomers exacerbated racial tensions that had been percolating for several years. The overcrowded conditions, lack of adequate housing, and the combustible mixing of the races on the shop floor led to fights, violent demonstrations, and labor walkouts. *Life* magazine wrote of the growing unrest: "Detroit can either blow up Hitler or it can blow up the U.S."

On the evening of June 20, 1943, a muggy Sunday, the tinderbox exploded. A fistfight between white sailors and black teenagers on Belle Isle spilled over onto the bridge to the mainland. An apocryphal story spread through Paradise Valley that a black woman and her baby had been thrown off the bridge, provoking attacks on whites by blacks. Whites responded in kind. By Monday morning, businesses were being torched, cars overturned, and unwary members of both races brutally attacked, some fatally.

"The 1943 riot was a *race* riot," emphasized Fred Williams, a retired police officer who remembers watching whites stone the streetcars. "In 1967, the riot was just blacks and whites looting. In 1943, blacks and whites were at each other's throats."

Sam Mitchell, a black combat veteran of the First World War, was riding a Woodward Avenue streetcar when several whites smashed their way through the door with a crowbar, shouting, "Are there any niggers in there?" As Mitchell fled from the trolley, he was struck in the side by three bullets. He staggered toward some police officers, who pulled him into the middle of the street. "I begged them not to let the rioters attack me," said Mitchell. "While they held me by both arms, nine or ten men walked out of the crowd and struck me hard blows. Men kept coming up to me and beating me, and the policemen did nothing to prevent it."

Martial law was declared and 5,000 federal troops were rushed in to restore

⋏ *Salvaging and rationing were integral parts of life on the home front during World War II. This salvager is collecting old tires for their scrap rubber.*

➤ *Pages 268-269: The NAACP held an emergency meeting in Detroit in 1943 to address racial tensions at the Packard plant. Two weeks later the city erupted.*

◄ A black youth is beaten as he tries to make his way through a crowd of whites during the '43 riot. Later, Detroit's overwhelmingly white police force was criticized for brutalizing black citizens. Twenty-five of the riot's 34 victims were African-American; many had been shot in the back.

◄ Opposite page: A streetcar burns on Woodward during the 1943 riot.

order. By the end of nearly three days of violence, 34 people had been killed. Twenty-five of those were blacks, 17 of whom were victims of the nearly all-white police force. Several had been shot in the back. Mayor Edward J. Jeffries empaneled an Interracial Committee that concluded what had long been obvious, at least to black citizens: Housing for Detroit's Negroes was inadequate and public transportation was overcrowded. Despite the emergence of a strong black middle class, conditions would improve only marginally over the next two decades.

Arthur Bray, an employee of the British Consulate during the war, marveled over the city's resilience in the wake of what was one of the deadliest civil disturbances in the nation's history. "If it were a normal town," he wrote, "the various types of social disturbance which are so obvious would spell its decay and ruin in the first month after the war. But this is not called Dynamic Detroit for nothing. Few towns have had such a growth, from 250,000 population at the turn of the century to some two million now."

⋏ *Mobilized federal troops roll into Detroit to help quell the 1943 race riot.*

➤ *Kapsen's Shoe Store was one of hundreds of businesses looted during the violence. Property damage was estimated at $2 million.*

Detroit reached its pinnacle in both prosperity and population during the 1950s. More cars than ever rolled off the assembly line, and for a time it seemed that anybody who wanted a job needed only to fill out an application at any local factory before starting work that day. Reflecting the optimism and affluence of the period, carmakers designed powerful gas-guzzlers featuring outlandish tailfins and a nearly obscene amount of chrome.

However, the postwar prosperity shielded serious societal problems. The rush toward open spaces north and west of the city was well under way. The migration had actually started in the 1920s, but was slowed for nearly two decades by the Depression and war. Although urban renewal and the striking down of illegal housing covenants allowed blacks to break out of their east side ghetto and enter into traditionally white neighborhoods after the war, it was prosperity, not racism, that initially fueled white Detroiters' flight to suburbia.

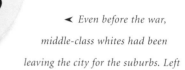

◄ *Even before the war, middle-class whites had been leaving the city for the suburbs. Left behind was a crumbling urban core, increasingly populated by blacks whose efforts to secure better housing were frequently sabotaged by realtors and mortgage lenders. Orville Hubbard, who served as Dearborn's mayor for 36 years, publicly advocated segregation.*

◄ *The war exacerbated the already severe housing problem in metro Detroit, with an estimated 300,000 newcomers pouring into the tri-country area between 1940 and 1943. While many workers and their families were squeezed into trailer parks, tent cities and public housing, Detroiters who could afford it continued to buy into subdivisions carved out of cornfields.*

The Mother of the Civil Rights Movement

Not only has Detroit had its share of civil rights pioneers, for nearly a half-century it has been home to one of the freedom movement's greatest symbols—a seamstress whose refusal to give up her seat on an Alabama bus sparked the Montgomery Bus Boycott, a seminal event in civil rights history.

On December 1, 1955, 42-year-old Rosa Parks of Montgomery, Alabama, was riding home from her job on a city bus when the driver ordered her to give up her seat to a white man. When she refused, she was arrested and fined $10 for failing to comply with the city's racial segregation ordinances. This ignited a 382-day boycott by local blacks that thrust a young pastor named Martin Luther King Jr. into national prominence. The nonviolent protest led to a U.S. Supreme Court decision desegregating public transportation and created for Parks the title of "mother of the civil rights movement."

However, in 1957 continual harassment forced Parks, her husband, and her mother to move to Detroit, where her brother, Sylvester, had been living for several years. They settled into an apartment on Euclid Street and Parks resumed her job as a seamstress. Although her active participation in the growing civil rights movement of the 1960s was minimal, she remained a potent symbol. In 1965 she was hired as an assistant in the office of U.S. Representative John Conyers, a position she held until 1988. Since that time Parks has received numerous awards, including 43 honorary doctorates and the 1996 Medal of Freedom from President Bill Clinton. In 1975, Detroit's 12th Street was renamed Rosa Parks Boulevard in her honor.

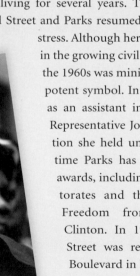

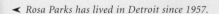
◄ *Rosa Parks has lived in Detroit since 1957.*

Unlike other major cities, where workers lived in high-rise flats and tenement buildings, Detroit had always been a city of single-family homes. Suburban sprawl was inevitable as Detroit households—most headed by someone drawing union wages from the flourishing postwar auto industry—continued their quest for bigger houses with attached garages and spacious backyards. Subdivisions, factories, schools, churches, office buildings, and bowling alleys sprang up in the meadows and cornfields ringing the city. Meanwhile, Detroit's population peaked at nearly two million in the early 1950s, then began its long, slow slide.

Angie Mattera of Sterling Heights is just one of hundreds of thousands of suburbanites who have an "old neighborhood" in their past. In this case, it was a street bounded by Forest and Canfield and within walking distance of St. Catherine Church and Eastern High School. Her father, Pasquale Battaglia, the first of three brothers to immigrate from Italy, moved onto the block in 1934.

"At the time, Dad lived with an aunt and uncle, sleeping in a small utility room off the kitchen of their upstairs flat," Mattera said. "His aunt was so miserly, he would tell us, that she would make chicken soup by tying a live chicken over a boiling kettle so it could sweat into the water."

In time Pasquale found a job, a wife, and a house, all in the neighborhood.

"Our family moved in 1956," continued Mattera. "The neighborhood exodus began slowly and then picked up speed. We were the fourth family to move to the suburbs. My grandparents stayed, and a few others refused to move. Eventually everyone was gone, one way or the other. Today, there is an empty lot where our house once stood."

◄ In the early 1940s, a half-mile-long "wailing wall" was erected near Mendota and Eight Mile Road to separate a black neighborhood from a newly built white subdivision.

In keeping with the Motor City's new-model syndrome, this migration to greener pastures was viewed as progress. However, the larger picture wasn't yet apparent. In 1954, for example, the J.L. Hudson Company opened Northland, the country's first suburban mall, on 161 acres of land in Southfield. Not coincidentally, that year the company's flagship store—a downtown fixture since horse and buggy days—posted its first annual loss. The Woodward Avenue store would never again finish in the black and would finally close in 1983, yet another victim of Detroit's changing socioeconomic climate.

One of the chief destabilizing factors was the freeway system, which carved up 19th-century neighborhoods in an ambitious attempt to provide expeditious access to and from the core city. In July 1951, a two-mile section of the Edsel Ford Expressway running from the western city limits east to Livernois opened to traffic. The *Detroit News*, which called it the "most modern and most costly highway in the world," determined that commuters saved three minutes and missed eight traffic lights by not traveling on adjacent Michigan Avenue. By the end of the decade the Lodge and Fisher freeways were feeding the ever-widening web of interstate highways.

Instead of tying the suburbs to downtown, however, these concrete conduits

Detroit's Changing Population

Year	Population	U.S. Rank	% Foreign Born	% Black
1701	100	–	–	–
1773	1,357	–	–	–
1778	2,144	–	–	–
1780	2,207	–	–	–
1783	2,291	–	–	–
1796	500	–	–	–
1810	1,650	–	–	–
1820	1,442	–	–	4.9
1830	2,222	35	–	5.6
1840	9,102	25	–	2.1
1850	21,019	23	47.7	2.8
1860	45,619	18	–	3.0
1870	79,577	17	–	2.8
1880	116,340	17	44.4	2.4
1890	205,876	14	–	1.7
1900	285,704	13	33.7	1.4
1910	465,766	9	33.5	1.2
1920	993,678	4	29.1	4.1
1930	1,568,662	4	26.0	7.6
1940	1,623,452	4	19.8	9.1
1950	1,849,568	5	14.9	16.1
1960	1,670,144	5	12.1	28.9
1970	1,511,482	5	7.9	44.5
1980	1,203,339	6	5.7	63.0
1990	1,027,974	9	3.4	76.0
2000	951,270	10	–	81.6

➤ *Detroit's freeway system was built in several stages between 1941 and 1989 at an aggregate cost approaching $1 billion. The Walter Reuther Freeway (I-696) alone took 30 years and $675 million to complete. The ribbons of concrete tore apart neighborhoods even as they expedited access to and from the core city.*

▼ *Ruth Regan-Spring as a tyke on Plainview Street in west Detroit, circa 1925, not long before the subdivision was completely built up and settled by white working-class families. Getting around by streetcars was common then, recalls Regan-Spring, who now lives in Redford, but by the 1950s most families in the neighborhood had one or two automobiles in their driveway.*

had the insidious effect of sucking away homeowners and businesses that could afford to leave for the greener pastures of Livonia, Lincoln Park, and Southfield. The deterioration of the already crumbling "inner city" accelerated in the late 1950s. Unemployment among blacks rose sharply as longtime automakers Hudson and Packard closed and Chrysler, the city's largest employer, slashed its workforce by more than half.

So, when a 33-year-old Irish-Catholic liberal named Jerry Cavanagh upset incumbent Louis Miriani in the 1961 mayoral election, the newcomer didn't figure to have it easy. The city's population was declining, the tax base was shrinking, the neighborhoods were deteriorating, and there was a $34-million deficit. But under President Lyndon Johnson's "Great Society" programs, the city received $42 million to fund its anti-poverty programs during the '60s. On June 23, 1963, Cavanagh linked arms with Martin Luther King Jr. as 125,000 black and white Detroiters marched peacefully down Woodward Avenue. The young preacher concluded the "Walk to Freedom" by giving his famous "I Have a Dream" speech for the first time. "That sort of thing can't happen here" was the common refrain after the Watts district of Los Angeles went up in flames in 1965. At about this time *Life* magazine touted Detroit as "the model city."

But "that sort of thing" did happen in Detroit. The immediate catalyst was a

WHEN I SEE RACISM I TALK ABOUT IT. I'VE BEEN DOING THAT ALL MY LIFE AND I HOPE I CAN STOP TALKING
ABOUT IT. YOU KNOW WHEN THAT WILL HAPPEN? WHEN I DON'T SEE ANY MORE RACISM. — *Mayor Coleman Young*

police raid on a 12th Street blind pig on June 23, 1967, but neighborhood blacks had been stewing for years over police brutality and the unofficial racist policies of city departments and area employers. The rock throwing that accompanied the raid that Sunday morning quickly blossomed into a full-scale riot that spread west to Grand River and Livernois and east to Mack Avenue. Before long paratroopers were riding DSR buses into the battle zone. The body count reached 43 before the violence was quelled. More than 2,500 stores were looted or burned and 7,231 arrests were made during what most observers described as a "rebellion." Cavanagh, devastated, decided not to seek another term.

The riot brought on seismic change in the Motor City. The gradual exodus of white families and businesses became a headlong race for the exits. In 1973, Detroit for the first time had more black than white residents. Voters elected the first black mayor, Coleman Young, a blasphemous, charismatic civil-rights firebrand who spent a contentious two decades in office. Young was an Alabama transplant who had experienced racism as a youth in Black Bottom, as a member of the Tuskegee airmen during the war, and as a union organizer at Ford. He immediately set about integrating city departments, especially the historically racist police force. Among his first reforms was abolishing the infamous STRESS (Stop the Robberies, Enjoy Safe Streets) undercover unit, which many citizens considered to be little more than an execution squad targeting young black males.

During his tenure Young watched much of the black middle class flee Detroit, leaving behind a dispiriting landscape of poverty and crime that his police chief,

◄ *White flight in the wake of the devastating '67 riot brought to power a new generation of black leaders, including longtime civil rights firebrand, Coleman Young.*

▼ *Attorney Ken Cockrel was a charismatic radical who joined the city council in 1977 and commenced shaking up the system. Among the many battles he successfully waged against Detroit's establishment was dismantling the STRESS undercover unit, which many citizens complained, unfairly targeted young black males.*

Daniel West: Detroit's Most Mysterious Politician

Everyone who knew Daniel West agreed that he was some guy. Exactly which guy, however, didn't become clear until December 5, 1964.

That snowy Saturday, news broke that the distinguished-looking 55-year-old Detroit Democrat, a man with one of the most impressive resumés in the State House of Representatives, had assumed the identity and professional credentials of a dead New York lawyer by the same name.

It was an astonishing exposé, even by the standards of big-city politics, but there was more. The laid-back legislator with the pencil mustache, who had just been elected to a second term, was charged with hiding an extensive criminal past, engaging in voter fraud, and bilking the government out of a cool $250,000 by filing bogus income tax returns. As the national media spotlight fell on Detroit, friends and fellow House members said they would suspend judgment until Representative West gave his version of events.

They're still waiting. West has been unavailable for comment for more than three decades, ever since he disappeared on the eve of his federal trial for tax fraud.

"He was a man who played many roles," said his friend and defense attorney, Peter P. Cobbs of Detroit. "He was always involved in something fascinating." This seems a charitable way of saying that his client, arguably the greatest scam artist ever to hold public office in Michigan, spent his entire adult life keeping one step ahead of the bloodhounds.

Daniel Harvey Laverne Wilson West—a name he used in various combinations, depending on where he was incarcerated—was born in 1909. Exactly where remains a mystery. On various documents he listed locations in four different states, including Detroit, as his birthplace.

He settled in Detroit sometime in the 1940s and married a local clerk, Susan Fikes, in 1953. Fikes later admitted she wasn't sure how many times he'd been married before, nor could she describe exactly what he did for a living. He worked as a bookkeeper for a couple of nursing homes ("sort of a manager," she said) before drifting into "real estate." While he may actually have managed properties, it's worth noting that numbers racketeers often used the term as a cover for their activities.

During the 1950s West became a familiar figure at local Democratic clubs. He had a quietly confident air about him that impressed people, though some privately wondered why this well-dressed Phi Beta Kappa graduate of Swarthmore College and Yale law school was running a dingy hardware store on the west side of Detroit.

"I came to doubt that he really was who he said he was," admitted Cobbs, who nonetheless enjoyed listening to West's stories about his experiences as a black attorney in the South. "But he was very cunning, a great impersonator, right down to the school rings he wore."

In 1962, those rings, along with the photo of him and John F. Kennedy that he kept in his store window (ostensibly taken at the 1960 Democratic Convention), helped get West elected to the legislature. Voters evidently were impressed by the credentials of Daniel W. West, the name that appeared on affidavits filed with election commissions. In addition to his lofty academic record, they showed that he was a retired attorney licensed to practice in New York and Tennessee and that he had held elected office in the Virgin Islands and the District of Columbia. The biography was reprinted in the 1963–64 edition of the *Michigan Manual*, the official compiler of data for all state officials.

Belying his august background, during his two years in Lansing West did little but sit tight-lipped in the back of the chambers. He didn't pal around with his colleagues. The only legislation he introduced—a bewildering, badly worded bill aimed at motorists who drove with one arm around a girl—was met with embarrassed chuckles. Civic Searchlight, a nonpartisan organization that evaluated political candidates, listed "No rating" next to West's name when he ran for reelection in 1964. This was tantamount to being called unqualified, said William O'Brien, the Detroit attorney who served as executive director.

"I interviewed West. He was a pretty sharp guy," said O'Brien. He recalled that West had once been asked in a questionnaire to describe specific improvements he would promote, if elected. The prison system needed reform, he had responded authoritatively.

It was Thomas O'Hara, an autoworker defeated by West in the '64 Democratic primary, who set West's downfall in motion. Checking voter registration cards, O'Hara discovered 14 families from outside the district who claimed to live at the same sparsely furnished apartment that West listed as his residence. When confronted by police investigators, all admitted that West had encouraged them to falsify registrations in order to vote for him.

This misdemeanor offense, to which West pled innocent when arraigned in Recorder's Court two weeks after the primary, did not affect his overwhelming victory over the Republican candidate in the November election. However, the Internal Revenue Service and Jack Carlisle, the veteran reporter of the *Detroit News*, were about to conclude investigations of their own.

For several years West had been working as a tax consultant, preparing returns for people who were encouraged to sign blank forms and let him fill in the details. He would typically file two separate forms. On one he would show the client receiving no rebate. On the other he would add fictitious dependents and other bogus deductions and have the refund check sent to his address. The IRS estimated he had swindled about 1,500 people and defrauded the government of $250,000 in phony rebate claims.

At the same time that the IRS was building its case, Carlisle, tipped off by O'Hara, was trying to resolve the discrepancies in West's biography. He found that a Daniel W. West had indeed graduated from Swarthmore and Yale. Further digging revealed that that particular West was a white attorney who had died at age 36 in Larchmont, New York, in 1961. As incredible as it seemed, Representative Daniel West, a felon whose higher education consisted of a mail-order diploma from a Chicago correspondence school, had assumed the brilliant attorney's background.

The news of West's outrageous hoaxes was a bombshell. As the national media picked up the details of the legislator's extraordinary double life, he remained unruffled and declined comment. The Monday following the revelations he was arrested by FBI agents and arraigned on 117 counts of income tax fraud. West was released three days later on a $10,000 bond. The uproar cost him none of his characteristic chutzpah. When the House, following its own investigation, refused to seat him, he filed to run in the special election to fill his vacancy.

By the time it came to cast ballots, however, Detroiters had been made aware of new details of his past, thanks to an FBI comparison of fingerprint records.

In 1928 in Minneapolis, an 18-year-old "bishop" claiming to be a descendant of Daniel Boone was sentenced to six months in prison for stealing a watch and some clothes from his "parishioners." Soon after his release, the dubious prelate was given another 18 months after pleading guilty to burglary. Having served time for two felony convictions, he was then picked up for creating a disturbance inside a whorehouse. The judge didn't buy his story that he was conducting an undercover investigation for the mayor of Minneapolis, and gave him 45 days.

The same glib fellow suddenly showed up in New York in 1935. He attached himself to Harlem's famous Father Divine and was identified in the preacher's publications as a member of the Minnesota State Legislature and the personal emissary of the governor. Over the next six years the self-described "overseer of young people of the Church of God in Christ for Minnesota, South Dakota, and Montana" was arrested for larceny in New Jersey, did time in a Virginia reformatory for housebreaking, and was sentenced to serve 15 years in the Iowa State Penitentiary for forgery.

Needless to say, these revelations were hardly a boost to West's campaign to win back his seat. He finished 15th among 17 candidates.

Meanwhile, the world was closing in. According to Fikes, after her husband was exposed "he didn't know what to do." Nobody would give him a job. He couldn't pay his lawyers. His car was repossessed. He was facing a maximum sentence of 755 years in a federal prison and $864,000 in fines. Beyond that were the misdemeanor charges for voter fraud and subornation of witness and the inevitable civil suits from the hundreds of taxpayers he had defrauded. Feeling the pressure, the normally jaunty West broke down and "cried like a baby," she said.

Then, on July 5, 1965, the day before his trial was to begin, he simply vanished. He left behind a wife and two sons.

"I don't know where he is," Fikes told the press, "but I know he's a good man. From what I know about him I'm sure he will turn himself in soon. He has everything to live for and we had everything to be happy about."

Her optimism, like the ink on the feds' fugitive warrant, gradually faded.

"He completely disappeared," Cobbs recalled. "I knew some people who knew him well, and they never heard from him again."

Authorities have always assumed West fled to Canada, a convenient refuge. Aside from its proximity, the country's extradition treaties do not cover the crimes with which he was charged, meaning he could not be forced to return to the United States to stand trial.

If alive today, West would be about 90. If dead—well, Cobbs provided an epitaph, of sorts, for the chameleonic con man, who skipped town owing him money: "Daniel West actually had great integrity," he insisted. "But he had a great imagination, too."

MID-JANUARY. "NO HOPEFUL SIGNS FOR THE ECONOMY." DETROIT IS HURTING BADLY; "AS DETROIT GOES SO GOES THE NATION." MORE AND MORE EMPTY HOUSES AND STORES, FOR LEASE AND FOR SALE SIGNS. "AS LONG AS SUPPLEMENTAL UNEMPLOYMENT BENEFITS PAY HOLDS OUT"—BUT THEN WHAT? AND TO THINK THAT TWO YEARS AGO ONE OF THE MAJOR ISSUES IN THE SHOPS WAS VOLUNTARY OVERTIME! — *Poet Lawrence Joseph, 1975*

William Hart, called "one big ghetto all the way to its borders."

Contributing mightily was the shocking evaporation of well-paying factory jobs, as automakers, buffeted by higher fuel prices and foreign competition, closed plants, laid off tens of thousands of workers, and automated as many manufacturing jobs as possible. Between 1978 and 1988, 50,000 Detroit auto workers lost their jobs.

Despite such controversial "successes" as the Renaissance Center and the General Motors Poletown plant, the city's manufacturing and retail base all but disintegrated. By 1990 the city's population of 1 million was half of what it had been in the 1950s. Three of every four Detroiters were African-American. Backed by studies that showed the metropolitan area to be the most racially segregated in the country, Young accused the prosperous suburbs that ringed the core city of intentional neglect.

"It occurs to me that people outside Detroit like to think of the metropolitan area as a doughnut," he said, "with the suburbs as the sweet meat and the city as the hole in the goddamn middle."

The national media plumbed the depths of that hole, whether touting Detroit's image as "Murder City" in the 1970s (when it had the nation's highest homicide rate) or playing up the Devil's Night debacles of the late 1980s, when fire buffs from around the world descended on Detroit to watch hundreds of houses burned up during an annual ritual of mindless arson. The community once touted as the place "Where Life is Worth Living" had become, within the space of a single generation, the kind of urban wasteland seen in Richard Roundtree movies.

The argument has been made that the city's socioeconomic deterioration was a largely inherited situation that Young exacerbated with his cronyism, paranoia, and profane, race-baiting rhetoric. For all of his faults, Young served a record 20

▲ *Henry Ford II, the auto tycoon's grandson, was the driving force behind the Renaissance Center, which opened on the riverfront in March 1977. Unfortunately for "Henry the Deuce" and his fellow well-intentioned partners, the fortresslike $337-million office-hotel-retail complex reinforced the division between races and classes in an already deeply fractionalized city.*

◄ *Opposite page: Some parts of the city were almost entirely consumed by the '67 riot.*

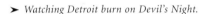

➤ *Watching Detroit burn on Devil's Night.*

▼ *The city's ongoing drug wars have produced the kind of random violence and outlandish characters that characterized prohibition. When "Maserati Rick" Carter was gunned down inside his hospital room in 1988, friends responded by laying out the 29-year-old drug kingpin in a $16,000 casket fashioned into a Mercedes.*

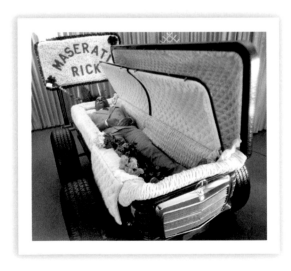

years before failing health kept him from running for a sixth term in 1993. The last of the big-city bosses remains Motown's Paul Bunyan, a legend who could easily be reelected—if he hadn't died in 1997. Even so, mayoral hopefuls have learned to keep one eye trained on Elmwood Cemetery.

Focus: HOPE, a nationally acclaimed civil rights organization that is one of the city's most important and unusual institutions, was one of the few positives to emerge from the 1967 riot. In 1968, 38-year-old Detroit native Father William Cunningham, the pastor at the Church of the Madonna, and Eleanor Josaitis, a former Michigan Bell employee and the mother of five, started the organization with a volunteer staff and a budget of $11,000. More than three decades after its founding, Focus: HOPE has blossomed into a multifaceted agency that continues to address the needs of an economically distressed inner city community.

The story of Focus: HOPE centers around Cunningham, the unconventional, liberal-minded priest who believed in truly practicing what he preached, particularly the obligation to help others. The son of an affluent Irish-Catholic real estate developer, Cunningham was raised with his two sisters inside a Boston-Edison district mansion before taking the vow of poverty and pursuing God's calling. Although the handsome, charismatic priest clearly was headed for the archdiocese's fast track during the 1960s, his primary focus became that of a simple parish priest after the riot.

As an English instructor at Sacred Heart Seminary, Cunningham had had a front-seat view of the violence and the looting. Immediately afterward, he met with Eleanor Josaitis, a suburban homemaker whom he had first met when he was an assistant weekend pastor at her church in Taylor. Both were concerned with helping to heal the city's wounds by developing programs that would help the socially and economically disadvantaged break out of their cycle of poverty and despair. The following year they took over an abandoned factory on Oakman Boulevard near Linwood. On March 18, 1968, they launched their interracial volunteer organization with this mission statement:

Recognizing the dignity and beauty of every person, we pledge intelligent and practical action to overcome racism, poverty and injustice. And to build a metropolitan community where all people may live in freedom, harmony, trust and affection. Black and white, yellow, brown and red from Detroit and its suburbs of every economic status, national origin and religious persuasion, we join in this covenant.

Focus: HOPE's first major project was the Food Prescription Program, which continues to distribute food to thousands of needy persons in Detroit.

Eventually the Oakman property expanded into numerous buildings spread over 40 acres, with the Machinist Training Institute and the Center for Advanced Technologies providing skilled job training for women and minorities. With the assistance of corporate sponsors, Focus: HOPE soon created a handful of for-profit companies, thereby establishing jobs for its graduates and revenue for its numerous programs. Beginning in 1975, Focus: HOPE's message of celebrating diversity and promoting racial harmony was publicized with an annual eight-mile fundraising march, with thousands of Detroiters and suburbanites strolling arm in arm through the streets of Detroit and Highland Park. Presidents George Bush and Bill Clinton, impressed by the organization's success, visited the site. Today, the

⋏ *For more than 40 years, until her death in 2001, Charleszetta "Mother" Waddles doled out food, clothes, advice and plain old-fashioned hope at her storefront Perpetual Mission. "Just dealing with her felt like you were going to church," one friend said of the former welfare mom, who had gained national recognition for her selfless work on behalf of Detroit's downtrodden.*

Bob-Lo: Detroit's Fantasy Island

If you grew up in the Detroit area, the chances are excellent that at some point in your life you took a boat ride to Bob-Lo Island. It might have been with your classmates, a Cub Scout pack, the Brownies, your family, or even a first date. But you never forgot the experience.

Located 18 miles downriver from the Ambassador Bridge, Bob-Lo Island was an escape from a hot concrete jungle, the closest thing generations of Detroiters had to a Disneyland or Fantasy Island. Baby boomers remember Captain Bob-Lo (Joe Short) greeting them at the dock and waving good-bye at the end of a long day filled with rides, laughter, and maybe even a stomach ache from too much cotton candy. The two-hour round-trip journey from the docks at the foot of Woodward or behind Cobo Hall on one of the two Bob-Lo boats provided a unique perspective of Detroit and neighboring Canada. For many Detroiters, it was their only boating experience on the Detroit River.

Named Bois Blanc ("island of white wood") by the French in the 1700s, the island later served as a military outpost for the British. During the War of 1812 it briefly was head-quarters for Tecumseh, the legendary Shawnee Chief then aiding the British army against the Americans. In the years leading up to the Civil War, the island—which is part of Ontario—became a stop on the underground railway for slaves escaping to Canada.

By the end of the 19th century, Bois Blanc Island had become a popular picnic destination for wealthy U.S. and Canadian visitors. After the island was sold by private owners to the Detroit, Belle Isle, & Windsor Ferry Company, Henry Ford hired his favorite architect, Albert Kahn, to build what was then the world's second largest dance hall in the middle of the island.

The Bob-Lo Excursion Line christened the steamers *Columbia* and *Ste. Claire* in 1902 and 1910, respectively. The triple-decked steamers each could hold up to 2,500 passengers and boasted a dance floor and a beer garden. Years later, WJR's J.P. McCarthy and television news anchor Bill Bonds captained each ship in an annual race against each other for charity.

By 1949, the island was transformed into an amusement park that in its heyday hosted up to 800,000 visitors a summer. However, as people became more attracted to larger and more sophisticated amusement parks like Cedar Point during the 1970s, attendance nose-dived. The island's ownership changed hands several times in attempts to keep it afloat. The park finally closed in the mid 1990s when the amusement rides and passenger boats were auctioned off.

When it was announced in 1994 that Bob-Lo was to close for good, Detroiters lamented its loss as another in a series of vanished traditions that once had connected them to the city. Joanna Gunn, then 80, fondly told reporters of going to church picnics there in the early 1920s, when it looked like a city park with just a few rides. After taking the late-night boat ride home, Gunn remembered, she and her friends would stop at the Vernor's waterfront plant for a glass of ginger ale. Ann Hunt's favorite memory was the dance hall. "The park had the most wonderful

▼ *Turned into an amusement park by a steamship company in the late 19th century, Bob-Lo Island had a park that featured rides and a cavernous dancing pavilion that could accommodate 5,000 patrons.*

Dancing Pavilion at Bob-Lo (Bois Blanc Island) Detroit River

dance floor on earth," she said. "It was divine, polished. It was just beautiful, big, and airy." She added that "if you got lucky and some fellow asked you to go, you'd have dinner on the boat or at the island and come back in the dark."

Not everyone had pleasant memories, however. In his autobiography, Detroit Mayor Coleman Young recalled the eighth-grade graduation party that had been scheduled for Bob-Lo in 1931. "As we were loading the boat to take us to Bob-Lo, one of the guides jerked the cap off my head to check out my hair and officiously informed me that black children were not permitted at the park." Despite previous encounters with discrimination, "I honestly wasn't prepared for that. And I was never quite the same person again."

Consequently, the mayor's office had no interest in helping to save Bob-Lo. Today, the island is a residential community of upscale homes while the steamers *Ste. Claire* and *Columbia* are privately docked, a foundation desperately seeking the millions of dollars in donations needed to save their rotting hulls.

∨ *The triple-decked steamers* Columbia *and* Ste. Claire *could each hold as many as 2,500 passengers. At its peak, Bob-Lo Island entertained 800,000 people a year.*

The Golden Voice of Detroit

He was often called the "voice of Detroit." Over a span of four decades, WJR's J.P. McCarthy woke up the city each morning at 6:15 with the words, "Hello, world!"

Sometimes it felt as if it were just J.P.'s world. But even if you weren't a golfer or a boater, you still listened to the one person who not only captured the pulse of the city, but seemed at times to keep its heart beating. Until his sudden and untimely death at age 62, the radio legend was one of the most influential persons the city has ever known, providing a forum for a who's who of local and national business, sports, entertainment, and political figures—all of whom he knew on a first-name basis.

Joseph Priestly McCarthy, whose family moved to Detroit from New York when he was 10, was nationally recognized with numerous awards, including the prestigious Marconi Award for career achievement and induction into the Radio Hall of Fame. "He was bigger than the people he covered and he was the one person everyone listened to," said longtime *Detroit News* columnist Pete Waldmeir. "He could call the governor at any time, and whether he was a Democrat or a Republican, he would talk to J.P."

With WJR's 50,000-watt signal carrying his voice to numerous states and Canada, McCarthy was Detroit's goodwill ambassador. On any given day, whether you were at the breakfast table or stuck on I-75 during a traffic snarl, McCarthy would undoubtedly be interviewing someone in the news with his inimitably smooth, nonconfrontational style. It could be a CEO announcing plans for his company, or Sparky Anderson, half awake, trying to explain what happened in the ballgame the night before. Often his interviews would create news, reported at the top of the hour by the WJR news department.

Everyday listeners became a part of his show, calling in on such regular features as "Winners and Losers of the Day" and "What's Bothering You?" The phone feature "The Answer Man" called for J.P. to adopt a nerdy comical voice to answer questions on any subject. At noon, listeners felt as though they were eavesdropping on J.P.'s conversations as he interviewed in-studio guests on his "Focus" show.

An indication of how important J.P. was to the city and Michigan was the hoopla surrounding St. Patrick's Day, when the proud Irishman hosted a

morning-long party. This holiday show originally aired from WJR's lobby, but it was later moved to the Pegasus Restaurant in the Fisher Building and then the Fox Theatre lobby after the invitation list topped 1,000 persons. McCarthy would stroll through the crowd and interview the numerous celebrities, business leaders, and politicians (many fueled with the appropriate libation) who had anxiously awaited their brief moment with J.P.

Other favorite J.P. rituals were broadcasts from the field each opening day at Tiger Stadium, the annual charity golf tournament benefiting the Police Athletic League, and Christmas caroling at Hart Plaza to open the holiday season. He would also occasionally broadcast from such locations as Wimbledon, the America's Cup race, PGA golf tournaments, and Churchill Downs.

A favorite character who appeared on his show hundreds of times over the years was "Fat Bob" Taylor, "the singing plumber." One day in 1967, Taylor called J.P. on the air, saying he could sing the opera song "Vesti La Giubba" better than McCarthy. For the next 28 years, Fat Bob was a fixture. Taylor might sing "Let Me Call You Sweet Heart" to a listener on Valentine's Day, or disguise his voice, calling himself "Mrs. Pennyfeather," an old lady with a biting sense of humor. Taylor continued to appear on the show until he suffered a fatal stroke one June day in 1995.

Just weeks after Taylor's passing, loyal listeners received an even greater shock. McCarthy was diagnosed with a blood ailment, myelodysplastic syndrome. The disease forced him off the air after nearly 40 years. Prior to his death on August 16, 1995, thousands of Metro Detroiters frantically had their blood tested in hopes of providing a bone marrow transplant. His funeral service, reminiscent of those given a fallen head of state, was covered live by all the local television outlets, while radio stations went off the air momentarily in a respectful moment of silence.

McCarthy's memory is kept alive today through the J.P. McCarthy Foundation, established to help research a cure for the disease that stilled one of the city's most distinctive voices.

▲ *Friends in high places: J.P. and the mayor.*

▲ *Downtown Hudson's represented many memories for Detroiters, including the world's largest flag (a seven-story-high banner unfurled for holidays and special civic occasions) and the annual Thanksgiving Day parade. Both traditions started in the 1920s, when the store—and the city—were at their zenith.*

◄ *Out with the old. Hudson's closed its downtown store in 1983 but it wasn't until 15 years later—October 24, 1998 — that the empty 25-story landmark was leveled in front of an estimated 50,000 spectators. A parking garage for the Compuware world headquarters is planned for the site.*

⋏ Top: For more than a century, farmers and vendors have brought their goods to Eastern Market on Russell north of Gratiot. It is the largest open-air wholesale-retail market in the country. On any given day, customers can be seen jamming the stalls and shops for fruits, vegetables, flowers and other products.

⋏ Above: The $200-million Greektown Casino opened in 2000, four years after voters statewide approved three casinos for Detroit.

organization has approximately 800 employees and 51,000 volunteers, contributors, and supporters.

In the spring of 1997, just two months shy of the 30th anniversary of the 1967 riot, Father Cunningham passed away after a lengthy battle with liver cancer. Thousands of mourners, from the needy to millionaires and politicians, came to pay their respects. "All of Detroit wept," the *Detroit Free Press* declared. At his funeral, Josaitis read a letter from President Clinton, who spoke of the priest's "legacy of compassion and achievement."

Stepping into Coleman Young's giant brogans was Dennis Archer, a former justice of the state Supreme Court whose greatest asset was who he wasn't. He wasn't Coleman Young, which made him immediately palatable to suburban power brokers turned off by his combative predecessor. Archer, who grew up in rural Michigan in even poorer circumstances than Young, came across as cerebral, humorless, and wooden. But during his first four years in office, he saw voters and developers come together on the issues of casino gambling (which had been repeatedly rejected at the polls during Young's tenure) and side-by-side downtown stadiums for the football Lions and baseball Tigers. Comerica Park opened in the spring of 2000, with the construction of Ford Field slated to be completed by the fall of 2002. These triumphs were accompanied by Washington's awarding of $100 million for a federal empowerment zone to boost business development, as well as a rash of new housing starts in the city.

There was a palpable sense of synergy and optimism. "To me, opera is just a lot of loud singing," admitted Arthur Stewart, an unemployed pipefitter, as the Detroit Opera House neared completion in the spring of 1996. "But anything that brings those bigwigs downtown again got to be a good thing." That same year, General Motors announced that it was buying the RenCen for $73 million and, after an extensive facelift, moving its giant white-collar workforce from the New Center area to the riverfront. This was followed by Compuware's decision to build a corporate headquarters downtown, the groundbreaking occurring in the fall of 2000.

Archer was easily reelected in 1997 but then took considerable public abuse, principally for failing to put a serious dent in problems that continue to afflict the community at large: demolished and abandoned houses, unreliable public services, drug-infested neighborhoods, and a failing school system. Despite his thin skin and slightly arrogant personal style, Archer remained the favored choice of many to continue the slow process of lifting Detroit out of its Third World doldrums—until he shocked the community by announcing that he would not run for re-election in 2001. Whoever succeeds Archer must contend with the hard facts of America's largest black-majority city. Over the last 50 years, the poverty rate in Detroit has doubled while the rate in the suburbs has been cut in half. A 1999 study by the Brookings Institution ranked Detroit a dismal 67th in job growth when compared to other cities. The real growth in Metro Detroit's economy is fueled by the suburbs, the think

▼ *Although Dennis Archer helped mend fences with the suburbs during his eight years as mayor, he decided not to seek a third term in 2001.*

➤ *Mayor Archer and Peter Karmanos at the 1999 announcement that Compuware Corporation would build its new world headquarters in downtown.*

➤ *Opposite page: In with the new. After spending the previous 104 summers playing ball at the corner of Michigan and Trumbull, the Detroit Tigers opened a new era on April 11, 2000 by playing their first game at Comerica Park, a $375-million facility heavily bankrolled with public dollars.*

▼ *Below: The Dr. Charles H. Wright Museum of African American History opened in 1999 at a cost of $38 million. The original museum started in the basement of Dr. Wright's home office on West Grand Boulevard in 1965.*

▼ *Bottom: An architectural sketch of Ford Field, due to open in the fall of 2002 next door to Comerica Park.*

tank reported. "The economic capital of southeast Michigan is Oakland County. That the region is still called Detroit is an historical artifact." The new mayor also must contend with fascinated sociologists and cultural historians who urge that certain derelict parts of the city be preserved as a kind of American Acropolis or skyscraper graveyard.

In 2001, as Detroiters and suburbanites participated in a year-long series of special events celebrating the city's 300th birthday, citizens continue to shrug off the jokes and stereotypes and watch Detroit continue its slow, fitful march back to respectability. Perhaps no major city in the world has gone through as many permutations. Cadillac's village. The Gateway to the West. Where Life is Worth Living. The Motor City. The Arsenal of Democracy. Motown. The Murder City. And finally, the Renaissance City, a Pollyanna-ish moniker from the '70s that can be seen to connect a pair of optimists—one white, one black—from across the centuries. The first is Father Gabriel Richard, who coined Detroit's motto following the devastating fire of 1805: "We hope for better things; it will arise from its ashes." The other is Dudley Randall, appointed the city's poet laureate by Mayor Young, who in his best known work, "Detroit Renaissance," echoed and expanded on the priest's simple message:

Cities have died, have burned,
Yet phoenix-like returned
To soar up livelier, lovelier than before.
Detroit has felt the fire
Yet each time left the pyre
As if the flames had power to restore.

First, burn away the myths
Of what it was, and is—
A lovely, tree-laned town of peace and trade.
Hatred has festered here,
And bigotry and fear
Filled streets with strife and raised the barricade.

Wealth of a city lies,
Not in its factories,
Its marts and towers crowding to the sky,
But in its people who
Possess grace to imbue
Their lives with beauty, wisdom, charity.

Together we will build
A city that will yield
To all their hopes and dreams so long deferred.
New faces will appear
Too long neglected here;
New minds, new means will build a brave new world.

⋏ *Dudley Randall: "Detroit has felt the fire...."*

➤ *Opposite page: Fireworks on the river that Cadillac quietly traversed three centuries ago.*

A number of individuals, libraries, and historical depositories were of great assistance during the researching and writing of this book, and it is my pleasure to acknowledge their help. I would like to thank the staffs of the following: the Burton Historical Collection of the Detroit Public Library, particularly its manager, Dave Poremba; the Archives of Labor History and Urban Affairs, Wayne State University, particularly Thomas Featherstone and Mary Wallace; Barbara Martin from the E. Azalia Hackley Memorial Collection of the Detroit Public Library; the Detroit Free Press, *especially Bill McGraw and Craig Porter; the* Detroit News; *and the William L. Clements Library of the University of Michigan. Bill Dow assisted in the researching and writing of several sidebars while many gifted photographers from the Detroit area contributed contemporary photographs to complement the historical images.*

2 Robert Stewart, **4** Balthazar Korab, **6** Balthazar Korab, **8** Christopher Scalise, **9** Burton Historical Collection, **10** Burton Historical Collection, **11** *Detroit Free Press*, **12** Christopher Scalise, **13** *(top)* Burton Historical Collection, **13** *(bottom)* Christopher Scalise, **14** Burton Historical Collection, **15** William L. Clements Library, University of Michigan, **16** Balthazar Korab, **17** *(top)* Burton Historical Collection, **17** *(middle)* Burton Historical Collection, **17** *(bottom)* Richard Bak, **18** Richard Bak, **19** William L. Clements Library, University of Michigan, **20** *(left)* Burton Historical Collection, **20** *(bottom)* Tom Sherry, **21** Burton Historical Collection, **22** William L. Clements Library, University of Michigan, **25** Ameritech, **26** Walter P. Reuther Library, **27** *(top)* Burton Historical Collection, **27** *(bottom)* David Woods, **28** *(right)* Burton Historical Collection, **31** State Archives of Michigan, **33** Burton Historical Collection, **34** Burton Historical Collection, **35** Burton Historical Collection, **36** *(top)* Burton Historical Collection, **36** *(bottom)* Burton Historical Collection, **37** Robert Stewart, **38** Burton Historical Collection, **39** Burton Historical Collection, **40** *(top)* Burton Historical Collection, **40** *(bottom)* Burton Historical Collection, **41** *(top)* Paul Mehney Collection, **41** *(bottom)* State Archives of Michigan, **42** Richard Bak, **43** *(top)* Richard Bak, **43** *(bottom)* Burton Historical Collection, **44** Burton Historical Collection, **45** *(left)* Burton Historical Collection, **45** *(right)* Burton Historical Collection, **46** Richard Bak, **47** *(top)* Susan Tyszka, **47** *(bottom)* Richard Bak, **48** *(top)* Richard Bak, **48** *(bottom)* Richard Bak, **49** Balthazar Korab, **50** *(top left)* Detroit Institute of Arts Reference Library, **50** *(bottom left)* Richard Bak, **50** *(right)* Burton Historical Collection, **51** *(left)* Henry Ford Museum, **51** *(right)* Henry Ford Museum, **52** *(right)* Richard Bak, **53** *(top)* Burton Historical Collection, **53** *(bottom)* Burton Historical Collection, **54** *(left)* Walter P. Reuther Library, **55** Burton Historical Collection, **56** *(top right)* Burton Historical Collection, **56** *(bottom right)* Burton Historical Collection, **57** Michigan Views, **58** *(left)* Richard Bak, **58** *(right)* Richard Bak, **60** Burton Historical Collection, **61** Richard Bak, **62** *(right)* Richard Bak, **63** Burton Historical Collection, **64** Manning Brothers, **65** *(middle)* Burton Historical Collection, **66-67** Robert Stewart, **68** Richard Bak, **70** *(top)* Richard Bak, **70-71** *(bottom)* Library of Congress, **71** *(right)* Richard Bak, **71** *(left)* Richard Bak, **72** Burton Historical Collection, **73** Richard Bak, **75** Burton Historical Collection, **76** Richard Bak, **77** *(top)* Burton Historical Collection, **77** *(bottom)* Richard Bak, **78** Richard Bak, **79** Richard Bak, **80** *(top)* Burton Historical Collection, **80** *(bottom)* Burton Historical Collection, **81** *(top)* Motor Vehicle Manufacturers Association of the United States, Inc., **81** *(bottom)* Burton Historical Collection, **82** *(right)* Burton Historical Collection, **83** Walter P. Reuther Library, **84** *(left)* Burton Historical Collection, **84** *(right)* Burton Historical Collection, **85** *(top)* Walter P. Reuther Library, **86** *(top left)* Richard Bak, **86** *(bottom left)* Richard Bak, **86** *(middle)* Richard Bak, **86** *(right)* Richard Bak, **87** *(left)* Walter P. Reuther Library, **87** *(right)* Richard Bak, **88** Richard Bak, **89** Burton Historical Collection, **90** *(top left)* Richard Bak, **90** *(bottom right)* Burton Historical Collection, **91** *Detroit Free Press*, **93** Balthazar Korab, **94** Walter P. Reuther Library, **95** Richard Bak, **96** Richard Bak, **97** *(left)* Richard Bak, **97** *(right)* Richard Bak, **98** *(top)* Burton Historical Collection, **99** *(top)* Richard Bak, **99** *(bottom)* Richard Bak, **100** Richard Bak, **101** Richard Bak, **102** Walter P. Reuther Library, **103** Walter P. Reuther Library, **104** *(top)* Walter P. Reuther Library, **104** *(bottom)* Walter P. Reuther Library, **105** Michelle Andonian, **106** Susan Tyszka, **107** Susan Tyszka, **108** Richard Bak, **109** Richard Bak, **110** *(top)* Richard Bak, **110** *(bottom)* Richard Bak, **111** *(top)* Walter P. Reuther Library, **111** *(bottom)* Richard Bak, **112** *(top)* *Detroit News*, **112** *(bottom)* Burton Historical Collection, **113** Manning Brothers, **114** Burton Historical Collection, **115** Burton Historical Collection, **116** Richard Bak, **117** Richard Bak, **118** Walter P. Reuther Library, **119** Richard Bak, **120** Robert Stewart, **121** *(top)* *Detroit Free Press*, **121** *(bottom)* Richard Bak, **122** Taro Yamasaki, **123** *(left)* Albert Kahn Associates, **124** Burton Historical Collection, **125** Burton Historical Collection, **126** *(left)* Richard Bak, **126** *(right)* Richard Bak, **127** Richard Bak, **128** Burton Historical Collection, **129** Balthazar Korab, **130** Burton Historical Collection, **131** Richard Bak, **132** *(bottom)* Burton Historical Collection, **133** Christopher Scalise, **134** *(top)* Burton Historical Collection, **134** *(bottom)* Burton Historical Collection, **135** *(top)* Richard Bak, **135** *(bottom)* Richard Bak, **136** *(top)* *Detroit News*, **136** *(bottom)* Burton Historical Collection, **137** *(left)* *Windsor Star*, **137** *(right)* Richard Bak, **138** *(left)* Richard Bak, **138** *(right)* Richard Bak, **139** *(top)* Richard Bak, **139** *(bottom)* Richard Bak, **140** Walter P. Reuther Library, **141** *(top)* Walter P. Reuther Library, **141** *(bottom)* Walter P. Reuther Library, **143** Walter P. Reuther Library, **144** Walter P. Reuther Library, **145** *(top)* Richard Bak, **146** Walter P. Reuther Library, **147** Richard Bak, **149** Walter P. Reuther Library, **150** Richard Bak, **151** *(top)* Richard Bak, **151** *(bottom)* Richard Bak, **153** Walter P. Reuther Library, **154** Walter P. Reuther Library, **155** Walter P. Reuther Library, **156** *(left)* Burton Historical Collection, **156-157** Burton Historical Collection, **158** Burton Historical Collection, **159** Justin Maconochie, **160** Walter P. Reuther Library, **162** *(left)* Richard Bak, **162-163** Walter P. Reuther Library, **164** Walter P. Reuther Library, **165** Burton Historical Collection, **166** *(top)* Walter P. Reuther Library, **166** *(bottom left)* Walter P. Reuther Library, **166** *(bottom right)* Walter P. Reuther Library, **167** Walter P. Reuther Library, **168** Walter P. Reuther Library, **169** *(top)* Library of Congress, **169** *(bottom)* Library of Congress, **170** *(top)* Walter P. Reuther Library, **170** *(bottom)* Walter P. Reuther Library, **171** *(top)* *Detroit Free Press*, **171** *(bottom)* Richard Bak, **172** *(left)* Walter P. Reuther Library, **172** *(right)* Walter P. Reuther Library, **173** *(left)* Burton Historical Collection, **174** *(right)* Burton Historical Collection, **175** Burton Historical Collection, **176** *(left)* Walter P. Reuther Library, **176** *(right)* Walter P. Reuther Library, **177** *(bottom)* State Archives of Michigan, **178** Walter P. Reuther Library, **179** Burton Historical Collection, **180** *(left)* Burton Historical Collection, **180** *(right)* Burton Historical Collection, **181** Walter P. Reuther Library, **182** *(left)* Walter P. Reuther Library, **183** Walter P. Reuther Library, **185** Walter P. Reuther Library, **186** Walter P. Reuther Library, **188** Manning Brothers, **189** Richard Bak, **190** Detroit Institute of Arts, **191** Detroit Institute of Arts, **192** *(top)* R.L. Montgomery, **193** *(top)* Richard Bak, **193** *(bottom)* Richard Bak, **194** Larry Peplin, **195** *(bottom)* Burton Historical Collection, **196** *(left)* Michelle Andonian, **197** *(left)* Richard Bak, **197** *(right)* AP/Wide World Photos, **198** *(top)* Burton Historical Collection, **198** *(bottom)* Burton Historical Collection, **199** *(left)* Library of Congress, **199** *(right)* Burton Historical Collection, **200** Richard Bak, **201** Richard Bak, **202** Burton Historical Collection, **203** Richard Bak, **204** Burton Historical Collection, **205** Justin Maconochie, **206** Pewabic Society, Inc., **208** *(top left)* AP/Wide World Photos, **208** *(bottom left)* AP/Wide World Photos, **208** *(right)* *Detroit Free Press*, **209** Richard Bak, **210** Burton Historical Collection, **211** *(left)* Richard Bak, **211** *(right)* Richard Bak, **212** Walter P. Reuther Library, **215** E. Azalia Hackley Memorial Collection, **218** *(left)* *Detroit Free Press*, **218** *(right)* E. Azalia Hackley Memorial Collection, **219** Milt Hinton, **221** Burton Historical Collection, **222** *(left)* Richard Bak, **222** *(right)* Richard Bak, **223** Richard Bak, **224** Michelle Andonian, **225** Richard Bak, **226** Richard Bak, **227** *(top)* Richard Bak, **227** *(bottom)* Richard Bak, **228** *(left)* Richard Bak, **228** *(right)* Richard Bak, **229** Richard Bak, **230** *(left)* Richard Bak, **230** *(right)* Richard Bak, **231** *(left)* Richard Bak, **231** *(right)* Richard Bak, **231** *(bottom)* Richard Bak, **232-233** Richard Bak, **234** Leon T. Daniels, Jr., **235** Leon T. Daniels, Jr., **236** *(top)* Richard Bak, **236** *(bottom left)* Richard Bak, **236** *(bottom right)* Richard Bak, **237** *(top)* Richard Bak, **239** Richard Bak, **240** *(top)* Richard Bak, **240** *(bottom)* Richard Bak, **241** Richard Bak, **242** Manning Brothers, **243** Walter P. Reuther Library, **245** Richard Bak, **246** Richard Bak, **247** Rebecca Cook, **248** Richard Bak, **249** Richard Bak, **250** *(bottom)* Richard Bak, **251** *(top left)* *Detroit Free Press*/Julian H. Gonzalez, **251** *(bottom left)* *Detroit News*/Dale Young, **251** *(right)* Richard Bak, **252** *(left)* Detroit Pistons, **252** *(right)* WNBA Enterprises, LLC, **253** *(left)* AP/Wide World Photos, **253** *(right)* David A. Smith, **254** *Detroit Free Press*, **255** Designated Hatter, **256** *(left)* Richard Bak, **256** *(right)* Richard Bak, **257** *(top)* Richard Bak, **257** *(bottom)* Richard Bak, **258-259** Larry Lester, **260** *(left)* Richard Bak, **260** *(right)* Michelle Andonian, **261** Walter P. Reuther Library, **262** *(left)* Richard Bak, **262** *(right)* Richard Bak, **263** Richard Bak, **264** Burton Historical Collection, **265** Burton Historical Collection, **266** *(top)* Walter P. Reuther Library, **266** *(bottom)* Walter P. Reuther Library, **267** Library of Congress, **268-269** Library of Congress, **270** Richard Bak, **271** Burton Historical Collection, **272** *(left)* Burton Historical Collection, **272** *(right)* Burton Historical Collection, **273** *(bottom)* Library of Congress, **274** Walter P. Reuther Library, **275** Library of Congress, **276** *(bottom)* Ruth Regan-Spring, **276** *(top)* Richard Bak, **277** *(left)* Burton Historical Collection, **277** *(right)* *Detroit Free Press*, **278** Walter P. Reuther Library, **280** Richard Bak, **281** Richard Bak, **282** *(top)* *Detroit Free Press*, **282** *(bottom)* *Detroit Free Press*, **283** *Detroit Free Press*, **284** *(top)* Walter P. Reuther Library, **285** Richard Bak, **286** Michael Shiels/WJR, **287** *(left)* Tom Sherry, **287** *(top right)* Burton Historical Collection, **287** *(bottom right)* Richard Bak, **288** *(top)* Robert Stewart, **288** *(bottom)* Greektown Casino, **289** *Detroit Free Press*, **290** *(top left)* Justin Maconochie, **290** *(bottom left)* Detroit Lions, **290** *(right)* Compuware Corporation/William E. Dwyer, **291** Justin Maconochie, **292** *Detroit Free Press*, **293** Robert Stewart, **294** Robert Stewart, **297** Robert Stewart

All postcards and memorabilia from the author's collection. The publisher will be pleased to rectify any photography copyright omissions or inaccuracies in the next printing.

Charles C. Alexander. *Ty Cobb* (Oxford University Press, 1984).

Frank Angelo. *On Guard: A History of the Detroit Free Press* (Detroit Free Press, 1981).

Steve Babson. *Working Detroit: The Making of a Union Town* (Adama Books, 1984).

Richard Bak. *Joe Louis: The Great Black Hope* (Taylor, 1996).

Richard Bak. *A Place for Summer: A Narrative History of Tiger Stadium* (Wayne State University Press, 1998).

F. Clever Bald. *The Great Fire of 1805* (Wayne State University Press, 1951).

John Barnard. *Walter Reuther and the Rise of the Auto Workers* (Little, Brown, 1983).

Norman Beasley and George W. Stark. *Made in Detroit* (Van Rees Press, 1957).

Malcolm W. Bingay. *Detroit Is My Own Home Town* (Bobbs–Merrill, 1946).

Malcolm W. Bingay. *Of Me I Sing* (Bobbs–Merrill, 1949).

Peter H. Blum. *Brewed in Detroit: Breweries and Beers Since 1830* (Wayne State University Press, 1999).

Sidney Bolkosky. *Harmony and Dissonance: Voices of Jewish Identity in Detroit, 1914–1967* (Wayne State University Press, 1991).

Kevin Boyle and Victoria Getis. *Muddy Boots and Ragged Aprons: Images of Working-Class Detroit, 1900–1930* (Wayne State University Press, 1997).

Clarence Monroe Burton (with M.M. Quaife). *When Detroit Was Young* (Burton Abstract and Title Co., 1951).

Ze'ev Chafets. *Devil's Night and Other True Tales of Detroit* (Random House, 1990).

Alan Clive. *State of War: Michigan in World War II* (University of Michigan Press, 1979).

Peter Collier and David Horowitz. *The Fords: An American Epic* (Summit Books, 1987).

Robert Conot. *American Odyssey: A Unique History of America Told Through the Life of a Great City* (William Morrow, 1974).

Ed Cray. *Chrome Colossus* (McGraw–Hill, 1980).

John C. Dancy. *Sand Against the Wind: The Memoirs of John C. Dancy* (Wayne State University Press, 1966).

Brian Leigh Dunnigan. *Frontier Metropolis: Picturing Early Detroit, 1701–1838* (Wayne State University Press, 2001).

Lawrence Englemann. *Intemperance: The Lost War Against Liquor* (The Free Press, 1979).

Reynolds Farley, Sheldon Danziger, and Harry Holzer. *Detroit Divided* (Russell Sage Foundation, 2000).

Silas Farmer. *History of Detroit and Wayne County and Early Michigan: A Chronological Cyclopedia of the Past and Present* (Gale Research Co., 1969). Originally published 1884.

W. Hawkins Ferry. *The Buildings of Detroit: A History* (Wayne State University Press, 1968).

W. Hawkins Ferry. *The Legacy of Albert Kahn* (Detroit Institute of Arts, 1970).

Sidney Fine. *Frank Murphy: The Detroit Years* (University of Michigan Press, 1975).

Sidney Fine. *Violence in the Model City: The Cavanagh Administration, Race Relations, and the Detroit Riot of 1967* (University of Michigan Press, 1989).

Peter Gavrilovich and Bill McGraw (eds.) *The Detroit Almanac: 300 Years of Life in the Motor City* (Detroit Free Press, 2000).

Nelson George. *Where Did Our Love Go? The Rise and Fall of the Motown Sound* (St. Martin's Press, 1985).

Laurence Goldstein (ed.). "Detroit: An American City." *Michigan Quarterly Review* (Spring 1986).

David Halberstam. *The Reckoning* (William Morrow, 1986).

Melvin G. Holli. *Reform in Detroit: Hazen S. Pingree and Urban Politics* (Oxford University Press, 1969).

Charles K. Hyde. *Detroit: An Industrial History Guide* (Detroit Historical Society, 1980).

David Katzman. *Before the Ghetto: Black Detroit in the 19th Century* (University of Illinois Press, 1973).

Robert Lacey. *Ford: The Men and the Machine* (Little, Brown, 1986).

David Allen Levine. *Internal Combustion: The Races in Detroit, 1915–1926* (Greenwood Press, 1976).

David L. Lewis. *The Public Image of Henry Ford* (Wayne State University Press, 1976).

David L. Lewis (ed.). "The Automobile and American Culture." *Michigan Quarterly Review* (Fall 1980/Winter 1981).

Nelson Lichtenstein. *The Most Dangerous Man in Detroit: Walter Reuther and the Fate of American Labor* (Basic Books, 1995).

Don Lochbiler. *Detroit's Coming of Age: 1873 to 1973* (Wayne State University Press, 1973).

John C. Lodge (with M.M. Quaife). *I Remember Detroit* (Wayne State University Press, 1949).

William W. Lutz. *The News of Detroit* (Little, Brown, 1973).

Philip P. Mason. *The Ambassador Bridge: A Monument to Progress* (Wayne State University Press, 1987).

Philip P. Mason. *Rumrunning and the Roaring Twenties: Prohibition on the Michigan–Ontario Waterway* (Wayne State University Press, 1995).

Dennis Alan Nawrocki. *Art in Detroit Public Places* (Wayne State University Press, 1999).

Richard Jules Oestreicher. *Solidarity and Fragmentation: Working People and Class Consciousness in Detroit, 1875–1900* (University of Illinois Press, 1986).

Lawrence D. Orton. *Polish Detroit and the Kolasinski Affair* (Wayne State University Press, 1981).

Stanley Pargellis. *Father Gabriel Richard* (Wayne State University Press, 1950).

Howard H. Peckham. *Pontiac and the Indian Uprising* (Princeton University Press, 1947).

Jean Madden Pitrone. *Hudson's: Hub of America's Heartland* (A & M Publishing Co., 1991).

David Lee Poremba (ed.). *Detroit in Its World Setting* (Wayne State University Press, 2001).

John Schneider. *Detroit and the Problem of Order, 1830–1880: A Geography of Crime, Riot, and Policing* (University of Nebraska Press, 1980).

Suzanne E. Smith. *Dancing in the Street: Motown and the Cultural Politics of Detroit* (Harvard University Press, 1999).

Thomas Sugrue. *The Origins of the Urban Crisis: Race and Inequality in Postwar Detroit* (Princeton University Press, 1996).

Richard W. Thomas. *Life for Us Is What We Make It: Building Black Community in Detroit, 1915–1945* (Indiana University Press, 1982).

Bernard Weisberger. *The Dream Maker: William C. Durant, Founder of General Motors* (Little, Brown, 1979).

Frank B. Woodford. *Lewis Cass: The Last Jeffersonian* (Rutgers University press, 1950).

Frank B. Woodford. *Mr. Jefferson's Disciple: A Life of Justice Woodward* (Michigan State College Press, 1953).

Frank B. Woodford and Albert Hyma. *Gabriel Richard, Frontier Ambassador* (Wayne State University Press, 1958).

Frank B. Woodford and Arthur M. Woodford. *All Our Yesterdays: A Brief History of Detroit* (Wayne State University Press, 1969).

Coleman Young (with Lonnie Wheeler). *Hard Stuff: The Autobiography of Mayor Coleman Young* (Viking, 1994).

Olivier Zunz. *The Changing Face of Inequality: Urbanization, Industrial Development, and Immigrants in Detroit, 1880–1920* (University of Chicago Press, 1982).